Modern
British Philosophy

Also by Bryan Magee

GO WEST, YOUNG MAN
TO LIVE IN DANGER
THE NEW RADICALISM
THE DEMOCRATIC REVOLUTION
TOWARDS 2000
ONE IN TWENTY
THE TELEVISION INTERVIEWER
ASPECTS OF WAGNER

BRYAN MAGEE

Modern
British Philosophy

A. J. Ayer   Gilbert Ryle
Stuart Hampshire   Ninian Smart
Alasdair MacIntyre   Peter Strawson
Alan Montefiore   Geoffrey Warnock
David Pears   Bernard Williams
Karl Popper   Richard Wollheim
          Anthony Quinton

St. MARTIN'S PRESS · NEW YORK

AFFILIATED PUBLISHERS: Macmillan & Company, Limited,
London – also at Bombay, Calcutta, Madras and Melbourne –
The Macmillan Company of Canada, Limited, Toronto

Contents

Preface   vii

CONVERSATION WITH ANTHONY QUINTON   1
Introduction

1   CONVERSATION WITH STUART HAMPSHIRE   17
    The Philosophy of Russell: I

2   CONVERSATION WITH DAVID PEARS   31
    The Two Philosophies of Wittgenstein

3   CONVERSATION WITH A. J. AYER   48

4   CONVERSATION WITH KARL POPPER   66

5   CONVERSATION WITH GEOFFREY WARNOCK   83
    The Philosophies of Moore and Austin

6   CONVERSATION WITH GILBERT RYLE   100

7   CONVERSATION WITH PETER STRAWSON   115

8   DISCUSSION AMONG KARL POPPER, PETER
    STRAWSON AND GEOFFREY WARNOCK   131
    The Philosophy of Russell: II

9   CONVERSATION WITH BERNARD WILLIAMS   150
    Philosophy and Morals

10 CONVERSATION WITH NINIAN SMART   166
    Philosophy and Religion

11 CONVERSATION WITH RICHARD WOLLHEIM   178
    Philosophy and the Arts

12 CONVERSATION WITH ALASDAIR
    MACINTYRE   191
    Philosophy and Social Theory

CONVERSATION WITH ALAN MONTEFIORE   202
Conclusion

Suggested Reading   218

Notes on Contributors   224

Name Index   229

Subject Index   231

Preface

This book originates in a series of conversations which were first broadcast on BBC radio during the winter of 1970–71. Since unscripted talk cannot profitably be published as it stands, and some revision of the transcripts was therefore unavoidable, I made a virtue of necessity by inviting the participants to amend their contributions to any extent they wished. They took me at my word, with the result that all the conversations have been revised extensively. As a book the series will be useful, I hope, in three ways. First, it constitutes a lively introduction to contemporary British philosophy – but I mean 'introduction': it does not pretend to be a comprehensive survey; a volume this size cannot cover so variegated a field of activity. Inevitably, philosophers and subjects have been left out that are as important as some of those included. It might well be possible to produce a series as good as this with a completely different set of contributors; and perhaps this will be attempted if the reception accorded to this volume warrants it. (Then the two books taken together might constitute a survey of the field.) Second, the light thrown by philosophers on their own work will be of interest to everyone seriously interested in the subject. Third, some ideas of importance are published here for the first time.

From a general survey of contemporary British philosophy I believe certain features would stand out which are already discernible in this volume. One is that, as in so many other spheres of activity in Britain today, there is, for the first time in a long time, no prevailing orthodoxy. The attitude has become widespread which was expressed by Karl Popper in his preface to the first English edition of *The Logic of Scientific Discovery*, a preface directed against the then (1959) prevailing orthodoxies of language analysis: 'It may perhaps be asked what other "methods" a philosopher might use. My answer is that although there are any number of different "methods", I am really not interested in enumerating them. I do not care what methods a philosopher (or anybody else) may use so long as he has an interesting problem, and so long as he is sincerely trying to solve it.' Young philosophers in particular seem ready to experiment with any approach and see what it leads to; and they tend to be summarily dismissive of colleagues who attack this as illegitimate. So there is a welter of reappraisal and experiment, most of which, in the nature of things, will lead nowhere, but all of which is tolerated, not to say welcomed. In consequence, whole areas of philosophy have become active after years of stagnation.

The hegemonies of language analysis and, before that, logical positivism – despite the intrinsic merits of the two schools, which were considerable – had the effect of stunting growth, though for different reasons. The logical positivists believed that any proposition which was neither empirically verifiable nor logically tautologous was cognitively meaningless. It was generally realized that characteristic statements in whole areas of traditional philosophy – morals, political and social theory, aesthetics, philosophy of religion – were neither verifiable nor tautologous, and these areas were duly depopulated. It was less generally appreciated that philosophical propositions as such were neither. Nevertheless, acceptance of criteria which, if consistently applied, pronounced all philosophical propositions to be meaningless (unless they were tautologies) profoundly inhibited the positive development of even the most central areas of the subject. Large numbers of philosophers were, very properly, reluctant to say anything at all.

The ensuing generation, the linguistic analysts, reacted by reinstating everything – 'each field of discourse has its own appropriate logic' – and held that philosophical problems are only muddles into which we are enticed by our misuse of language. There is no need to explain why serious philosophical problems were neglected by people who did not believe such things existed. But it did mean that for the second generation running there were whole areas of philosophy in which little work of substance was done. Nevertheless much positive good had been achieved: the logical positivists gave a powerful stimulus to philosophical interest in logic, mathematics and the sciences generally; the linguistic analysts raised the techniques of informal logic to an unprecedented level of sophistication. And there was even more negative good: each of the two schools, in its different way, exposed the inadequacy of large amounts of hitherto plausible philosophizing. So if they left much of the ground barren it must at least be said that they cleared it; and this is a contribution of great historical importance. The conditions are now present for new growth. And new growth is beginning to stir. Also, some of the older philosophers who were never orthodox are at last coming into their own. There are still plenty of language analysts about, and there are even a few characters who look suspiciously like logical positivists; but their numbers are decreasing, and with negligible exceptions they themselves no longer regard theirs as the only legitimate way to philosophize.

One result of this attitude is an unprecedented openness to influences from outside. In this respect the present volume could be misleading: it probably represents the last attempt that will be possible to discuss contemporary British philosophy solely in terms of British philosophers and their work. Even so, the living philosopher referred to by more contributors than any other in this volume is the American Chomsky. Another American, Quine, is described by Stuart Hampshire as 'the most distinguished living systematic philosopher'. Anthony Quinton discusses Australian materialism at some length. If this volume does have a successor it will have to give individual treatment to each of these. British philosophy is no longer autonomous in the way it once was – indeed, it seems on the way to becoming the chief province in a territory whose capital is elsewhere. A chance but expressive fact is that when the first letters of invitation were sent to the contributors to this volume it was found that six of the thirteen were currently in North America. Twenty years ago this would almost certainly not have been the case: today it is utterly unsurprising. Also, more and more of our philosophers are choosing to publish their most important papers in American journals. *Mind* may still be the leading philosophical journal in England but it is no longer the leading philosophical journal in English. There does remain a parochial element in British philosophy; but its significance has changed – parochialism is an unimportant fault when the most important events happen to be in one's parish (which was the case in England when Russell, Whitehead, Moore and Wittgenstein were at Cambridge together).

The need to go at some length into the recent background of philosophy in order to make the present clear means that this volume is by way of being an introduction not just to contemporary British philosophy but to British philosophy in this century. Stuart Hampshire calls the whole period 'the age of Russell'; and it is extraordinary how every important line of development stems from Russell, or is at least vitally nourished by him. He was part-creator of the very subject of mathematical logic. His Theory of Descriptions fathered the kind of logical analysis of ordinary-language propositions which has been one of the main concerns of British philosophy ever since. His friend Moore worked off him for much of the time. His pupil Wittgenstein, in the *Tractatus*, pushed to its extreme a doctrine first propounded by him – and that book in its turn became the text most influential on the Vienna Circle. To quote Hampshire again, 'Carnap and the logical positivist school associated with him started from Russell's programme of logical analysis and – abandoning his metaphysics – provided a simplified diagram of the structure of natural knowledge, and of mathematical knowledge, which Russell

did not accept. Quine . . . equally starts from and develops Russell.'
So does Strawson. And the quite different school devoted to the re-
construction of Humean empiricism – a school of which A. J. Ayer is
the most noted member – claims Russell as its immediate progenitor.
Popper, who is at odds with so many of his contemporaries about
so much, is at one with them in acknowledging Russell as a major
influence. Even philosophies abominated by Russell, like those of the
late Wittgenstein and other schools of linguistic analysis, were, as has
so often been pointed out, directly descended from his work.

It is ironical that the era which began with Russell's (and Moore's)
breakaway, as young men, from the German tradition in philosophy
should be ending with, among other things, a revival of interest in
that tradition on the part of so many intelligent young people. To me
it seems the greatest possible mistake to regard the two traditions as
being necessarily opposed. The reason why both so obstinately
thrive is that each gives a central place to valid considerations which
are underestimated by the other. No systematic philosophy (and
perhaps no philosophy) can be satisfactory which does not draw on
both. Wittgenstein's certainly did – and so does the philosophical
practice of many of the contributors to this volume, in ways that can
differ as widely as Strawson's and Popper's. Even Russell was more
Kantian than he knew. Impatience on the part of the young with
recent British philosophy is, while only partially, nevertheless vitally
mistaken. And philosophy itself is impoverished by the mistake. A
striking amount of the most valuable and influential philosophy has
been produced by young men. To take examples only from the British
tradition: all the works for which Berkeley is now famous were
published when he was in his twenties; and what is arguably the
greatest work of philosophy in the English language, Hume's
Treatise of Human Nature, was completed when the author was 25.
The period covered by the present volume yields many examples.
G. E. Moore was 30 when he published *Principia Ethica*. Russell was
31 when he published *The Principles of Mathematics* and 33 when he
published his Theory of Descriptions; the whole of *Principia Mathematica* was written while he was in his thirties. Wittgenstein was 32
when he published the *Tractatus*, having finished it when he was 29.
Karl Popper was 32 when he published *The Logic of Scientific Discovery*. A. J. Ayer was 25 when he published *Language, Truth and
Logic*. There are no such figures now – indeed, it says something
both about the recent state of the subject and about the attitude
towards it of the gifted young that there have been no such figures for
more than a generation. But we are, I am convinced, about to see a
change in this.

A word about the provenance of the present volume. My original intention had been to make each conversation a genuine dialogue, turning often into argument. But this proved impracticable – first because, for an audience which could not be presumed to be already familiar with the subject matter, most of the time had to be given over to exposition anyway; and second because time was not then sufficient to allow two different and opposing views of the same subject matter to be put clearly and unconfusingly. So, once having chosen which subjects to deal with, and which contributors to invite, I cast myself in the role of an interlocutor whose task was to elicit from a protagonist a single, coherent view.

Conversations 1 to 7 focus on the work of individual philosophers (in four of them that of the protagonist himself) and 9 to 12 on various recognized fields within philosophy. Between these two groups I have inserted a discussion among Popper, Strawson and Warnock about aspects of Russell's philosophy which were not covered in the foregoing conversation with Hampshire. For reasons set out earlier in this Preface, Russell's work and influence call for more extended treatment than those of any other philosopher of our period. Hampshire himself ends by expressing the wish that he could have covered more ground, in particular the Theory of Descriptions, which is taken up at length in the discussion. (The theory is in fact discussed at three different points in the book, and I know some readers will find this helpful: not only is it the most influential philosophical theory in English of this century, it also happens to be difficult.) I have put the discussion in its present position rather than immediately after the Hampshire conversation because the reader will see more of the implications of what is said, and be able to read more between the lines, if he is familiar with the conversations of which Popper, Strawson and Warnock are themselves the sole protagonists, and also the conversation about the two philosophies of Wittgenstein. There are also the small but legitimate points that, coming where it does, it marks the change from one kind of subject matter to another, and also provides a refreshing contrast of form between two series of conversations.

My warmest appreciation goes to the Head of BBC Radio 3, P. H. Newby, for making this whole project possible, and to the Producer, George MacBeth, for leaving me to do it all in my own way – thanks to both of them, responsibility for any fault in the series is mine. I would like also to thank Drusilla Montgomerie and Enid Robinson for sharing the arduous burdens of transcribing and typing.

B.M.

Conversation with Anthony Quinton

Introduction

MAGEE: People coming to contemporary British philosophy for the first time will probably find it helpful if we start with a general survey of the ground to be covered, before we get down to cases. I've already made the point that if we want to understand what living philosophers are doing we can't consider only the living: the work of certain recently dead philosophers is in the forefront of attention – I'm thinking particularly of Wittgenstein and Austin, and also Russell and Moore. These names come up over and over again whenever philosophers are writing, teaching, or discussing among themselves. In order to understand what's going on today we've got to know what they were doing, and that means going back some way to find the starting point for this series of conversations. There's usually a problem in deciding where to break into a continuous history, but in this case, fortunately, something like a natural starting point occurs where two of the people I've just mentioned, Russell and Moore, broke away from the German Idealism which had dominated British philosophy up to then.

Anthony Quinton, can we take the story on from there?

QUINTON: Yes, I think it's always useful to explain something by contrast with something quite different. I think everyone would agree that there is a genuine continuity in British philosophy since the great year of 1903 when Russell's and Moore's first vitally important works came out. That continuity consists in the fact that all the variations of philosophical style that have existed since that time have had the common property of taking philosophy to be an essentially critical activity. This wasn't a conviction that sprang fully formed from the first reflections on philosophy of Russell and Moore, but it was something into which their very strong reaction against the Absolute Idealism of the late nineteenth century developed.

MAGEE: Can we start with what they were reacting against? Is it possible for you to give a concise outline of the orthodoxy from which they broke away?

QUINTON: As I said, the main theme of all these continuously related styles of philosophy in the twentieth century has been the view of philosophy as a critical, or as people sometimes say analytic, undertaking. One needs a corresponding term to explain what's basic to Absolute Idealism. It's clear to start with that Absolute Idealism was an exceedingly ambitious way of doing philosophy. It was above all not critical so much as constructive. The Absolute Idealist conceived the philosopher to have at his disposal a method of thinking which was altogether superior to the styles of thinking that people investigating particular departments of reality had at their disposal. There's an old distinction, inherited ultimately from Kant, between reason and understanding. Understanding is the method of thought used by scientists, by historians, and even more by ordinary men in their practical dealings with the world round them. But reason is thought of as a higher kind of thinking, and what for the Absolute Idealist is characteristic or definitive of the philosopher is that he employs reason. Now this is a very antiquated notion in some ways. You can trace it back, possibly, to Parmenides – the first really full-blooded, argumentative metaphysician there ever was, or that we know of. The idea is that the philosopher with his special method of reason can find out the truth about reality, while ordinary men deal only with appearance. And so the philosopher is raised up by this version of what his powers and responsibilities are to an altogether higher status than other types of thinker.

MAGEE: When Russell and Moore went up to Cambridge as undergraduates, this prevailing orthodoxy gave them their first philosophical education. But they broke away from it as very young men, Moore leading the way, Russell following closely. What were the breaking points?

QUINTON: They were quite different for the two of them because they both had quite different initial expertises. Moore began as a classical scholar, and as a properly trained classical scholar had a very exact sense of the precise meaning of words. Constant training in translations, proses, the construction of Greek verses, develops a very precise sense of what words definitely mean. But this perhaps had more to do with Moore's technique than with his fundamental attitude. His attitude was one of massive common sense. He persisted in a complete refusal to be hypnotized, to be taken in by vast masses of edifying and exciting-looking expository verbiage. Armed with his solicitor-like precision in the use of words, and with a very simple, straightforward, commonsensical conviction that certain things at any rate were quite indubitable, whatever the elaborate contraptions of philosophers might suggest to the contrary, he simply found the whole Idealist structure looking to him like a fraud. Now Russell has never been so fond of common sense as this: he has said, for example, that common sense embodies the metaphysics of savages. Russell has constantly attacked the latest developments of the philosophy that so largely springs from him because of this commonsensicality and has condemned it as intellectually torpid, unadventurous and generally deplorable.

MAGEE: There's a phrase in *The Problems of Philosophy*: 'The truth about physical objects *must* be strange.'

QUINTON: Yes, that's highly characteristic. Russell's point of entry into philosophy was quite different from Moore's. His initial training was in mathematics, and in mathematics the very precise separation of conceptions from one another is essential. Mathematical reasoning is a very exact, rule-governed process that has to be of the utmost explicitness at all times. There's no reliance on vague analogies and metaphors in the reasoning, however much they may figure in the creative work of the mathematician. What he found was that mathematics could not be reconciled with Idealism, for all its enchantment. I think he's a much more impressible figure than Moore: his whole career has shown him to be immensely sensitive to a vast range of intellectual influences, and because he's a more impressible figure I think he felt the fascination of Idealism much more than Moore ever did. But the fact that he was a highly gifted mathematician made it impossible for him to swallow Absolute Idealism in the end. So coming from these two quite different directions – from what is in some ways the most abstract, sophisticated, remote and unpedestrian of intellectual activities, in Russell's case, and from the everyday solid confidence in the definite reality of chairs and tables in Moore's case – there was a curious convergence of the two against the consoling idea that philosophy could somehow rise above the harsh reality of innumerable things separate from one another and merely contingently arranged, and could give a totally new picture of the world as a rational unity.

MAGEE: They did still believe, though, that we could arrive at substantial knowledge of fact by pure reason.

QUINTON: Yes, though the kind of fact that they thought could be attained was of a rather specialized kind. Perhaps one might just call it abstract fact, or – to bring in a philosophical technical term – facts about universals. When he had rejected the whole idealist attitude towards the nature of thought, Russell was left with the problem of giving some alternative account of mathematics, and this drove him back to the kind of account that you find in Plato, where mathematics isn't like botany or geology or what have you, isn't about concrete, perceptible objects, but is about a class of special abstract, totally perfect objects which in their perfection aren't fully present in – but only more or less approximated to by – things in the observable world. So the mathematician was seen by Russell, in his earliest writings on the nature of mathematical knowledge, as a kind of geographer of this realm of abstract entities. The account of mathematical knowledge which he gives is that it is a description of the relations of abstract entities, things accessible to the intellect but not directly accessible to the senses. Having vindicated a non-empirical knowledge of this sort for the mathematician, it was then natural to extend it and say that the philosopher's stock-in-trade is knowledge of essentially the same kind. And in what, I suppose, is still very much the best guide to the kind of ideas that Russell and Moore had in the first decade of this century – Russell's *Problems of Philosophy* – this is a very central theme.

MAGEE: What sort of positive view of the world – not of philosophy, but of the way things are – did Moore and Russell arrive at after their rejection of their predecessors?

QUINTON: That can be put quite straightforwardly in quite a small number of propositions. The first of these is that the world isn't in any substantial sense a unity, but consists of a vast number of things of a number of different kinds: each of these things is perfectly capable of being conceived to exist on its own. That the world consists of so many things, and of things of so many different kinds, is just a brute fact. This is the pluralistic element in their point of view. The other side of it – one had better call it realistic – is that things of different kinds have just as good a claim to being regarded as real as each other. They didn't want to give any preferential status to minds and mental states as contrasted with material objects. As far as Moore and Russell were concerned, there is the physical world, consisting of material objects. Then there is the mental world, parcelled out between an indefinitely large number of minds. The physical world impinges on these minds, causes ideas, sensations, experiences to occur in them. It is in virtue of this causal influence of the material world on minds that knowledge of that world is achieved by these minds. Thirdly, there is another kind of reality, which they were perfectly prepared to admit and to which they accorded an equal status to that of the mental and the physical: this is the realm of the abstract or logical, of those universals of which I was speaking. They thought that there is a timeless world of abstractions which the mathematician most conspicuously, but the philosopher too, perhaps, in a more faltering, stumbling kind of way, tells us about the contents of. Finally, there's a fourth order of reality, if I can call it so – the order of values. Moore maintained that goodness and badness are pro-perties of things, but he insisted that they are non-natural properties – that's to say properties that we can't find out about by relying on the senses. This, of course, totally detaches them from human experiences of pleasure and pain.

MAGEE: Moore and Russell themselves became very much the dominating figures on the English philosophical scene, and remained so well into the thirties. The next really large-scale innovation from an English philosopher came with the publication of A. J. Ayer's *Language, Truth and Logic* in January 1936.

QUINTON: We need to go a little more into the connecting tissue here. On the whole, up to about 1914, Russell and Moore, despite the differences between them, were operating more or less on the same basis and supporting each other. Russell was then converted away from Moore's views about value. Perhaps the most important thing that happened was the arrival of Wittgenstein in Cambridge, in the years just before 1914, to work with Russell. A very fruitful mutual influence developed between them. What particularly drew Witt-genstein to Cambridge was not so much Russell's philosophy – the thing he shared with Moore – but Russell's work in logic. By using Russell's logic, Wittgenstein convinced Russell that mathematical propositions were really tautologies, that they were purely conceptual truths, that they didn't state pieces of information about a world of universals. This is an idea that Russell was rather unwilling to accept from Wittgenstein, as indeed many people have been, because it seems, though it shouldn't, to undermine the claims of mathematics to being important. It doesn't really imply this at all: it merely argues that the reasons why the most complicated discoveries of pure mathe-matics are true are in the end the same reasons that make it true that all wives are women: the antecedently assigned meanings of the terms involved in these propositions are such that any denial of the proposition involves a contradiction. This view had been suggested in various ways by many people beforehand in the reasonably remote philosophical past – by, for instance Hume and Leibniz – but it wasn't until Russell's logic had argued that the whole of mathematics was strictly continuous with the most elementary parts of logic that this idea, which had previously been a more or less reasonable conjecture, could be presented as a solid and reasonably coercive argument. From the time of Wittgenstein's arrival in Cambridge Russell deviates from Moore a good deal. Moore sticks to the rather narrow range of problems (particularly those of the perception of the external world and of the meaning and justification of moral judgments) which have always been the central stock-in-trade of British philosophers, whereas Russell is concerned with a more wide-ranging collection of problems: most importantly, the problems which would nowadays constitute the subject of philosophical logic – problems about the nature of meaning and of truth, problems about the necessity of propositions, of what it is that makes some propositions necessarily true. This body of interests has become a philosophical discipline in its own right. The first really comprehensive book on the subject is Wittgenstein's very difficult *Tractatus Logico-Philosophicus*, where the whole question of what it is for a sentence to have meaning is raised, and a rather surprising answer is given: namely, that for a proposition to have meaning it must picture a fact. Either a proposition is a single picture or else it is a collection of pictures, and any proposition, therefore, that isn't by itself a single picture of some fact or possible fact must be decomposable or analysable into a set of elementary propositions of this kind – propositions that in themselves have a direct connection with the world. This was all done in a very general, abstract way by Wittgenstein: he didn't say what the facts themselves were like, what kind of facts they were, just that there must be an array of facts for the basic sentences of language to correlate with.

Now the logical positivism which developed to a very large extent out of Wittgenstein's *Tractatus* arose from taking this abstract structure that Wittgenstein had put forward, and giving it a particular application. The essential step is the idea that the elementary or basic propositions of language describe sense experiences, immediate experiences – the occurrence of colour patches in the visual fields of observers, the hearing of sounds, the smelling of smells. And when you make this application of Wittgenstein's fundamental doctrine about meaning, what you get is something that is well-known as the central thesis of logical positivism – the verificationist doctrine that for a form of words to have a meaning is for it to be correlated with some type of experience which makes it true, and whose failure to occur would falsify it. And this has been used by the logical positivists as a general critical weapon in philosophical activity. It has all sorts of consequences – some destructive, some explanatory.

MAGEE: By now we've arrived at a view which is not only unlike that held by the Idealists but also unlike that held by Russell and Moore – namely, the view that no knowledge of fact can be arrived at by reason alone, that all knowledge of fact must be based on observation. Is that right?

QUINTON: Certainly. All knowledge of substantial matters of fact about the world not only must be based on observation, but really is a more or less complicated reporting of the contents of observation. It doesn't tell one about quite independent things that cause these observations, although it may look as if it does so. To talk about a material world is to talk about a kind of order that experience may exhibit, a lawful regular order that can exist in one's observations. That is the positivist account of empirical reality. But there's also to be explained the abstract reality, which Russell and Moore in their early days had taken mathematics to describe. Mathematical knowledge is accounted for by the positivists as purely conceptual in character. There isn't an order of independently existing fact which it describes. Essentially, mathematics is a technique of inference: mathematical propositions tell you how to get from one piece of information – for example, that you have two things and another two things – to another piece of information, or really the same piece of information differently stated – that you have four things. No one's going to find that very interesting in the case of such a very elementary mathematical truth. The more exciting part of the doctrine is that the same thing, despite appearances, is the case with all the propositions of mathematics. So the propositions of mathematics don't tell you anything substantial about the world. But this doesn't mean that they aren't vitally useful for the organization of knowledge.

MAGEE: My impression is that even today, in the 1970s, a lot of people – well educated but not educated in philosophy – are under the impression that contemporary philosophy is logical positivism. Some are even hostile to it on the basis of that false assumption. But when I studied philosophy at Oxford there was an examination question: 'Does anything now survive of the influence of logical positivism?' And that was getting on for twenty years ago. Obviously logical positivism is even more a movement of the past now than it was then. Why was it rejected?

QUINTON: Perhaps an explanation of the point of view of the people you are speaking about is called for. I think there's perhaps one quite literary explanation for it – namely, that no book has supplanted Ayer's *Language, Truth and Logic* as an ideally accessible book on more or less contemporary philosophy. There it is, beautifully written, exquisitely lucid, and nothing has come out to take its place as a book in which to find out what's going on. Of course, what it reported was what was going on in 1936. Ayer himself, in fact, has remained broadly loyal to many of the fundamental theses of that book, but he's qualified them a good deal. It's perfectly correct to say that the general movement has been away from them. There are two main factors which have led in this direction. The first is the development by Wittgenstein of a completely new point of view in philosophy. Before 1914 Wittgenstein was at Cambridge. In the 1914 War he was with the Austrian Army. He was taken prisoner. While he was a prisoner he wrote up the ideas he'd developed when working with Russell before the War. These were published in the very early twenties. Then Wittgenstein gave up philosophy until 1929 or thereabouts. He returned to England and in due course became Professor of Philosophy in Cambridge. And around 1929 it would appear that his views were actually much closer to positivism than the views expressed in the *Tractatus*: that's to say, he was prepared to come very near to accepting what the positivists had done with the *Tractatus* – the particular application they had made of it. And then he moved away from this altogether. One might say about positivism that it is a philosophical defence of the intellectual pre-eminence of science and mathematics. It takes these as the supreme ways of exercising human rationality.

MAGEE: And of gaining knowledge about the world.

QUINTON: Yes. And any form of thought or discourse that doesn't essentially amount to mathematics or science is, as it were, noise or exhaust. Now it was this excessively partisan commitment of the positivists that came to be abandoned in due course. First of all it was contended that the verification principle itself was impossible to formulate in a way that would really do what the positivists wanted it to do. This is a fairly technical difficulty, but a serious one, which produced a certain loss of nerve in positivists themselves. Then some of the particular philosophical applications were thought to be just strictly incredible: the view that the most ordinary statements about material things in one's neighbourhood are really highly complicated theoretical statements about the possible course of one's sense-experience, the idea that all judgments of value (that the deliberate

infliction of human suffering is wrong, for example) are just expressions of emotional tendencies, and in general the type of scepticism about that which was not mathematics and science, strictly
speaking – these just seemed incredible. At this point, Moore's rock-
like common sense is brought into play. So, on the one hand, the
technical arguments and analyses of the positivists ran into all sorts
of specific difficulties, and, on the other, the broad implications
about what could be taken as literally true about the world seemed
quite unacceptable. There's a well-known remark of the late eight-
eenth-century Scottish philosopher, Thomas Reid, about the beliefs
of common sense: that they're older and of more authority than all
the arguments of philosophy. The basis of the reaction to positivism
was a point of view that that remark of Reid's expresses. Its insistence on giving an account of the real meaning of statements
came into collision with the specific accounts it gave of the meaning
of certain sorts of statements: it seemed that we just couldn't mean
by our ordinary beliefs about our material environment what,
according to positivism, we should have to mean. In a very general
way this is what the reaction amounted to. But it is a quite inadequate
account of the later philosophy of Wittgenstein. One way of present-
ing that would be to say that Wittgenstein abandoned his earlier
conviction that Russell's logic somehow represented the essential
skeleton, or bone structure, of any human thinking worthy of the
name. Russell's logic was perhaps an account of the structure of
certain kinds of formalized mathematical thinking, but formalized
mathematical thinking, though a very remarkable thing, was just
one kind of thinking. Wittgenstein's reaction against his earlier
rather programmatic work can be seen as a reaction towards a new
kind of empiricism – an empiricism about thought and language. He
agrees that what we're concerned with in philosophy, first of all at
any rate, is the understanding of meaning, but to understand meaning we have to see what people actually do in what they take to be
the meaningful use of terms. When we do investigate this, we find all
sorts of different activities going on – most of them very different
from the presentation of mathematical theorems or the development
of scientific theories. Meaning is not to be explained as a correlation
between words and immediate experience, but in terms of the use of
words in all the varied circumstances of life in which they are used.
This reversion to a more empiricist attitude to meaning goes with a
readiness to admit that there can be a vast variety of different ways
in which language can be effectively employed, and goes also with a
hostility, generated by that recognition, to the presentation of any
very general theories of meaning. Wittgenstein saw his own earlier
work as the result of an obsession with the idea that you could

produce some unified omnicompetent theory of meaning. And what he practised in his later writings was an immensely piecemeal *ad hoc* investigation of different kinds of problematic utterance.

MAGEE: So now we've arrived at something that comes under the umbrella term of linguistic philosophy – which could be described as any philosophy based on the assumption that the subject-matter of philosophy is linguistic. (Incidentally this is an assumption that Russell vigorously rejected to the end of his life.) Who were its major practitioners?

QUINTON: Wittgenstein was the dominating figure, of course, in Cambridge, and despite his extreme cageyness about publication during his lifetime his ideas did spread among philosophers in general. In Oxford the leading figures were Ryle and Austin. And despite the immense differences of style between Wittgenstein's writings and Ryle's, Ryle's main work, *The Concept of Mind* – a remarkable literary object and perhaps the best book to read to get an idea of the linguistic philosophy of the period 1945–60 – is essentially on the themes of Wittgenstein's later philosophy. The starting-point of Wittgenstein's later views, as I said, is a totally new attitude to the question of investigating meaning. This leads into the subject that was most preoccupying philosophers in that post-war period – the philosophy of mind. The meaningful use of language, or thinking, is a mental activity. Hitherto that had always been conceived as operations going on inside the mind of the meaner or thinker. Wittgenstein's insistence that one should ascertain the meaning of a word or sentence by seeing how it is actually used in real public circumstances is backed up by a lot of argumentation: for example, that there couldn't possibly be a wholly private language, that language is of necessity a public phenomenon. This is a support for his attitude to the investigation of meaning. It also leads into the view that not just meaning and thinking but all mental phenomena must be discovered by considering the activities and circumstances of the persons to whom they're ascribed. Now people have often characterized the philosophy of mind that emerges in the writings of Wittgenstein and Ryle as behaviouristic. And it is in a way. This needs to be qualified to some extent, but at any rate it's not a grotesque misrepresentation to say that it leans in a behaviouristic direction. In Ryle, indeed, this tendency is pretty pronounced. Ryle says that to talk about anyone's mental state, your own or somebody else's, is to talk about what they're likely to do, what their dispositions to behaviour are. This was the most canvassed area of philosophy in the fifteen years after 1945, and it took up a subject which had not been utterly ignored before, but had not been thought of as one of the central fields of interest. The idea that necessary truth is analytical, verbal or conceptual, continues to prevail in some form or other, though it has been interestingly criticized by the American logician and philosopher Quine. The phenomenalist theory of perception that was characteristic of positivism – the idea that all our beliefs about the material world, although they may not look like that, are in fact beliefs about the potential course of our experience – was abandoned, or widely criticized and not very much supported. This was one of Austin's main interests. Perhaps Austin's most accessible book is *Sense and Sensibilia*, which is a penetrating attack on the assumptions of phenomenalism.

MAGEE: And is in fact a criticism of Ayer's second book, *The Foundations of Empirical Knowledge*.

QUINTON: Yes, for the most part it confines itself to the main contentions of Ayer's book on perception. Austin is very careful not to advance a positive theory co-ordinate with Ayer's and in direct competition with it. That caution of Austin's is part of a resistance to general theorizing that critics of linguistic philosophy found particularly objectionable.

MAGEE: Wittgenstein has been dead for twenty years. It's over twenty years since *The Concept of Mind* was published. Austin has been dead ten years. What's happening now?

QUINTON: Curiously, quite a number of things happened together in 1959. In the first place two books were published in that year – Strawson's *Individuals* and Hampshire's *Thought and Action* – which nobody could object to on the score of desultoriness, or lack of comprehensiveness, or lack of theory. These were both very large and ambitious works which covered a great deal of ground. The main point of Strawson's was to identify what the fundamental subjects of discourse had to be in order that the other things that we talk about should be capable of being talked about at all. This takes in a very large area indeed, and the doctrine presented has a pretty systematic character. Hampshire's book covers much the same ground in the first and admittedly the longest of its four chapters – and then goes on to a large number of other issues. Now what has happened in the last decade? One thing is the resurrection of a certain kind of scientism in philosophy. I said earlier that positivism was a kind of philosophical defence of mathematics and science as the ideal forms of human thinking. Something like that has come about again, there's a doctrine called the identity theory which, in defiance of one of the most firmly rooted philosophical convictions, says that as a matter of fact the mental states of human beings are literally identical with certain conditions in their brains or nervous systems generally. For some reason or other this was first propounded by and has received its most energetic support from philosophers in Australia, so that it's sometimes even called 'Australian Materialism'. But it's certainly been one of the more widely discussed issues of recent times. It has quite a large set of cultural implications, because one of the things that was most characteristic of Wittgenstein's account of the mind was his view that human actions, human decisions, human intentions, the whole area of man's life as an agent – his activities, and the decisions and intentions that lead up to his activities – aren't capable of being causally explained. The implication of this is that there couldn't be a science of human behaviour, that there could be no such thing really as psychology or sociology as these are usually conceived by their practitioners. To put it in more metaphysical language, man isn't a part of nature. It all started, this idea of Wittgenstein's, from a very simple initial point. What, he says, is the difference between my arm going up and my raising my arm? Now somebody might say: my raising my arm is caused by an act of will, whereas my arm just going up may be due to some small muscular seizure somewhere around my shoulder, and the difference between the two events will be a matter of the difference between their causes. Wittgenstein said that there is no act of volition which precedes one's arm going up and turns it into a case of one's raising one's arm. To say a man raised his arm is to say something very much more complicated than that he raised his arm as a result of an act of will: it's to say something about the sort of thing he would say if you asked him what he was doing and what the circumstances were. Now out of this apparently small point, a very large-scale philosophical collision can develop between those who say man is a part of nature and that what is most important about man as an active being is embodied in the scientific picture of the world (a view strongly supported by the identity theory I mentioned a moment ago) and those who take the opposite view that human actions need to be understood as a kind of thing quite different from natural happenings.

Another thing that's happened recently is the recognition by philosophers of the relevance of recent developments in the science of linguistics. I'm thinking here most conspicuously of the work of Chomsky. It's natural enough that a science of linguistics should be taken account of by a kind of philosophy that thinks of itself as very centrally concerned with the phenomenon of human language. The type of linguistics that Chomsky practises, which is not just a history of the changes of language but an endeavour to give a cross-sectional analysis of whole languages, an account of their fundamental structure, is of obvious relevance to a philosophical interest in language. An interesting thing about Chomsky is that there's a certain affinity between his account of human nature, considered from the point of view of linguistics, and the more or less Wittgensteinian doctrine that man isn't part of the causal operations of nature. This isn't to say that Chomsky doesn't think that what he's doing is science: it's presented as a science and it endeavours to adhere to the recognized principles of scientific method. But his main philosophically interesting conclusion is that the human power to learn and use language can't be explained behaviouristically: you can't take human beings as plastic objects that from birth onwards are subjected to certain more or less linguistic stimuli and are conditioned by these into becoming things which can understand the speech of others and speak themselves. What Chomsky maintains is that the human power to use language in a way that's characteristic of humans, to make totally new sentences out of bits of familiar linguistic material, can be explained only if we credit human beings with some kind of innate mental structure which allows them to acquire the languages that they do. This is something very fundamental in human beings which differentiates them from the rest of nature, even if it isn't as fundamental a differentiation as the Wittgensteinian one which holds that the methods that are appropriate to the investigation of non-human nature just won't work on men. Furthermore, there is a very close connection between Chomsky's views about human nature as derived from the study of human language, on the one hand – this purely neutral, impersonal, intellectual field of interest of his – and his well-known moral and political views, on the other. One of the things that Chomsky has most violently attacked in recent American policy is the application of social science for politically dominative purposes, the endeavour to apply the findings of social science to the pacification of peasant populations in South-East Asia. This might be thought to have nothing whatever to do with Chomsky's technical work in linguistics, nevertheless they do seem to support each other. Both embody an idea of the special uniqueness of man, who on the one hand is the only true language-user and on the other is the moral agent *par excellence*, the type of entity in the world about which moral issues primarily arise. These two uniquenesses are linked in Chomsky's case by a bond of sympathy. This is particularly interesting because, as I said, his starting-point is of a rigorously scientific character.

Now the type of philosophy that I call scientistic, by which I mean positivism in the thirties or the Australian materialism of more recent years, is the type most disliked by highly progressive or radical people – the New Left, broadly speaking, at the present time. The hostility of the more articulate radical students towards official academic philosophy is strongly directed at its scientistic aspects, and yet their hero, as undoubtedly Chomsky is and with very good reason, is himself, in his technical work, scientistic. Of course, the New Left is also hostile to linguistic philosophy of the immediately post-war kind, although the moral extremism of the New Left is as much present in Wittgenstein's attitude to the world, even though it doesn't take quite the same form. A widespread view about linguistic philosophy is that it's complacent, quietist, conformist, utterly satisfied with the world as it is and with language as it is, viewing the task of the philosopher as a kind of marginal tidying-up. A placatory message of this kind is seen as the broad social implication of linguistic philosophy. There's nothing very much positive for philosophy to do. There are these well-established intellectual procedures – morality, science and so forth – which are basically all right, so that all the philosopher has to do is to clear away confusions about them that people have. Now that is something the radical-minded strongly oppose. But they oppose scientism even more strongly, because what they see, and not altogether incorrectly, in scientistic philosophies like positivism is what they regard as propaganda for technology. The hatred of a technologically dominated civilization extends to what looks like its philosophical justification. Indeed it is frequently alleged by people on the far critical Left that analytic philosophy as a whole is a hand-maiden for science, that science is a destructive monster, and that the blame for its monstrosities which attaches to science also attaches to the philosophy which plays the part of its supporter or rhinoceros-bird or jackal. So one might say that both phases of analytic philosophy, its positivistic phase and its linguistic phase, are objects of hostility to the more radical elements of the student population. In that group there's a much greater interest in and sympathy for the type of philosophies practised on the continent of Europe. There's a great deal of enthusiasm for Marx of a quite understandable kind, and it inevitably focuses on the younger and more explicitly moral and humanitarian Marx – the Marx that's in closest relation to Hegel. It's towards a thickening of philosophy with at any rate the interests of, even if not the explicit doctrines of, philosophers like Hegel and Marx that the younger critics of the orthodox state of affairs in philosophy are looking.

MAGEE: One striking thing about the whole account you've given is that it moves from German Idealism to German Idealism. We started at the beginning of the century with a predominantly Hegelian orthodoxy from which a couple of brilliant young men broke away – and now in the 1970s we're finding that the intelligent young have a renewed interest in precisely those rejected philosophers: Hegel, the young Marx, and then more recent German Idealists.

1
Conversation with Stuart Hampshire

The Philosophy of Russell: I

MAGEE: If any one individual is to be regarded as the founding father of the modern movement in philosophy it is unquestionably Bertrand Russell.

He wrote more than 60 books; and even allowing for the fact that less than one-third of them are works of technical philosophy I don't think any other great philosopher – not even Plato – has been so productive over so long a period. Inevitably, many of his ideas changed over time. Often he himself was the first to point to a flaw in something he had published. So whereas most great philosophers seem to have managed to write one or two masterpieces in which their fully developed views are presented, Russell wrote no such masterpiece, in my opinion, but, instead, umpteen flawed and superseded books. His whole life's work was an open-ended, ongoing, continuously self-critical process – one of the many extraordinarily impressive things about it.

He was born in 1872, which means of course that his first full decade of adult life was the nineties. At Cambridge he studied first mathematics, then philosophy; his first book of lasting importance, published in 1900, was a study of the mathematician-philosopher Leibniz. In 1903 came *The Principles of Mathematics*, and in 1910 the first of the three massive volumes of *Principia Mathematica*, which he wrote in collaboration with Alfred North Whitehead. Up to this point, then, it was all mathematical philosophy. He did not turn to general philosophy until his little book *The Problems of Philosophy*, which was published in 1912, the year he became 40. After that he pursued the two together and in conjunction. A few of the most important titles are *Our Knowledge of the External World*, published in 1914, *The Philosophy of Logical Atomism*, 1918, *The Analysis of*

Mind, 1921 – and one might mention *The Analysis of Matter*, 1927. Then comes a gap, the interwar period during which he was immersed in political, social and educational activities. Then in 1940 *An Enquiry into Meaning and Truth*; and in 1948 his last original work of philosophy: *Human Knowledge – Its Scope and Limits*. He himself tried to sum up his half-century of philosophizing in a book published in 1959 called *My Philosophical Development*, which is invaluable as an authoritative retrospect.

Mr Hampshire, when Russell died it emerged that a lot of people were under the impression that he is regarded as a great philosopher because of his writings on social problems, politics, morals, education and so on – and of course this isn't the case at all. So I'd like to start our discussion by asking you to take on the difficult task of explaining why Russell really is a great philosopher.

HAMPSHIRE: I think one must start from his work in logic. *Principia Mathematica*, which he wrote with Whitehead, was the supreme intellectual achievement of his life, and, as he states in his autobiography, the most exhausting one. It was the source-book of modern mathematical logic and a great classic. It set out to show the foundations of mathematics in a few central notions of logic, and it was the beginning of a new science which has made extraordinary progress in the years since *Principia Mathematica* was published. He re-created the subject, and established his notation for it. He attempted to derive the whole of classical mathematics from a few elementary truths. And he attempted to show, for example, in his definition of number, that the central notions of mathematics could be defined in terms of logical notions, the notion of number in terms of the notion of class. But I don't intend in this discussion to dwell on Russell as a logician, for two reasons, the first of which is that I'm not a logician myself, and the second of which is that as a philosopher, as opposed to a pure logician, Russell's greatest achievement was to apply the discoveries that were made in formal logic to the analysis of propositions that we assert in our ordinary knowledge claims, our ordinary speech about the world.

MAGEE: So when he moved from mathematical logic to general philosophy it wasn't an arbitrary move but an attempt to apply techniques developed in mathematical logic to problems in general philosophy.

HAMPSHIRE: He took philosophy to be the search for the skeleton forms of different types of proposition and an attempt to discover the systematic relations of dependence between these different types. It was always his belief that there were standard or canonical forms buried beneath the various casual grammars of the natural languages. So his continuing enterprise was to use logic to clarify our ordinary knowledge claims within a systematic theory of logical form; and he believed that this would lead to new discoveries in metaphysics, that the raising of answerable questions about the ultimate elements in reality depended upon an analysis of propositions and the division of them into types. I think perhaps the best way of classifying what this enterprise was is to consider that early work which you have just mentioned, his study of the philosophy of Leibniz. I think probably it's the best work ever written by one philosopher about another; and it comes early in Russell's life, after a work on geometry and after his first book, which was itself brilliant and original, a set of lectures on German Social Democracy, which were given in the first session of the London School of Economics. *The Philosophy of Leibniz* is a study, superbly clear and beautifully written, of the logical doctrines upon which, as Russell believes, Leibniz's metaphysics was founded. Leibniz himself, Russell claims, believed that the picture of the world as consisting of independent substances, monads, was forced upon him by an analysis of the claims to truth that we make in simple propositions of the subject-predicate form. Russell criticized Leibniz's metaphysics by criticizing this central tenet of his logic. He set out to show that if you analyse propositions into the subject-predicate form, as Leibniz did, and required that all propositions should assume this form, you would be led to an untenable metaphysics of the Leibnizian kind. He took from Leibniz the idea that there is a deep structure of syntax or grammar below the ordinary structure of spoken language; and he took from Leibniz the idea that it's the work of philosophical analysis to reduce complex notions to their simple constituents, and to reduce unanalysed sentences to their canonical forms. Like Leibniz he believed that if we carried out this enterprise, then our reasoning could be made systematic, and the whole structure of our knowledge of the natural world would be laid out before us in an inclusive map or grid. Where he differed from Leibniz was, as I have mentioned, over the claim of Leibniz that propositions should be all analysed as being fundamentally of subject-predicate form, with its corollary that we have to employ the notion of substance in our metaphysics. That's one central point in which he differed with him. And the other point in which he differed from him was that Russell took the simple notions, which are the bricks out of which all our knowledge is built, to be elements with which we're acquainted in our experience. They were not innate ideas or the primary notions of thought, as they had been for Leibniz. He was an empiricist throughout his life, while Leibniz took it that the simple elements of our knowledge were not elements derived from experience, but were the innate notions which we brought to experience. Nonetheless he took from Leibniz the notion of analysis, of reducing a complex notion to simple ones, as the proper method in philosophy: and, secondly, the insistence that any metaphysics must be founded upon an improved logical grammar (Leibniz himself was an originator in formal logic).

MAGEE: I take the point you made just now that you don't want to go into the mathematical logic in detail, but there is one thing about it I want to raise before we leave it altogether. On page 100 of *My Philosophical Development* Russell writes: 'It has seemed to me that those who are not familiar with mathematical logic find great difficulty in understanding what is meant by structure, and owing to this difficulty are apt to go astray in attempting to understand the empirical world.' He is very close here to suggesting that you can't understand the empirical world unless you know mathematical logic.

HAMPSHIRE: Yes, I think there are two things he believed which could be glosses on that statement. The first is that unless you understood mathematical logic you wouldn't have a clear idea of what the possibilities are for a systematic logical syntax as opposed to an ordinary descriptive grammar of ordinary language; and, secondly, that unless you understood mathematics, and understood the search for structure which is characteristic of mathematicians, you wouldn't understand modern physics, and you'd have a naïve idea of how physicists reason and indeed of the structure of physical theory itself. He believed both these things. He was always aiming at finding a deep structure beneath ordinary speech and ordinary propositions, beneath the ordinary knowledge claims that we make: and it was never of very great significance to him that the structures which he suggested as being the true structures of a range of empirical propositions, or the true structures of a range of mathematical truths, were not the ones which intuitively we would seize upon when asked to write a grammar of our statements. This would not disturb him. He was not greatly interested in our unsystematic intuitions about ordinary language.

MAGEE: But just as he accused Leibniz of developing a metaphysic out of his logical commitments – whether consciously or unconsciously doesn't matter – Russell then went on to do the same thing himself, didn't he: because surely logical atomism is a metaphysical system derived from a logic?

HAMPSHIRE: Derived from two sources. One is logic, but the other is his theory of knowledge. Logical atomism was for him both a theory of meaning and a theory of knowledge. He made it an unalterable principle that the terms in the basic propositions, upon which all our knowledge rests, must stand for distinct elements in our experience. All empirical truths, whether the ordinary common-sense propositions about chairs and tables and houses, medium-sized objects, or the sophisticated propositions of mathematical physics, all these are inferred in accordance with fixed rules of inference from the data of immediate experience, which are things like sounds, colours, smells, shapes, whatever we perceive directly. That they are perceived directly entails that we can give no clear account of why we believe that, for example, a red patch is in front of us, other than that we actually experience it. He thought that there must be a bottom level of knowledge claims which are so far not questionable by reference to any other knowledge claims, and which have to be validated simply by a matching of the proposition with experience. If we carried out an analysis of the forms of propositions, and if we could identify correctly the terms that occur in basic propositions, then we would know that the ultimate constituents of reality are those things that are designated by the terms that occur in the elementary or basic propositions, on which all our knowledge rests. This was the picture of knowledge that he carried with him, and if you ask 'Does it entail metaphysical conclusions in the sense that it entails that we discover by this method what the ultimate structure of reality is?' the answer is, yes; but he didn't cling to a metaphysics consistently all through his life. He took different views at different times as to what the ultimate elements in reality were. Most empiricists, and Russell was no different in this respect, point to those peculiar elementary propositions, such as 'The large red patch that I see in front of me is to the right of the small blue patch,' the sort of thing one might perhaps say to an oculist, which refer to my own sensations and appear to be direct reports of them, and claim they neither need nor can be given any further verification; I know them to be true by acquaintance, in the sense that I'm the man who has the red patch in front of him and I know that it is to the right of the blue one. The proposition is not in any way the conclusion of an inference. So that my answer to the question 'Why do you believe this to be true?', is 'I see it there.' That's all there is to it; on the other hand if I talk about persons or physical objects and say, 'The man in the iron mask had a long life,' or 'The man in the next room is bald,' then I make a knowledge claim, or express a belief, that has to be justified in some way by something like an inference, not from direct experience. I have to answer the question, how do you know, or why do you believe this, and give some steps of evidence; because I could be wrong, and these steps will always lead me back (so the suggestion goes) to my own sensations. This is a point common to Russell and other modern empiricists; but what's original is that he combines this distinction with a general distinction between two kinds of knowledge: knowledge by acquaintance and knowledge by description. And then he uses this distinction in a theory of meanin and of the understanding of words and sentences. There are certain words or phrases which one understands because one is directly acquainted with what the words or phrases designate. There are other words and phrases which one understands only because one can supply some identifying description of what it is that they desig-nate: that is, one can associate certain descriptions with a name or phrase, and through these descriptions one may pick out the object, or an object, which satisfies the descriptions. For example, Russell would say that if I talk about the man in the iron mask, and if I know what I mean by that phrase, I must be able to analyse the phrase into terms which stand for things with which I have been acquainted.

MAGEE: You must know what a man is, you must know what iron is, you must know what a mask is, and so on – and this knowledge again has to have been derived from experience at some time in the past.

HAMPSHIRE: Yes.

MAGEE: Does that mean he allowed memory as a form of knowledge by acquaintance – direct knowledge?

HAMPSHIRE: Sometimes he did, and sometimes he didn't. I don't think he was consistent here, throughout his life.

MAGEE: This one-to-one correspondence between propositions and reality presumably commits him to a correspondence theory of truth. In fact, it *is* a correspondence theory of truth.

HAMPSHIRE: Yes. The correspondence theory of truth is part of his doctrine of logical atomism, which is also a theory of meaning. In this phase of his thinking, the correspondence between proposition and fact holds in its simple form at the bottom level of empirical knowledge, and applies to those basic propositions which aren't to be questioned by reference to other propositions: these basic propo-sitions correspond to elements in our immediate experience. And the more theoretical and inferred propositions, which commit us to more than these basic propositions, have to be derived from, and justified by reference to, these basic propositions.

MAGEE: By logical processes.

HAMPSHIRE: Yes, though he never could show that inductive reasoning could properly be assimilated to a logical process.

MAGEE: But whatever the form of logical derivation might be, it proceeded from elementary propositions which mirrored elements of reality.

HAMPSHIRE: Yes, and it was that doctrine that Wittgenstein tried to make more precise in the *Tractatus*. But in order to understand the whole enterprise one must talk about the Theory of Descriptions, and Russell's theory of names and other referring expressions, because this is his most famous and greatest and most original contribution to philosophy. I think that the article in 1905 in *Mind*, 'On Denoting', is a landmark in the history of philosophy, like Descartes' *Meditations* or any other landmark you choose to think of. It's a classic and a new beginning. It's exceedingly obscure and it's not clear that anyone – or very few people – have ever really understood it completely, including its author; it's exceedingly obscure in the way that Plato's *Parmenides* or *The Sophist* are obscure. It's an enormous effort of original thought, difficult to understand because the article represents thought in the making, and really original thought. The Theory of Descriptions, very briefly and non-technically stated, starts from a mystery in the theory of meaning, or theory of signs; there are intelligible noun phrases, such as 'the present King of France' – which *is* an intelligible phrase, and one which we all understand – and we find such intelligible noun phrases standing in subject positions in sentences as substantival phrases; yet they may stand for nothing at all; there is no present King of France. So there can be discourse about subjects which do not exist, such as the present King of France, or the Loch Ness monster (presuming he doesn't) or the golden mountain. We understand propositions that have these subject terms referring to non-existent things, and this had led philosophers, who had a naïve conception of the relation between signs or words and what they stand for, to say that in the case of substantival or noun phrases, which stood for non-existent things, they stood for subsistent things, which Russell found offensive to his sense of reality and of clarity in explanation.

MAGEE: Wasn't the theory that, since there wasn't a physical something, there must be a non-physical something?

HAMPSHIRE: There must be, as it were, a Platonic something – another realm of being.

MAGEE: Yes, but 'be' is the operative word – there must *be* something that the sign stands for.

HAMPSHIRE: Yes, because it's natural to think of meaning as a direct relation between word and object, where noun phrases, or anything that looks like a name, or substantival phrases, are concerned. And 'the present King of France' does look like a name; strictly speaking it's a title, plus a temporal adjective. But it looks like a name, and how can we understand a name if there's nothing that it names? So what is needed is logical analysis, and this Russell gives; and the analysis depends upon the use of notions from mathematical logic – of a propositional function and the existential operator. But perhaps the idea can be explained without recourse to these technical terms.* Suppose we consider the statement that the present King of France is bald, uttered when there doesn't exist a King of France, then a suggested analysis of this, a translation of it into its canonical form, is as follows: 'The description "present King of France" is satisfied, and is satisfied uniquely, and whoever satisfies this description also satisfies the description of being bald.' Russell makes this phrase – 'the present King of France is bald' – assert the instantiation of a set of properties and the unique instantiation of one set of properties. One has a paraphrasing sentence which translates the plain language sentence 'the present King of France is bald' into another form, translates it not in the sense that it reproduces the surface meaning and intuitive sense of the original sentence – it doesn't. It transforms the sentence in such a way that we find that we're no longer referring to a pseudo-substance at all. What we've achieved is an elimination of the subject term, and hence we don't need to postulate pseudo-substances to correspond to this subject term. Russell applies this procedure, this rule of translation, to all sentences which have substantival phrases, with the definite article, in the subject-place; all subject-predicate sentences of this form are eliminated, and replaced by an existential proposition which states a unique instantiation of a certain property. In the case of the King of France as opposed to *a* King of France, unique instantiation is claimed, because he thought that the function of the definite article here is to claim uniqueness. This analysis can be disputed on many

* A more accessible explanation than the one that follows begins on p. 145—Ed.

grounds, and the whole doctrine has been often disputed on the ground that this so-called analysis doesn't correspond to the ordinary way in which we interpret these phrases. Ordinarily, so it's said, we wouldn't say that the statement 'the King of France is bald' is false, and give as our ground, or as what makes it false, the fact that there is no King of France. On the contrary, so it's said, we would hesitate to use either 'true' or 'false' of a statement which refers to a non-existent entity in this way. Rather we would suspend judgment, and ask what the speaker meant or was referring to. This is a very important dividing point, from the point of view of this series of conversations on contemporary philosophy. Russell, unlike Moore, and unlike many philosophers influenced by Moore in Oxford, doesn't accept intuitive linguistic correctness as a proper criterion of satisfactory logical analysis, where correctness is interpreted as 'giving an accurate description of ordinary usage', ordinary English, or ordinary French or ordinary German. For him, philosophical analysis must look through ordinary grammar to find a systematic logical syntax which will at certain points be counter-intuitive. He holds that any scientific enquiry, whether physics or logic, yields counter-intuitive results. He doesn't think that the ordinary forms of natural languages have to be reproduced as deep structure. In philosophy you're not describing – on the contrary, you're improving: you're trying to get a logically clear language which will permit the transitions of reasoning made in the sciences to be absolutely distinct. Controversy still continues over the whole project of finding a logically clear syntax. I agree that Russell's Theory of Descriptions is a systematization of ordinary usage which does at certain points involve some counter-intuitive results – that is, doesn't consistently reproduce our ordinary way of interpreting sentences.

MAGEE: But, as you say, he would have said that that's not a criticism of it.

HAMPSHIRE: Yes. And I would agree with him that it's not a criticism of it. He is looking for the structural relations to be used in exact reasoning in the sciences and in philosophy. What's important for this purpose, I think, is that he has eliminated the need to look for quasi-substances to act as the meanings of substantival terms. And he carries this very much further, and very importantly further with proper names – I mean, ordinary names like 'de Gaulle', or 'Shakespeare', or 'Homer'; perhaps these are not very ordinary names, but 'John Smith' or 'Jones', these are ordinary proper names certainly, but they get their sense, their meaning, from the associated descriptions that give the name meaning. And we can see this once again by thinking of the application of existence to a name. I can ask – people have asked – still are asking – 'Did Homer exist?' 'Did Shakespeare exist?' When I'm asking that question – says Russell – what I'm asking is: 'Was there a man who satisfied a certain set of descriptions which are the descriptions which I associate, or which are generally associated (there's some oscillation between these two views) with the name "de Gaulle", or "Homer", or "Shakespeare"?' It's a real question whether Shakespeare exists, which it couldn't be if the name 'Shakespeare' simply designated an individual, and got its meaning from the designation. When I speak of Shakespeare I'm indirectly speaking of that X which instantiates a certain set of definite descriptions – the man who lived at Stratford and who wrote those plays. And if I discovered that no one man wrote those plays who lived at Stratford, well, I don't know how much latitude I have in choosing the essential descriptions, but if none of the associated descriptions were satisfied, then I would say Shakespeare didn't exist. If the name 'Shakespeare' stands for the individual Shakespeare, and if the name gets its sense from this designation, the question whether or not Shakespeare existed would be the same as the question whether or not the name was intelligible.

MAGEE: The name could even only be used if Shakespeare existed.

HAMPSHIRE: Yes. So Russell holds that ordinary proper names are not proper names in a technical sense of 'proper name' which he introduced. Proper names, in his strict sense, stand for directly perceived elements in our experience, and get their meaning entirely from what they stand for, not from associated descriptions.

MAGEE: I think it's permissible to say, broadly speaking, that those views of his that you've now set out, from the theory of Definite Descriptions onwards, are those that were to come under the heading 'logical atomism', the philosophy to which he subscribed in the second decade of the century. It was probably at that time that his views were at their clearest and most coherent – he himself was later to say this in *My Philosophical Development*. Can you sum up what the total position arrived at was?

HAMPSHIRE: Yes. I'd like to sum it up by stating what he never changed, what is constant in his philosophy from beginning to end. First, the proper method of philosophy is analysis of the forms of propositions – looking for the true underlying form, and syntax, of valid knowledge claims, the syntax which will lay bare the logical connections between different types of empirical knowledge. This he always held to be the proper method in philosophy. Secondly, this analysis involved very considerable departure from the description of ordinary speech and of the grammar of natural languages. This programme of logical analysis became a great issue afterwards, in the 1930s and up to the present day. Wittgenstein emancipated himself from Russell by questioning this notion that there was a logically clear language to be discovered, and a universal structure of knowledge, or universal syntax of knowledge, beneath the ordinary grammars of natural languages. Russell I don't think ever doubted that it was the proper work of philosophy to look for it – it may be very difficult to find. Secondly, he asserted all his life that all our empirical knowledge rests upon reports of direct experience, in some definable sense of 'direct experience', sometimes taken more widely, and sometimes more narrowly. Thirdly, the discoveries incorporated in physical theory represent the most systematic knowledge we have, but they also rest ultimately on this common basis of direct experience – the reported experience of individual observers, on the hard raw data of their observations. I don't think he ever hesitated about any of those propositions in spite of the unclarity of the logical and epistemological relations that are involved, and that are concealed, by such words as 'based on' and 'derived from', which I have been using. Finally, his importance is just that the method of analysis that he introduced set standards of clarity in argument, and delineated a programme, which almost every philosopher of lasting value (I would say) in the English-speaking world has followed up to a point, then criticized and emancipated himself from. Moore devoted much of his lectures and writing to criticizing Russell, and took many of his topics, in the theory of knowledge and of language, from Russell. Moore and Russell learnt from each other in Russell's early, most productive years. Wittgenstein equally gradually emancipated himself from Russell's and his own logical atomism, and Russell was, so to speak, his father in philosophy in that sense – a rejected father.

MAGEE: And what remains Wittgenstein's most famous book, the *Tractatus*, pushes to its extreme a doctrine first propounded by Russell.

HAMPSHIRE: Yes and Carnap, and the logical positivist school associated with him, started from Russell's programme of logical analysis and – abandoning his metaphysics – provided a simplified diagram of the structure of natural knowledge and of mathematical knowledge, which Russell did not accept. Quine, who I think is the most distinguished living systematic philosopher, equally starts from and develops Russell, disagreeing with him at many essential points, such as the distinction between necessary and contingent truths, which was important to Russell at various times in his life; and about the nature of elementary reports of experience. But still, it's in Russell's logical analysis that all these philosophical ambitions have their roots, and he has set the framework in which all modern philosophy of the analytical kind has flourished.

MAGEE: In view of this fact, and this enormous range of influence – and also in view of his own enormous output – one of the surprising things about Russell is what he did *not* do. For example, for most of his adult life he was active in politics (he even stood for Parliament twice) and he probably wrote more books about politics than he did about philosophy; and yet he never made any original contribution to political philosophy. Or, to take another example, history: his knowledge of history was vast. I think he knew more history than any non-professional historian I've ever met – in fact he wrote one substantial and distinguished work of nineteenth-century history himself, *Freedom and Organization*. And yet he never made any contribution to the philosophy of history. And so one could go on: nothing original in morals or ethics, nothing in aesthetics. Why is it that with all his interest and concern in these subjects, and his knowledge of them, and his extensive writing about them, this great philosopher never contributed to the philosophy of these subjects?

HAMPSHIRE: I think he had, as a mathematician, an abstract and generalizing mind, and that he hadn't a delicate perception of concrete things, which I think he probably needed for writing interestingly about politics, or writing interestingly about ethics. He assimilated all forms of argument, as far as he could, to the abstract arguments of mathematics and logic. In part the extraordinary power and consistency and beauty of his prose style depend upon this distinct propositional way of reasoning, and not only of reasoning but of writing on all subjects, even personal and intimate subjects; he naturally generalized and he had a nobly abstract conception of what was required in political thought, which omitted the variety of kinds of reasoning and kinds of persons and kinds of sentiment that there are. He always looked for simple structures, in psychology or in historical explanation; which was, of course, what made him a genius in one sphere, but made him relatively unproductive in the other, I think.

MAGEE: You've touched on the quality of his prose – and he did, after all, win the Nobel Prize for Literature in 1950. This alone has had a serious influence on philosophers, hasn't it? For instance Karl Popper was once talking to me about the influence on him of Russell's style and he said: 'It's not just a question of clarity, it's a question of professional ethics.'

HAMPSHIRE: Yes. It's a question of not obfuscating – of leaving no blurred edges; of the duty to be entirely clear, so that one's mistakes can be seen; of never being pompous or evasive. It's a question of never fudging the results, never using rhetoric to fill a gap, never using a phrase which conveniently straddles, as it were, two or three notes and which leaves it ambiguous which one you're hitting. Russell's prose excludes even the possibility of evasion and of half-truth and if one looks back to the writing of the eighties or looks back to, say, Mill, I must agree with Karl's phrase about professional ethics; even in Mill, who was a very intellectually scrupulous man, one can be worried and perplexed as to which of two things exactly he means, and the fluent style allows him to leave this open; what he says is much more plausible because it's left open, while in Russell's writing there's always this extraordinary nakedness of clear assertion. His doctrines and arguments stand out in a hard, Greek light which allows no vagueness.

MAGEE: Your mention of Mill (who, incidentally, was Russell's godfather, wasn't he – a sort of lay-godfather) reminds me of another question I wanted to put to you. Unlike his friend Moore, and his pupil Wittgenstein, Russell was deeply rooted in a specifically British tradition of philosophy. Can you comment on this?

HAMPSHIRE: It's true that he very self-consciously thought of himself as Mill's heir and that he had this intense sense of the English tradition and intense patriotism – an intellectual patriotism, one might say. But I wish to emphasize that the connection that he made with European rationalism is also important, that what he brought to traditional empiricism was a more rigorous logic and a deeper understanding of mathematical reasoning and discovery. In my opinion this is what has been most productive in analytical philosophy since Russell, in the age of Russell; I am not referring only to the development of mathematical logic, which is a vast subject which without him would have scarcely developed so rapidly as it did – here he was the proto-originator, now superseded – but in philosophy itself the standards of rigour which he imposed are not standards at which Locke or Hume would have dreamt of aiming. Hume had a totally different conception of what philosophy can be.

He didn't think it could be, or should be, a precise discipline. To look for precision, he thought, was an intellectual error. No, I think one mustn't over-emphasize the empiricist strain in Russell to the exclusion of the Leibnizian strain.

MAGEE: In other words you think he was too big to be fitted into a single tradition?

HAMPSHIRE: Yes, and I think that the pursuit of rigour in argument, and the departure from common sense entailed by it, is what is permanently valuable in Russell.

MAGEE: Would you say he's a great philosopher in the narrowest sense of the word 'great' – the same sense as Plato, Descartes or Kant?

HAMPSHIRE: Yes, certainly. I only wish we could have discussed the Theory of Descriptions adequately and at length, and his Theory of Names, and the other hypotheses that he threw out in the theory of meaning, and I think this greatness would be evident.

2
Conversation with David Pears

The Two Philosophies of Wittgenstein

MAGEE: During the three years 1908–1911 the young Ludwig Wittgenstein, an engineering student from Austria, was studying aeronautics at Manchester University. He became interested in the foundations of the mathematics he was using, and this led him to read Bertrand Russell's *Principles of Mathematics*, which had not all that long been published. The book had a tremendous effect on him. In fact it resulted eventually, via a meeting with Frege, in his going to Cambridge in order to study philosophy under Russell – who later wrote: 'Getting to know Wittgenstein was one of the most exciting intellectual adventures of my life.'

In his teens Wittgenstein had read Schopenhauer and come under his spell, as have so many men of genius. And what happened now was not, as one might have expected, that he abandoned the metaphysics of Schopenhauer for the logic of Frege and Russell, but that he effected the almost unimaginable – a marriage between the two. This was in his book *Tractatus Logico-Philosophicus*, which he finished when he was 29. He honestly believed – in fact he wrote in the Preface – that on all essential points this book finally solved the problems of philosophy. This being so there was not much to go on being a philosopher for. So he turned away and did other things.

Alas, and of course, the confidence was misplaced. As the years went by he came to feel that the *Tractatus* was radically in error. And he believed that what had led him into this error was a mistaken theory of language. Ironically, in the Preface to the *Tractatus* he had said that the only reason we pose philosophical problems at all is that we misunderstand the logic of our language – and now he came to view the book itself as an example of precisely this mistake. So he started philosophizing again, but this time in the form of detailed investigations into specific ways in which language misleads. His writings in this second period were voluminous, but almost none of them were published until after his death in 1951. The most important book, *Philosophical Investigations*, was published in 1953.

So here we have what I think must be a unique phenomenon – a philosopher of genius producing two different philosophies in the course of his life, each one of which dominated a generation. The *Tractatus* was the text most influential on the Vienna Circle, and indeed on logical positivism as a whole, which was at its height between the two world wars. And *Philosophical Investigations* has had more influence on post-war philosophy, at least in England, than any other book.

Mr Pears, in addition to having written two forthcoming volumes on Wittgenstein you are one of the translators of the *Tractatus*. It's a very short book – less than 80 pages of text in your translation. Is it too much to ask you in one question what Wittgenstein was trying to do in it?

PEARS: Well, in the *Tractatus* he was trying to do a number of related things. I suppose there were three main things. First, as you say, he was trying to produce a definitive solution to the main problems of philosophy. Secondly, he was trying to draw the limits of factual discourse, the idea being that everything that you can say in factual propositions would find a place inside those limits. Thirdly, he wanted to investigate the foundations of logic, in order to explain adequately what logical necessity really is.

MAGEE: In the Preface he says that his book deals with the problems of philosophy, but he then goes on to say that its aim is to plot the limits of language – and you've just mentioned both these aims. Did he think they were the same thing?

PEARS: No, they're not the same thing, and he didn't think so, but they are connected. To determine the limits of language is to draw a boundary around all conceivable factual propositions enclosing both the factual propositions of science and the factual propositions of everyday life. Inside this boundary, once it had been drawn, would lie all the things that could be said in factual language. Outside it would lie the things that cannot be said in factual language.

The connection with the traditional problems of philosophy is this. Wittgenstein believed that there are at least two kinds of thing that cannot be said in factual language. Some things that cannot be said in factual language are sheer nonsense and of no interest. But there are also important things that we try to express in factual language although they are not the kind of thing that can be expressed in that way. Examples of this second category would be the truths of religion and morality and philosophy itself. Wittgenstein's idea was that there are deep truths here which are distorted when we try to express them in factual language. In the case of philosophy what happens is this. People feel that it must be some kind of super-science, perhaps a special kind of investigation of the human mind. This feeling, according to Wittgenstein, is mistaken, and it leads to all sorts of confusions and misunderstandings. Important insights are given the wrong kind of expression, forced, as it were, to wear the wrong clothes. For example, solipsism expresses itself as a factual proposition, but really the point that the solipsist makes ought to be revealed through language, and not stated in language. That was what Wittgenstein thought about the connection between the problems of philosophy and the limits of language.

MAGEE: Why does he start the book with – what would seem to be yet a third thing – a discussion of the foundations of logic?

PEARS: Yes, that certainly sounds like something quite different. But, in fact, the investigation of the foundations of logic isn't un-connected with the other tasks. Wittgenstein thought of logic as the framework of all factual language. So if he could discover how this framework is constructed he would know in advance what the limits of the possible developments of factual language are. I mean, any factual language would have to fit this framework like the cladding of a building with a steel structure. Now the point of connection is this. Logic, according to Wittgenstein, is the study of everything that can be known in advance of experience, or to put this into Latin, everything that is *a priori*. So anyone who investigates logic is really investigating the essential nature of language, which dictates the limits of its possible developments. That gives the connection between the foundations of logic and the limits of factual language.

MAGEE: What sort of explanation does he provide of logical necessity?

PEARS: What he says is that logic presents the scaffolding of the world. His idea is that corresponding to each factual proposition there will be a factual possibility. All these possibilities taken to-gether constitute, as it were, the space – the logical space – in which the world of facts takes shape. I mean, there is a space of possibilities, some of which will be realized as facts, while others will not be realized. The realization of a possibility is like the occupation of a point in space – one more fact where previously there had been only a possibility, a space for a fact. So the world of facts takes shape, like a building, within this scaffolding, which is fixed by logic. But that's hardly a complete answer to your question.

MAGEE: Well, no, I don't think it does fully answer it. How does the theory of logical necessity actually work?

PEARS: The theory is that a logical proposition is a tautology. For example, it is a tautology that either it is raining or it is not raining; and no experience is needed to establish that. It can be said in advance – *a priori*. Here Wittgenstein is using the word 'tautology' in his own special way, like this: It was his view – actually a view derived from Frege – that a factual proposition must say something absolutely definite, that it must have a definite sense. So the proposition that it is raining, which is a factual proposition, says that certain factual possibilities are realized, and that certain others are not realized; and it must be absolutely definite which possibilities are said to be realized, and which are said not to be realized. Since this factual proposition has an absolutely definite sense it follows that, if you add to it the words 'or it is not raining', thus producing 'Either it is raining or it is not raining,' you will be saying something that is necessarily true – true by logical necessity. For nothing whatsoever is excluded by what you are saying. The two factual propositions, the positive one and the negative one, when they are joined together with the logical connective 'or', exactly cover the whole field of possibilities, because they have absolutely definite senses, which are, as it were, contiguous and exhaustive. Therefore, this 'either-or' proposition excludes nothing.

Of course each of the two factual propositions, taken by itself, does say something about the way in which the world of facts takes shape inside its scaffolding. The proposition 'It is not raining' says that the relevant possibility is not realized, and the proposition 'It is raining' says that it is realized. Because the senses of these two factual propositions are definite, contiguous and exhaustive, the combination of them, 'Either it is raining or it is not raining,' must be true. It must be true because of the essential nature of propositions.

This explanation depends on the idea that a factual proposition must say something absolutely definite. It must leave nothing hazy or uncertain. Perhaps the easiest way to appreciate this dependence is this. We may say that a factual proposition such as 'It is raining,' and its negation 'It is not raining,' divide the field between them, and divide it with a sharp and definite line. The world of facts has, as it were, a choice. It can occupy the field on one side of the line, or it can occupy the field on the other side of the line. But what it cannot do is refuse to play. But if this explanation of logical necessity is going to work, then it's evident that the line must be sharp and definite. All factual propositions must have absolutely definite senses. This is Wittgenstein's fundamental idea, taken over, as I said, from Frege.

MAGEE: Let me make sure I've got things clear up to this point. Logic, in Wittgenstein's view, was a map of all possibilities, of everything that could conceivably be the case, and must therefore show us the limits of everything that can conceivably be said. So in plotting the map of logic one is making manifest both the limits of language and the limits of all possible worlds.

PEARS: Yes, that's it. There is a series of equations here. Logical propositions, which are tautologies, reveal the structure of language and so, at one remove, reveal the structure of the world. The idea is that these two structures are the same. The structure of language is the mirror-image of the structure of the world. Both structures are disclosed by logic. But you must remember that when we say this we are not saying that language necessarily provides a true description of the actual world, a true report of the facts. That, of course, would be absurd because naturally there must also be the possibility of false reports and incorrect descriptions. Wittgenstein's thesis, that language mirrors the structure of the world, is to be taken as a thesis about possibilities. All the possible choices that the actual world may make are already reflected in language. Every possibility is matched by a factual proposition with a sense, which must be definite. So, to use Wittgenstein's metaphor again, the world of facts can only take shape within a logical scaffolding fixed in advance.

Thus we arrive at the following result. Logic reveals the structure of language and at one remove the structure of reality. How can it do both these things? Simply because the two structures are the same, like a man and his shadow.

MAGEE: So we've got on the one hand logical statements, which are necessarily true, because they are compatible with all possibilities, and on the other hand factual statements, which rule out possibilities and, as it were, draw a line round the actual. What was the connection between this and Wittgenstein's theory of truth functions?

PEARS: The idea is that, as you say, factual propositions rule out possibilities. This does not mean that they make possibilities into impossibilities, but only that they say that they are not realized. To say that it is raining rules out the possibility that it is not raining. Or, to put it slightly differently, a factual proposition blocks out the related space so that reality cannot take shape at that point. Since a factual proposition must have an absolutely definite sense there must be a closed list of possibilities that it blocks out, while the rest, of course, remain open.

Now, to answer your question about truth functions, a complex proposition will be related to a large number of possibilities, a large number of points in logical space. So we can say that a complex proposition is a compound message made up of a number of simpler messages each of which is related to a point in logical space. Then the truth or falsehood of the complex message will depend entirely on the truth or falsehood of the simpler messages. Or, to put this in the usual terminology, the complex message will be a truth-function of the simpler messages. Furthermore, according to Wittgenstein there must be a rock bottom of simplicity. There must be some propositions which convey absolutely simple messages. This last thesis is Wittgenstein's version of logical atomism. It is closely related to Russell's logical atomism and, much more remotely, to the psychological atomism of Hume.

MAGEE: What about Wittgenstein's famous picture theory of meaning – the theory that a proposition has meaning because it is a picture of the reality which it is about?

PEARS: Well the picture theory of meaning is rather a difficult thing to explain. The theory is, as it were, a dazzlingly obscure theory. I mean that it's so convincing that we don't ask ourselves exactly what it is that we are being convinced of. It has to be seen as an attempt to explain how a factual proposition gets its sense. Now a proposition consists of words, and the words are attached to things. But the question is this: How is it that when we put words together in a certain way we get a proposition with a definite sense? How is this result achieved? The achievement is difficult to explain, because a word has a one to one correlation with the world, whereas a proposition has a one to two correlation with the world. For a word is attached to a thing, which is a unit, whereas a proposition is attached to a possibility, which may or may not be realized – a duality. How, then, can we succeed in producing propositions merely by stringing words together? That is the problem.

Wittgenstein's solution is that propositions are constructed out of words in much the same way as pictures and diagrams are constructed out of points. An arrangement of points in a diagram will represent a possible arrangement of things in reality: for example, a picture of a stage in a game of chess will represent a possible arrangement of actual chessmen on an actual chess board. In fact, some kinds of spatial pictures cannot fail to represent spatial possibilities. In much the same way, according to Wittgenstein, propositions represent the possibilities with which they are correlated.

But how close really is this similarity? If a spatial picture cannot stray into spatial nonsense, that will be because it is in the same medium. But words are not kept safe in this way, because language is not in the same medium as the reality with which it is concerned. So what prevents words from straying into nonsense? Wittgenstein, of course, allowed that words can stray into nonsense, and that in this respect strings of words are unlike some spatial pictures.

Nevertheless there remains a point of analogy. The point of analogy between propositions and pictures is this; when words occur in nonsensical strings, they have lost their connections with the things to which they were originally attached. Or to put this the other way round, when a word is attached to a thing, it absorbs into itself all the possibilities in which that thing can participate. It absorbs all these possibilities into itself like a chameleon which has to be able to match the colour of the thing on which it sits through all its possible changes. But if a word is obliged to preserve and respect all these possibilities, it may fail in this undertaking, unlike the points in the diagram which cannot fail to respect spatial possibilities, because, of course, they are in the same medium, space. In the case of words the failure would produce nonsense. So the analogy between propositions and pictures or diagrams is this. A point in a diagram automatically absorbs and retains the spatial possibilities open to the thing with which it is correlated. A word absorbs and retains the possibilities open to the thing with which it is correlated, but not automatically. For in this case both the absorption and the retention require human intellectual effort, and in both these things we may fail.

MAGEE: It's easy to see how a proposition about a matter of fact can be said to picture the state of affairs it's about, but it's difficult to see how propositions which are not about matters of fact – propositions about morals, say, or aesthetics; value judgments of any kind – can picture a state of affairs, since there is no factual state of affairs. How does the theory cope with propositions of this kind?

PEARS: Well, a large part of the point of Wittgenstein's theory of factual propositions is that the so-called propositions of morality, religion, aesthetics and indeed philosophy itself lie outside the boundary of factual discourse. Strictly speaking, according to

Wittgenstein, they are not really propositions. Now it might look as if, when he puts them outside the boundary, he must be condemning them as utter nonsense in an intolerant, positivistic way. But this is simply not so. He believed that all these things lack factual sense, and so are non-sense, but he didn't mean this as a condemnation. On the contrary, he thought that it is only when they masquerade as factual propositions that confusion begins. They are not factual propositions, and to say this is to take the first step towards understanding them. Wittgenstein's endeavour was to preserve them from the encroachments of factual discourse and particularly, of course, the encroachments of scientific discourse.

MAGEE: But the *Tractatus* itself is full of philosophical propositions – and you might think these are ruled out by the theory expressed in the book. Mind you, I don't myself see why Wittgenstein should maintain, as he does, that a proposition in any language has a structure concerning which *in the language* nothing can be said. It seems to me easy to construct sentences that make empirically verifiable statements about themselves. For instance the sentence 'The sentence I am now uttering contains nine words,' is empirically true.

PEARS: Yes, I agree. I think you've raised a very difficult question there. How can Wittgenstein have said anything so implausible? I think that what I shall try to do is not to give a complete answer to this question of interpretation but only half an answer to it.

Suppose that you grant to Wittgenstein that philosophy is a critical analysis of language which is, as you implied in your opening remarks, similar in aim to Kant's or Schopenhauer's critical analysis of human thought. Then a philosophical thesis will either be about factual language as a whole, like the picture theory, or it will be about a sub-division, a department of language, such as statements ascribing beliefs to people. But what will the status of a philosophical thesis be? For example, what is the status of the philosophical thesis that a given proposition has a certain sense? It cannot be a mere matter of fact, because, if that proposition did not have that sense, it would not be that proposition; indeed, it might not have a sense at all – it might be just dead. The point is that the analytical philosopher, according to Wittgenstein, is not talking about dead words, about, as it were, spare parts, but about a living language with a living vocabulary. So this kind of philosophical thesis will not be expressible in a factual proposition, because it won't be something which might or might not be true. It will be a proposition which is in some way necessarily true.

Somewhat similarly, the things that Wittgenstein says about factual language as a whole in the *Tractatus* cannot be factual propositions. They, too, according to him, will have a certain necessity. They're not, of course, tautologies, and they don't fall under his theory of logical necessity, but they do purport to give the essence of language, something to which any language must necessarily conform. They are, as it were, boundary statements. The boundary of language, like the boundary of your field of vision, is something that you cannot see, and yet something that you know must be there. This is an analogy taken from Schopenhauer which Wittgenstein himself sometimes used. I don't know if that answers the question. I think it's very difficult to answer it fully, but perhaps that does something . . .

MAGEE: Actually I think that's as good a brief answer as can be given. Can I now ask you to say something about the way the book is written? This is probably the first thing that strikes most readers: it's not written in sustained prose but in separate numbered paragraphs, some of them only a few words long. Why did he do that?

PEARS: Well, the *Tractatus* is a carefully selected excerpt from much lengthier notebooks which he kept, starting in 1914 and going on – well, we don't quite know how long, since the later ones unfortunately don't survive. What he did was to write in these notebooks day by day, and then he made selections winnowing out a lot of material, and in some cases omitting the details of his arguments, until finally he arrived at a version of the *Tractatus*, which he then revised again and published in the form in which we now have it. As a matter of fact, it's a great pity that the later notebooks don't survive, because often a passage which is obscure in the *Tractatus* becomes clear when we compare it with the parallel passage in the notebooks.

MAGEE: I suppose it must be one of the most influential books in the history of philosophy. What aspects of it were, in fact, the influential ones, and whom did they influence?

PEARS: What happened is rather strange. The influence that it exerted in the next twenty years was really that it gave a tremendous impetus to the analytical school of philosophy, and it did this not so much through its specific theory of factual language but, rather, through the general idea that it must be possible in some way to draw a limit to factual discourse. So the book gave the philosophers of the Vienna Circle a kind of programme. If philosophy was an

analytical activity, the next thing to be done was to apply Wittgenstein's general ideas in detail, and to analyse particular kinds of
propositions, such as empirical propositions about the physical
world, and to see exactly what their basis is. Similarly, if all *a priori*
propositions are tautologies this needed to be demonstrated by a
detailed analysis of particular *a priori* propositions. This was the
kind of way in which the book influenced people. The specific theory
of language, though it exerted some direct influence, did not exert
much, because it was too recondite and too abstract.

MAGEE: Who specifically was this an influence on?

PEARS: Primarily on the philosophers of the Vienna Circle, and
then later, during the 1930s, on philosophers in England, and
then in America.

MAGEE: And of course while the book was influencing other people
Wittgenstein was growing increasingly dissatisfied with it. What
did he himself come to think was wrong with it?

PEARS: Yes, as you said in your opening remarks, he gave up
philosophy after writing the *Tractatus*, and then gradually returned
to it and came to see that what he had written was mistaken, but
not completely mistaken, nor mistaken in a single way. His later
philosophy has several different but related points of departure.
Evidently, the most vulnerable point in the theory of language of the
Tractatus is this: one might ask how he could possibly have known
that all language necessarily has the structure that he assigned to it.
It was especially difficult for him to answer this question, because
it was hard to accommodate within the system of the *Tractatus*
necessary truths that are not tautologies. What could the status of this
necessary truth about language possibly be? And how could it
possibly be established?
   These difficulties led Wittgenstein to reflect that, since language
is an ordinary human phenomenon, it might be studied empirically.
Now an empirical study of language would soon show that it's not
constructed on the simple rigid framework described in the *Tractatus*.
There are enormously many varieties of discourse, with different
functions and different ways of fulfilling them. From this later point
of view Wittgenstein's verdict on the *Tractatus* was that it illegit-
imately selected one form of language and then projected it on to the
world. That's to say he thought that he had gone wrong because he
had constructed an excessively simple and rigid theory of language,
and then, looking through this theory like a pair of spectacles, had

supposed that he could see its independent basis in reality. But he now thought that that was an illusion: the apparent independent basis in reality was merely the result of looking through those spectacles.

MAGEE: What else did he think was wrong?

PEARS: I think that the other main point of departure was in the philosophy of logic and mathematics. About 1930 his view of logical and mathematical necessity began to undergo a radical change. He had believed that these necessities are imposed on us, and that we have no option about them. That was the theory of the *Tractatus*. But he came to believe the exact opposite – that we create them as we go along, and that we can modify them at any point if we wish without inconsistency, because we ourselves set the standards of consistency and can change them as we go along.

It's important to see that he didn't think that we have any *real* option, since, if we didn't ratify these necessities, our thoughts would be chaotic. Nevertheless we have a theoretical option, because it is we who ratify them, and so if we believe that they are already there independently of us as an objective feature of reality, that is an illusion. The apparent independent basis of logical necessity is merely a projection of our natural habits of thought. In short, man now stands in the centre of the system of necessary truths, and he supports them on his own. If he cannot accept this view of the situation that is only because he's suffering from the natural vertigo of the space traveller who suddenly realizes that all the old landmarks have gone.

MAGEE: To what extent is Wittgenstein's later philosophy an investigation of empirical facts about the use of language?

PEARS: To a great extent, and that's really a very striking feature of the later writings. It seems extremely paradoxical that so much of Wittgenstein's later philosophy should consist of ordinary empirical observations about language. People wonder where the philosophy has gone. The *Tractatus* may be a very difficult book to understand, but at least it's obviously and non-controversially a philosophical work in the old style. But in the later period, as Wittgenstein himself remarks, although it's much easier to understand what he's saying, it's correspondingly much more difficult to see the point of his saying it.

In order to understand the point of it, we have to go back to one of the tasks that he set himself in the *Tractatus* – plotting the limits of language. In the early period he had thought that the boundary could be drawn with a single sweeping line. Later, with his new respect for the varieties of discourse, he came to think that the boundary could only be drawn piecemeal, bit by bit. Also, in the later period he became much more interested in the boundaries between different areas of discourse, and much less interested in the far-out boundary which, according to him, enclosed the whole of factual discourse. For example, much of his later work was in the philosophy of mind, a special subject that scarcely makes an appearance in the lunar landscape of the *Tractatus*. In *Philosophical Investigations*, he tries to draw the line between discourse about material objects and discourse about sensations, thoughts, intentions and other mental entities. His point is that people are apt to stand with one foot on each side of this line, and to talk about sensations as if they were very like material objects, the only difference being the small one signified by the adjective. Sensations seem to be objects all right, but not material objects – mental objects. But this, he argues, is a great mistake, in fact the main mistake made by the British empiricists from Hume to Russell.

MAGEE: I'm not sure that what you've said really answers the question I put. Or rather I don't see from what you've said why any investigation of the empirical uses of language is necessitated in the later philosophy.

PEARS: It's necessitated in the following way. If you want to know the limits of language about sensations, and in particular if you want to know the location of the line that divides that language from language about material objects, then you will presumably start with an empirical investigation of the two languages as they are actually spoken. Where else could you start? The point of this empirical investigation is that it will provide a corrective for certain illusions. For these two languages, or parts of language, when they're put side by side suggest new and exciting possibilities. For example, might not sensations exist unowned by any person? Might they not migrate from person to person as some people have thought that consciousness might migrate? But when this suggestion is made about sensations, it is an illusion, a kind of dream suggested by language. It's certainly not an idea which would result from a sober empirical investigation of the way in which language about sensations has actually developed, and actually works.

What Wittgenstein wanted to do in his later period was to encourage such dreams and then to show what was wrong with them. This particular dream is a natural one, indeed a profound one, and not just a foolish, childish mistake. Nevertheless it is a mistake, and the remedy, according to him, is to take the dreamer back to the empirical facts about language, and to lead him slowly and methodically along the line which divides discourse about sensations from discourse about material objects. The illusion has to be hunted to extinction.

But one might ask, who would ever have such dreams? They seem so absurd. But it's not impossible to be taken for a ride by a philosophical theory and to end in absurdity. Hume, for example, suffered from the illusion about sensations that I described. His system was a sort of psychology without bodies, and he treated sensations as if they had a criterion of identity rather like, indeed too like, the criterion of identity of material objects. And many other philosophers have made the same kind of mistake.

MAGEE: It seems to me that a distrust of language is all-pervading in the later philosophy. It's looked on as the source of all our ills. Why?

PEARS: I think that it's not exactly that he distrusted language or thought that it should be improved or made into an honest broker. It was a kind of love-hate relationship with no wish for change. To be more precise, his idea in the later period was that you had to plot the logical boundaries of language or of some part of language by what might be called a method of oscillation. You don't just sit down and say 'That's where the boundary runs.' What you have to do is first of all to feel the temptation to cross the boundary. You have to actually experience the seductiveness of these dreams of language, and really make the attempt to cross. Then, according to Wittgenstein, you will find that you are forced back by the very nature of the part of language from which you started. So what happens is that first you deviate into nonsense – a very natural, indeed profound kind of nonsense – and then Wittgenstein's remedy is to recall you to the facts about the part of language from which you started. You come back to those facts with a better understanding of them.

MAGEE: It's very striking that, as you say, the end of each philosophical investigation is a return to the starting-point. With Wittgenstein you always seem to end up just where you began. Doesn't this embody an extreme linguistic conservatism?

PEARS: I don't think that it does indicate conservatism in Wittgenstein's case. I see your point – people have said this about Wittgenstein, and it's undoubtedly true of some kinds of linguistic philosophy.

But I don't think that it's an accurate comment on Wittgenstein's method or aims. You see, he wasn't opposed to modifying a part of language. What he was really against was treating it as if you had already modified it, although in fact you hadn't modified it. For example, instead of keeping the usual criterion of identity for sensations, you could improvise a new criterion, according to which it would make sense for two people to have one and the same sensation. It would then be possible to devise a criterion that allowed sensations to migrate from person to person. Naturally, such a novel criterion would have to be carefully formulated and consistently used. But Wittgenstein wouldn't object to it. What he objects to is the idea that you can stretch existing language to include the dream without modifying the basis of existing language. That would be like trying to move outside the relevant logical space without changing the language which was the point of origin of that very logical space – an impossible feat.

MAGEE: An analogy that's often been made – and which I must say strikes me as valid – is between psychoanalysis and Wittgenstein's view that we can cure our philosophical ills by a deep analysis of language. Do you think there's anything in it?

PEARS: Yes, I think there's something in it, but it has been greatly exaggerated. The valid point in the analogy is very much on the surface, and deeper down, I think, the analogy isn't close. For Wittgenstein's point was that these deep misunderstandings of language are not just a disease of the intellect, which ought to be avoided, if possible: they are an essential preliminary to achieving philosophical understanding. You will notice that it's always against the background of some dream or illusion that he assembles the empirical facts about the relevant part of language. This is a conscious philosophical method, and it's as much part of this method that you should begin with a deep misunderstanding as it is that you should end by getting things straight. Philosophy, in other words, is a kind of retrieval. If you have never strayed, or, at least, felt the urge to stray, you will never achieve philosophical understanding. Instead, you will suffer from what Wittgenstein calls 'loss of problems'. The point is that before you're retrieved, you must feel the urge to stray, and then you indulge in the dream, and finally you're brought back to language as it is. So philosophical understanding is achieved by two movements – first, the voyage out from the language that we all speak, and then the voyage back.

MAGEE: Some very good philosophers – for instance Russell and

Popper – have applied the analogy pejoratively. They see the later philosophy of Wittgenstein rather as Karl Kraus described psycho-analysis: an illness that mistakes itself for its cure. You've made it clear why you think they're wrong. But the later Wittgenstein does take possession of people in a peculiar way; it 'gets' them and eats into their lives. Can you explain this?

PEARS: It's difficult to explain anything as complex as that. I mean, one can't really give a complete explanation of that kind of influence in a few words. But there is one point that I would like to emphasize. Part of the explanation of the influence of his later philosophy is the very personal, romantic nature of his work. I am thinking of the torment of misunderstanding and the gradual retrieval to under-standing – a process which each person who reads his works is expected to go through. He invites his readers to elicit these dreams from their own minds and to work them out alongside the part of language that produced them. Now this is a very personal thing. Anybody who did it would have to be committed in some way to what he was doing. It's not like reading systematic philosophy, where you can sit back in a cool hour and assess the system without any personal involvement whatsoever. You see, the point about Wittgen-stein's later method is that these strange illusions and dreams are the essential background, which must be in the mind of anyone who's going to understand him. So it's always against this background that Wittgenstein assembles the facts about language, and this gives those facts an extraordinary depth. You could say that Wittgenstein saw the mysterious as an extra dimension of something perfectly ordinary. That, I think, is part of the secret of the way in which he captivates people, and also repels those who can't take it.

MAGEE: We've talked about some of the differences between the later and the earlier philosophy, but there are also important similarities. Can you say something about these?

PEARS: Yes. It's because the differences are so striking that Wittgen-stein wanted to include the text of the *Tractatus* in the same volume as *Philosophical Investigations*. He thought that his later ideas could best be understood against the background of his early ideas, because they grew out of them by a natural and continuous process of development. Perhaps the best way to trace this line of develop-ment is to see that in both his periods of philosophical activity his aim is to draw linguistic boundaries. In the early period he tried to draw one sweeping boundary around all factual discourse, with little said about internal boundaries. In the later period he turns his attention to the myriads of internal boundaries that run between different areas of discourse. This concern with linguistic boundaries is the main thing that remains constant in all his philosophy. As I have explained, the method of drawing the boundaries is totally different in the two periods. In the first period it's done in the old *a priori* way, and in the second period it's done by this very strange method of oscillation. But the general aim is the same – to draw the lines at which sense ceases, and nonsense begins, not in order to help people to communicate with one another more efficiently, but in order to help them to achieve the kind of theoretical understanding that we call 'philosophical'.

But we've talked a lot about Wittgenstein's philosophical method. There is also an important constant element in the philosophical doctrines that he maintained in the two periods. He believed that the dominance of scientific thought since the Renaissance is a disaster. For it drives us to assimilate other modes of thought to science, and, as a result, we misconstrue them and misunderstand them. I mentioned his resistance to the thrust of science earlier in this conversation, when we were talking about the *Tractatus*. But I would like to emphasize that it remained constant in his later work, and is especially conspicuous in his later philosophy of mind. It seems to me that this constant feature of his philosophical doctrines is just as important as the constant features of his philosophical method.

MAGEE: There are some people – and again Russell was certainly one – who regard the earlier philosophy as far greater than the later. How do you personally assess their relative merits?

PEARS: I think that they're both products of genius, and the extraordinary thing is how closely they're related to one another, in spite of their superficial differences. So, though I can understand Russell's judgment, that Wittgenstein ceased doing philosophy after he had written the *Tractatus*, I don't agree with it. I think that his later philosophy, properly understood, is a fascinating development from the earlier philosophy.

MAGEE: At Oxford the later Wittgenstein was the orthodoxy of a whole generation, but in some circles there's now been a reaction against it, and it's no longer the only way philosophy is done. What do you think are the valid alternatives?

PEARS: I don't think that Wittgenstein's later philosophy ever dominated Oxford, although, of course, its influence was present there as everywhere else. The main alternative, systematic philosophy, never lacked supporters even there. Wittgenstein's later philosophy is so extremely unsystematic. He believed that to systematize and to assimilate one thing to another is always to distort, so that even if you had a true general view about the whole of language, you'd be so far above the actual phenomena that almost nothing interesting could be picked up. The opposition today is between this very piecemeal, personal way of doing philosophy, and impersonal systematic philosophy, such as the philosophy of Russell, early Wittgenstein, Carnap, and Quine, and Strawson in Oxford. That's the opposition; and in different parts of the world, of course, the thing has gone in different ways. Sometimes Wittgensteinian philosophy dominates, and sometimes it produces a strong and perhaps excessive reaction.

3
Conversation with A. J. Ayer

MAGEE: In 1922 Moritz Schlick was appointed Professor in the Philosophy of Science at Vienna University. And around him gathered people who were quickly to form one of the most famous groups in the history of philosophy, the Vienna Circle. Most of them weren't philosophers at all by training: they were scientists or mathematicians. But unlike most scientists and mathematicians they had a serious interest in the philosophy of their own activities. The best known members of this group, besides Schlick, were Rudolph Carnap, Friedrich Waismann, Otto Neurath, Philip Frank, Karl Menger and Kurt Gödel. And the philosophy they developed came to be known as 'logical positivism'.

Two other figures of lasting importance in the Vienna of that day stood outside the Circle but were well known to its members, and had, or were to have, a profound influence on it. These were Ludwig Wittgenstein, the subject of the last conversation, and Karl Popper, who's to be the protagonist of the next one.

Most of the people I've named either held left-wing opinions or were Jews – or, of course, both – so with the coming of the Nazis they were scattered to England and America, where their physical presence greatly enhanced the influence of their work. However, as to the introduction of logical positivism into England, they were beaten to that by a young graduate from Oxford who had gone out to Vienna, spent some time with them there, and then returned to England and written what is probably the most explosive philosophical work in English of this century: *Language, Truth and Logic*. The young man was A. J. Ayer, 25 years old in January 1936 when the book was published – and now, I suppose, of all living English philosophers the one best known to the general public. To this day there are many professional philosophers who, when asked to recommend an introductory book by someone who thinks he might become interested in philosophy, recommend *Language, Truth and Logic*.

Ayer's second book, *The Foundations of Empirical Knowledge*, was published in 1940. Then, after the war, came the book that he himself regards as his best, *The Problem of Knowledge*, in 1956. Then in 1968 *The Origins of Pragmatism*, and in 1971 *Russell and Moore: the Analytical Heritage*. In addition he has been prolific of articles, many of which have been collected in volume form.

I think one can say that his development has proceeded in a clear, continuous line from that original logical positivism. Because of that – and because of its historic importance for philosophy in this country – we must start there.

Professor Ayer, the central doctrines of *Language, Truth and Logic* were baldly and clearly stated. What were they?

AYER: They were very simple. They derived very much from Hume. In fact, logical positivism, as its name would suggest, is a blending of the extreme empiricism of Hume with the modern logical techniques developed by people like Bertrand Russell. In outline the main principle that I put forward in the book was that significant propositions can be divided into two classes. The first class consisted of those that relate to matters of fact – as Hume put it – and for them I took it to be essential that they be testable by observation; I maintained that unless their truth or falsehood made some observable difference they were not significant. The other class of propositions were the formal propositions of mathematics or logic, and they were held to be tautologies – I thought of them as being merely rearrangements of symbols which did not make any statement about the world. Anything which didn't fall into either of these two classes was regarded as metaphysical, and so as nonsensical. I took this to include a good deal of what had passed for philosophy in the history of the subject, and also all theology – all theological propositions, anyhow in so far as they affected to be about a transcendent being, were held to be meaningless.

In *Language, Truth and Logic* I also developed a special view of ethical propositions: which was that they were expressions of emotion, rather than statements of fact. But this, of course, was not necessary to the general position of logical positivism. Schlick, for example, had a view of ethics which was a utilitarian one; however, it was necessary for the general position that every moral proposition should either be construed naturalistically, as being about human happiness, or in the sort of way I construed them. And apart from that, I think that all there was in my book was an attempt to show that in so far as philosophical problems of a traditional kind were genuine they were problems of a logical character, that is to say problems about the analysis of concepts. I think the book has had its success because of a certain passion with which I wrote it – and also because of its simplifying quality. I mean, to have all metaphysics cut away at one stroke was very gratifying to a certain type of mind, including mine at that time.

MAGEE: In *Language, Truth and Logic* you said that the proper task of philosophy was analysis. How did you conceive analysis at that time? Was it, for example, in the way that G. E. Moore, a dominating figure in philosophy then, was practising it?

AYER: I don't think I was at all clear about what I did think analysis was. But it's certainly true that I was very much influenced by Moore, and also influenced by the problems in which Moore was interested – not the Moore of *Principia Ethica* but the later Moore, who was very much concerned with the problem of perception, for example. And one of the unresolved problems in the Vienna Circle was the status of observation statements themselves. They held that everything had to be reduced to observation statements, that in the end what science was about was what was observable, but they weren't at all agreed on what was observable. They were divided between one wing, headed by Schlick, who wanted to reduce everything to so-called sensation statements, that is statements recording people's actual and possible sensations, and another wing led by Carnap and Neurath who wanted to stop at statements describing physical objects. And I too was always very much interested in this so-called basis problem, the problem of the foundations of knowledge, and in fact my second book is actually called *The Foundations of Empirical Knowledge*.

MAGEE: You took the basis problem to be chiefly the question whether the basic constituents of empirical knowledge are physical objects or sensations?

AYER: Yes. I did see this in terms of the analysis of statements – that is to say I thought that these problems could be presented as problems about the relation, the logical relation, of one class of statements to another. For instance, in my second book I was mainly concerned with a problem which I'm not sure I've even yet solved, that of the relation of statements at the common-sense level, referring to physical objects, like chairs and tables, to the statements about people's sense experiences on which I then thought, and still think, that these statements about physical objects are founded. At one time I thought there could be an equivalence; then I became doubtful of this, and this is one problem of analysis that has occupied me throughout my career.

Another similar problem would be the problem of the relation of scientific statements, statements about atoms and electrons, and so on, to statements about the objects of common sense. Now, you could call this semantic in the sense that one is dealing with the relation of classes of statements to one another. I wouldn't call it linguistic in the narrow sense at all. It's not a question about how words are used. And, of course, all sorts of other considerations come in. For example, considerations of one's theory of knowledge enter into any form of analysis of this sort.

MAGEE: But specifically about your commitment to analysis: can you say clearly *now* what you regard analysis as being, even if you weren't clear when you wrote *Language, Truth and Logic*?

AYER: Well, I think that there are an enormous number of different things which are comprehended under the heading of analysis. There is straightforward definition, which on the whole plays a very small part; there might be some examples in the philosophy of law, but apart from that, I think, very few philosophical problems are resolved simply by giving a straightforward definition. There is what's called definition in use, which is giving rules for translating one set of statements into statements of a different form; and the classical example of this would be Russell's Theory of Descriptions. Now, here, of course, the interest is not so much in the performance itself as in what lies behind the performance. If we take Russell's Theory of Descriptions as an example, he was worried by the fact that expressions which don't denote anything – expressions like 'the present King of France' – nevertheless have a meaning. He started from the assumption that nominative expressions of this sort could only be meaningful if they denoted something, and therefore when faced with this puzzle he tried to show that these weren't genuine nominative expressions; he gave a rule for translating out expressions of this kind so that they ceased to be nominative. Thus 'The present King of France is bald' becomes, as you know, 'There is one thing and just one thing that now rules France and it's not the case that anything now rules France that isn't bald'; and so on. Now this looks like a rather trivial verbal exercise but in fact it can be quite important, in as much as it shows you how you need not be committed to a certain sort of entity that you might find objectionable. And I think that this form of analysis nearly always has some further motive – either a motive deriving from one's theory of meaning, or a motive deriving from one's theory about what there is. People try to get rid of certain sorts of entities. Another very striking example of this would be Russell's whole attempt to reduce mathematics to logic, to get rid of numbers as entities in favour of classes.

Then there's another form of analysis that I was talking about a little while ago, where one is interested in what are really epistemological problems, and these I think tend to form a certain regular pattern, which I tried to bring out in the book you mentioned earlier, *The Problem of Knowledge*. I think there is a certain kind of sceptical argument that runs through the whole of philosophy, right back to the ancients, which tends to show that we can't really know lots of things that we think we know. And it takes the form first of all of showing, or trying to show, that a certain sort of entity is inaccessible, known only indirectly. For example, it will be held that other people's thoughts and feelings are not known to us directly, that I don't perceive anything going on in your mind, I only infer it from what I observe of your behaviour, from your facial expressions, from the gestures you make, from the noises you utter, the words you say. Then this inference is attacked. It's argued that it's not a deductive inference. That is to say, from the fact that you're behaving in a certain way, even from the fact that you cry out, it doesn't follow logically that you're in pain. It's not a contradiction to say that you're crying out but that you are not in pain, that you are pretending, or whatever. Then it is said, 'Well all right, if it is not a *de*ductive inference, it must be an *in*ductive one.' That is to say, there must be some *de facto* empirical correlation between people's saying certain things and their having certain thoughts, between their having certain facial expressions and their having certain feelings, between their making certain gestures and their having certain emotions; and so on. But then it's argued that it isn't a valid inductive inference either, because you can never observe the two together. Inductive inference is a generalization from observed concomitance, but in this case there is no observed concomitance, and therefore you reach a sceptical conclusion.

Now this argument can be resisted in all sorts of ways. I think you can even distinguish different epistemological positions by the different attitudes that people take towards different steps in the argument. Thus, intuitionists deny the first step. They say that we know directly what's going on in other people's minds. In perception they are naïve realists. They hold that we directly see physical objects without the intervention of sense data. Similarly they say that in memory we are directly acquainted with the past. Reductionists deny the second step. They say that your feeling so-and-so is nothing more than your behaving in such-and-such a way and that statements about the past are equivalent to statements about the evidence for them that may be obtainable, evidence in the present and the future. That is what the pragmatists held. Scientifically-minded philosophers tend to deny the third step. They say, in each case, that it is an inductive inference but a valid one. And finally linguistic analysts argue that although these points are quite valid nevertheless the sceptical conclusion doesn't apply, because we use words in such a way that these phenomena just are evidence for what the words express, and evidence is what it is taken to be.

Now I think that under analysis – and this shows how broadly I would use the term – I would comprehend the whole attempt at this problem. I mean that a successful analysis here would show exactly what the relations are in these various domains, how these statements are related. And in this way it would also show what we are justified in believing. So I think that there is a third form of analysis in which it runs into justification, in which the analytical philosopher's task is one of justifying ordinary or not so ordinary beliefs.

Again there is what might be called constructive analysis, as practised particularly by people like Carnap, where you don't bother so much with actual usage, or with justification, but you take some concept which is in ordinary or scientific use and re-define it in such a way as to sharpen it and perhaps make it more useful scientifically. This is what Carnap tried to do with the concept of probability and with the concept of confirmation; and it might also be said that Tarski did it with the concept of truth. You give a particular meaning to a concept, you sharpen it. And this is very like a scientific activity. It's exactly what Einstein did, for example, with the concept of simultaneity. You can either say that Einstein was telling us what we all meant by simultaneity or that he was producing a new concept which replaced the old defective one. And on the whole I think it more correct to say the second.

Finally, there is one other thing to which I attach much less importance (here I disagree with some of my colleagues) and that is the study of ordinary usage. I think that some recent philosophy has consisted in the careful study of ordinary usage. But for me this has not on the whole proved philosophically fruitful. I think that one sphere in which it might be useful would be the philosophy of law. But in the ordinary way I think ordinary usage isn't very interesting.

MAGEE: Well, now, we've talked about the Vienna Circle, about logical positivism, about your introduction of it into England, and about analysis. What I'd like to do is to get a clear view of your own development since those early days. And I think we can best do this by following a rough-and-ready chronological order (we needn't stick to it absolutely). You came to feel yourself that *Language, Truth and Logic* was inadequate, didn't you, in certain important ways, and you wrote a famous introduction to the Second Edition in 1946 in which you modified it. What were your chief modifications?

c

AYER: They were more attempts at an improvement and refinement, I think, than modifications. I tried to get the verification principle properly stated. The principle in its crude form being that a statement is significant only if it's either tautological or empirically verifiable, the problem then was to give a precise meaning to 'empirically verifiable'. I had given one version in the original edition of *Language, Truth and Logic* which was open to the objection that with some ingenuity you could smuggle anything in. And then I tried to improve on this and on the whole I don't think I altogether succeeded. I gave a weaker version of it, which certainly was less open to attack than my original one but ingenious logicians have found holes in this too. And I'm not sure to this day that all the gaps have been mended. I don't think this condemns the principle, since I think that a principle may be intuitively clear and effective even though you don't get a water-tight formal statement of it. But of course it would be much nicer to get a water-tight formal statement of it, if this were possible.

That was one change. I preserved the theory that *a priori* propositions, the propositions of pure mathematics and logic, were analytic, that is to say devoid of any empirical content, and true simply in virtue of the meaning of the symbols concerned. And possibly I should have been more critical of this theory. I now have some doubts whether I didn't deal with propositions of this sort a bit too summarily, and whether this whole analytic-synthetic distinction may not be less clear than I then thought it was. Anyhow, I didn't at that time query it. I retained the ethical theory too, and still would retain it. I still think this is correct. I abandoned two views I'd held in the original edition; and had indeed already abandoned them in my next book. One was the very implausible view which I had taken from the pragmatists – from C. I. Lewis I think – that propositions about the past were in fact about the evidence that might be obtainable for them at some present or future date. And this does seem to me too contrary to common sense as well as being open to obvious logical objections, so I gave it up. And I also in my second book gave up the view that I had held about other people. In the first edition of *Language, Truth and Logic* I had maintained that propositions about oneself, one's own feelings, were to be taken at their face value, so that when I was talking about my own thoughts I *was* talking about thoughts, feelings and so on, but that propositions about the mental states of other people were propositions about their behaviour. This was a fairly natural deduction from the principle of verifiability, but I came to see that it was wrong and in fact even inconsistent, that it could be shown to lead to a contradiction, and that these two classes of propositions had to be taken symmetrically. And once you take the view that they have to be symmetrical then either you can treat yourself behaviouristically, which means, as Ogden and Richards once put it, feigning anaesthesia, or you can ascribe thoughts and feelings to others in the literal way in which one ascribes them to oneself. And this is the view that I took in my second book and have held to ever since – though of course with considerable qualms about the problem which it creates about our knowledge of other minds, one difficulty being the weakness of the basis which one has for inferring to other people's thoughts and feelings.

I suppose these were the main changes. I also, in the introduction to the second edition of *Language, Truth and Logic,* took a more liberal view of the function of philosophy. I said that what I was still calling analysis might comprehend rather more than I had implied when I first wrote the book. I still did not take this quite so far as I now do, but I took it a little further then than I had previously.

MAGEE: The year of that second edition, 1946, is already a quarter of a century ago. How do your views stand now in relation to the whole book?

AYER: I still think that the approach of the book was right, but I am a little more charitable towards metaphysics. That is to say I am not any more charitable to what I described in the book as metaphysics, but I think that people called metaphysicians were perhaps not doing exactly what I described in the book. At least not to the extent that I then thought they were. In my last book of essays which is called *Metaphysics and Common Sense* I have a couple of essays in which I do talk about metaphysicians and I there argue that some metaphysics can be construed as an expression of dissatisfaction with our ordinary conceptual system and a groping towards putting something in its place. And this would be particularly true, I think, of metaphysicians who were associated with science. For instance, I think it could be descriptive of people like Spinoza and Leibniz, and in our own times Whitehead. I think the metaphysician can be seen, in some cases anyhow, as groping towards a conceptual system into which the science of his day could then be fitted. And this would seem to me perfectly permissible, and, if successful, clearly a very important and worthwhile activity.

MAGEE: In *Language, Truth and Logic* you denied the right of any metaphysics to be called philosophy. I take it from what you've just said that you would no longer do that.

AYER: No, let us put it this way. After all, these are library classifications. Something at least, perhaps much, of what comes under metaphysics as a library heading, might come under what I am calling constructive analysis. That is to say, attempting to fashion new concepts. To alter our way of looking at the world. To provide a system of a radically different kind into which our observations can be fitted. And some metaphysics, I think, is a matter of drawing attention to quite important logical points.

MAGEE: I suppose the most controversial aspect of *Language, Truth and Logic*, both when it came out and ever since, has been the principle of verification, which you've already said a lot about. And as you've said, nobody's ever satisfactorily formulated it. So obviously I can't now: but nevertheless it attempts to say something to the effect that every true statement must be either a tautology or a deduction from an observation. As people were very quick to point out, the principle of verification is itself neither of these things. What was its status?

AYER: Well at the time I don't think I was very clear. It seems extraordinary that I shouldn't have been. Afterwards, when this question was put to me, I said it was a stipulative definition. And of course if it is a stipulative definition, it's always open to anyone not to accept the stipulation. But one has to start somewhere and I suppose that if a statement is to be either true or false there must be some way of deciding it. There must be some decision procedure. I don't know how to justify this. I tried to do it by saying that I did not understand how a statement could have any claim on one's credence, could be put forward as something to believe, unless there was some criterion of its acceptability.

Now it may be said that I put forward a rather narrow criterion and I suppose that it might have been more prudent, and perhaps wiser, to have done what Popper subsequently did with his principle of falsification, and say not that one was putting forward a criterion of meaning but that one was putting forward a criterion of demarcation. The claim would then be that only statements which satisfied this criterion were to be accounted scientific. Now I don't very much mind having the principle watered down in this way, though clearly the book would have been less effective if I'd said that from the start. If one accepts this, there is still the problem which faces both verificationists and also the followers of Popper – because I don't think that his principle of falsification is adequate either for all that he wants – the problem of getting the criterion properly formulated. But let us suppose that this problem has been solved. Then someone might say: 'All right, you've demarcated scientific statements, what is there outside? Why shouldn't there be other forms of statement that are equally capable of being true?' And I suppose now in my more reasonable and tolerant old age I would say: 'Very well, I won't prejudge this question. Put your statements forward and give me some criterion for deciding them. If you wish, let it not be a criterion of observation, but what other one is there? What other one can there be? What are you proposing?' I'd throw the ball into the other court.

MAGEE: But of course it's not only the verification principle that doesn't fit its own criteria, almost all philosophical assertions don't fit that criterion either. So not only was your book full of statements which were neither empirical statements nor tautologies, the whole of philosophy seems to consist of such statements.

AYER: Well, I'm not sure about this. One would have to look at actual examples, but I think quite a lot of philosophy does take the form of logic, in the sense that it consists of assertions that this does or does not follow from that. And – I wonder, it's very difficult to say. A lot of it, I think, consists in giving what one might call persuasive definitions – that is to say laying down some rule for the use of an expression which carries certain implications – and in developing them: and then a lot of it consists simply in following out the argument, which would be a matter of applied logic. I don't know – I'm rather puzzled by this. I agree that philosophical statements don't fit neatly into any category. If I had to categorize them I would call them analytic in the sense that it seems to me that if they are true they are necessarily true, and if they are false they are contradictory, except in so far as they might be straightforward historical statements. But I agree that this then broadens the concept of analytic so much that it perhaps ceases to be very useful. So perhaps one should not try to classify them in this sort of way. One might prefer to say that philosophical statements were in some sense *sui generis*. I think the negative point is perhaps the important one, that in the main they aren't statements which are testable by observation, and on the positive side that they are statements which explain and clarify concepts. I admit that the notions of what it actually is to clarify a concept or to explain a theory or to justify a belief are obscure, but it is certainly into this area that philosophical statements fit.

MAGEE: But if they are analytic statements of any kind, that has the curious consequence that the whole of philosophical argument, debate, discussion, is argument about necessarily true statements.

AYER: Well, that is not so very surprising, is it, because think of the disputes that there are in mathematics.

MAGEE: That's true.

AYER: I mean, if one is employing the concept of necessary truth so widely that it covers mathematics then —

MAGEE: — then there's nothing odd about it covering philosophy?

AYER: Yes.

MAGEE: Towards the end of *Language, Truth and Logic* you reached the conclusion that philosophy is properly the logic of science – this being the only job left for it to do. One would therefore expect you to go off at that point and start devoting yourself to science, or rather to the logic of science. Did you in fact do that? Did you set yourself to find out a lot about science?

AYER: I have done a certain amount of amateur reading in science, and I have certainly in recent years been interested in problems entering into the philosophy of science. I am at the moment working on a book on probability and induction and that whole field. I never went very deeply into science, partly because I don't think I was very well equipped to. I was brought up, like most English philosophers, as a classical scholar, and never had any very great aptitude for mathematics or physics; I was therefore only capable of acquiring an amateur knowledge of science, and I think it probable that to do good work in the philosophy of science you need to approach it from the inside. I mean you need to have had a scientific training; so this is how I was personally handicapped. And also I found that a lot of problems which I'd thought I'd solved in *Language, Truth and Logic* still gave me trouble, like all these epistemological problems I've been talking about, and I have gone on being concerned with them. I've gone on being concerned with trying to get a theory of perception that satisfied me, a theory of memory that satisfied me, a view of other minds that satisfied me. I am still working away on that. And in my recent books I've been interested – much influenced here by Quine – in questions of ontology, in questions of what entities one admits in a theory and how far this is an arbitrary matter. And also in questions of meaning, not in the sense of getting a criterion of meaning like the verifiability principle, which would be a criterion of demarcation, but in trying to give an analysis of meaning itself. In my book on *The Origins of Pragmatism*, working on a basis supplied by the greatest of all pragmatists, Charles Sanders Peirce, I tried to develop a behavioural theory of meaning, a theory of meaning in terms of our dispositions to do certain things, and so on.

I was trying to get away from the Platonic model of the sign as mirroring something else, in favour of the Wittgensteinian notion of the sign as a tool, and to develop this. Not with total success, I must say, but this is the sort of thing I've been concerned with.

MAGEE: I think we've now got to move, as you did, away from logical positivism. But before we do there's one observation I'd like to make and one question I'd like to ask. The observation is that there was always one striking difference between positivists on the Continent and positivists in Britain. Positivists in Britain weren't ever very interested in mathematics and science – I think you suggested the reason earlier when you referred to the education system – while on the Continent they were never very interested in epistemology. The question I'd like to ask is this. A couple of generations of educated non-philosophers seem to have thought of contemporary philosophy as logical positivism, and even to have thought that this was the same thing as linguistic analysis. How do you suppose this very widespread misconception among the educated came about?

AYER: I suppose it is partly just because of the success of *Language, Truth and Logic*. This is a book more widely read than most philosophical books, and one that I suppose has been pretty influential on what has happened since. Beyond that, although logical positivism is certainly only one strand in the whole contemporary movement, it has certain features which I think are common to the whole movement. I think it is true not only of the logical positivists but also of most British and American philosophers since the beginning of the century that they have been hostile to metaphysics in the old system-building sense. Moore and Russell, who started the whole thing off, were both consciously reacting against the neo-Hegelians – against people like Bradley and McTaggart – and were in their different ways trying, as it were, to bring philosophy down to earth. To make it deal with concrete problems and make it deal with testable questions and so on. I think this is true of the whole movement. It's been diversified in various ways. In England we have had this fashion for ordinary language study, which I don't think has been much echoed elsewhere, and which I myself regard as something of a blind alley, though I think Austin's own work is interesting; but I don't think that the method has been very fruitful except in his hands.

MAGEE: Since so much contemporary philosophy is linguistic, can I interrupt at this point to ask why you're not a linguistic philosopher? And why you think linguistic philosophy is a blind alley?

AYER: Well I think that in my own case, even in my most positivist period, I've always been mainly interested in the theory of knowledge. I think that philosophy for me always has been a question of searching for proof or for justification – asking the question which runs through British empiricism: 'What ground do we have for these claims to knowledge?' I think this has always been my dominant interest, as it was Russell's, who is the philosopher whom I follow most closely. I believe it can be shown that all Russell's philosophy has been based on this quest for reassurance. It is sceptical in the sense that it questions all claims, but it also tries to find a solid base for them. The reason why Russell was always attempting to reduce things was to give fewer hostages to fortune. And it never seemed to me that the study of the usage of words contributed very much, except incidentally, to the resolution of this problem. I think it can be made useful. For example, Ryle in *The Concept of Mind* did use linguistic techniques but he used them in the interests of a thesis. Ryle had a very definite, very controversial, thesis, which, although he probably wouldn't like me to put it so crudely, was fundamentally a behaviourist one. And he used linguistic techniques to further this. I couldn't see that the study of the usage of words, as it were, *in vacuo*, was of philosophical importance. I don't say it's an activity people shouldn't engage in, but it didn't seem to me to illuminate any problem that I was concerned with. And I still think this.

MAGEE: In the preface to your second book, *The Foundations of Empirical Knowledge*, which came only four years after *Language, Truth and Logic*, you actually say that what you're going to deal with is the classical English problem of 'our knowledge of the external world'. What did you actually try to accomplish in that book?

AYER: In the main, I was trying to make what's known as a phenomenalist programme work. I was trying to achieve what I suppose Berkeley and Hume had, in a sense, set out to do, and show that all propositions about physical objects could be exhibited as propositions about sense data. Then I later came to the conclusion that I hadn't succeeded, and the view I now hold is that our talk of physical objects is a theory with respect to sensory statements. And in *The Origins of Pragmatism* and my books of essays I've tried to show exactly in what way this theory operates.

MAGEE: Since this is the view you now hold, can you expand on it?

AYER: Yes. I think that you can't effect a translation but I think you can show, for example, that a system of physical space and time can be built up on the basis of spatio-temporal relations that are directly given in our sense experience. In much the same way as Kant followed in his *Critique of Pure Reason*, you can build up – let's call it a picture of an objective physical world in terms of stable patterns of data reached by constant sensory routes. I mean, it is essential to our being able to have our physical picture as a theory that, to put it crudely, most things stay put; that you get the same blocks of data recurring in stable relations to each other. Now I tried to show in detail what kind of imaginative projection from the fragments we are given leads to this picture, which I think is our picture of the physical world. The new twist that I have added in my recent work is to separate priority in knowledge from priority in being. Hitherto nearly everyone has assumed that the data you start with are, as it were, what there fundamentally is. I now say that we can disassociate these questions and speak of what there is only at the level of theory. So I have a physicalist theory of being which gives primacy to physical objects, and an empiricist-sensory theory of knowledge. In this way I try to get the best of both worlds.

MAGEE: You said earlier that you're also working on questions concerning memory and questions concerning other minds.

AYER: Well, I'm not in fact working on those now. I've come to something of an *impasse* there. I haven't really advanced beyond the views I put forward in my *Problem of Knowledge*. It seems to me now, looking back on this book, that on the whole the sceptic won and I then by an arbitrary act deprived him of his victory. It does seem to me that I'm in the position, which I think Russell also reached, of saying that one can't really justify one's belief in the past, that one can't really justify one's belief in other minds. Well in the case of other minds I think one can work the 'argument from analogy' but it's a very dubious tool or bridge. It doesn't quite bear the weight one puts on it. But in the case of the past one simply has to say that one can only justify one memory statement in terms of another. It's simply impossible to ask for a justification of memory as a whole – which is a slightly unsatisfactory position. For the time being, at least, I feel that I have taken that group of problems as far as I can. I'm now working partly on the things I've just been talking about, on this idea of the physical object language as a theory with respect to sensory experiences, and also on questions of ontology, asking at what level one raises them and how they are related to questions about what one knows. And I've also gone on to this other area which I spoke about, of being interested in evidence in the scientific sense, and trying to find out what is a good reason for accepting one scientific hypothesis rather than another, and whether one can resolve this whole problem of going beyond one's evidence in terms of probability. In a sense this fits in, I suppose, with my general conception of philosophy, which I more and more come to regard as being, if you like, the study of *proof*; and what I'm doing is applying this in various fields. And having done all I can do on the common-sense level I'm now trying to move on to a slightly different level and try and take up the problems there. Because they are different in different cases.

MAGEE: When you say philosophy is the study of proof, what do you mean?

AYER: I mean really the study of what is a valid reason for what. If I had to sum up philosophy in a sentence I'd say that philosophy is the theory of the form of the proposition '*p* supports *q*'. The support at its strongest being entailment, you have there the whole of deductive logic. Logic can be said to be the theory of deductive argument. And I think the rest of philosophy can be comprised, at one level or another (well perhaps not the whole of the rest of philosophy because there are other things too – I suppose ethics doesn't quite fit into this mould) of what is good evidence for what, and why. Often, indeed, this is purely defensive work. As I said earlier, a sceptic comes along and says: 'But surely this isn't good evidence for that.' And then you have to make clear why you think it is. And do justice to the problems. And I think very often the answers you get in philosophy are quite platitudinous. Very often the answer just is that what we all think is so, is so, but it's the scenery you visit by the way that's important and interesting. This is of course the trouble, that one isn't sure one is going to be able to come out with anything that is going to be more than an assurance to people to do what they would have done anyway.

MAGEE: Like all good philosophers you seem to have doubts about the subject!

AYER: One always has that, I think. I think one always has doubts about the subject just because you don't get clear advances. I mean science isn't by any means always a bed of roses, but still in science you do put up a hypothesis and you get a test and the test is positive or negative. And then if it's positive you're pleased, and if it's negative you try again. In philosophy one never quite knows where one is, one never quite knows when one has got a problem solved –

whether one's got the problem properly *posed*. And of course some
people now think there aren't any genuine problems. I suppose this
might be a rather crude version of Wittgenstein, but certainly there's
a strain in Wittgenstein of assuming that the whole thing is a muddle.
I don't believe this, I believe there are genuine problems and I
believe there are true or false answers to them, otherwise I wouldn't
pursue the subject. But it's awfully hard to get the problems clearly
seen and clearly stated, and it's awfully hard to see even what the
criteria are for what are the correct answers to them. This I think
makes one despair at times, but then one goes on, and perhaps one
gets something one thinks may be right, and then one feels better
again.

MAGEE: You yourself have remarked to me – I don't know how
casually the remark was made – that the book of yours that you
regard as the best is *The Problem of Knowledge*. Why do you think
so?

AYER: Partly because I think it's the most original. I think that
Language, Truth and Logic is in a sense my most effective book – I
mean it obviously is, from its reception. It was written with great
passion. But I do think that in *The Problem of Knowledge* I did set
the whole theory of knowledge in a new light, at least a light that was
new to me, and that I hadn't seen produced elsewhere. And I do
think that it does make it intelligible what the subject is about, and
also how one might look for solutions to the various problems. I
think in this sense it was a seminal book.

MAGEE: It did seem to me, reading it recently, that it kept leaving
everything as it was. I mean, its characteristic mode of procedure is
to take a common-sense viewpoint, consider the sceptical objection
to it, rebuff the objection – and therefore one is constantly being
plonked back where one was before one read the book.

AYER: In a sense, in this field, it would be very startling not to be
left where one was. I mean, if one did come up with a proof that one
had no reason to believe the things that one does believe about the
past, or about other people's minds, and so on, it would indeed be
much more exciting, but at the same time very disturbing. I think
that you would need a very strong argument to be convinced of this.
Perhaps I had too much respect for common sense. This might be so.
Perhaps I was too much under common-sense control when I wrote
this book. But I wouldn't regard it as an objection to philosophy
that it left things where they were, because . . .

MAGEE: Because that's where they are.

AYER: Because that's where they are. The point is to clarify, to elucidate, to justify. If such fundamental beliefs as these seem to be are capable of justification, the thing is to find it. I don't think I did altogether find it in that book. As I said, the weakness in the book is that to some extent it cheats. The sceptical arguments are triumphant and not sufficiently met, so that I should perhaps have ended on a more sceptical note than I did.

If you want a philosopher to be constructive in the sense of not leaving things where they are, then I think you've got to marry him to a scientist. I don't see how one is to effect changes except by changing one's conceptual outlook, and I don't think one can do this except in conjunction with scientific theories. Here again Einstein is a good example. He didn't leave things where they were because he changed our whole concept of time. I should call this a philosophical achievement. But it had to be done in the light of a scientific theory. Apart from the whole scientific context of the Michelson-Morley experiment, and the breakdown of the evidence for the ether and so on, it wouldn't have been possible. And the same with the quantum theory, and its revision of the concept of causality; this had to be done in a scientific context. I don't think you're going to get major philosophical revisions, things being moved on by philosophy, except in conjunction with science – except in conjunction with scientific evidence which calls for a new way of looking at the world, which calls for a new conceptual structure. And if you're operating at the level of common sense then you are going to leave things as they are, unless you move over into science – as for example Russell did when he came to reject common-sense concepts in favour of scientific ones. For instance, he wanted to say that the common man is simply mistaken in thinking that the sky is blue.

MAGEE: We've discussed your three best-known books, and we've also talked about some of the things that you're working on at the moment. To end with, is there anything you'd like to say about the immediate future of philosophy?

AYER: I think that there has again to be a *rapprochement* of philosophy and science. They diverged in the nineteenth century, partly in consequence of the romantic movement and partly because science got too difficult, and now there are some signs that they are coming together again. And I see the future of philosophy as lying after all where I put it at the end of *Language, Truth and Logic*, in its being the logic of science.

MAGEE: So you think that the future for linguistic philosophy is bleak?

AYER: I think that the future for pure linguistic philosophy is very bleak. But of course in another sense it is not so at all. There is still the whole study of language, the work that people like Chomsky are doing. But the point there again is that they are approaching it scientifically.

4
Conversation with Karl Popper

MAGEE: Karl Popper was born in Vienna in 1902, and lived there till he was in his thirties. He was never one of the members of the Vienna Circle, for although he shared most of their interests he disagreed with their doctrines. One could almost say that his first book, *Logik der Forschung* – which means literally 'The Logic of Research' – was written *against* the Vienna Circle. Unfortunately, although it was published in the autumn of 1934, it didn't appear in English translation till a quarter of a century later (under the title *The Logic of Scientific Discovery*). I can't help feeling that the philosophy of a whole generation here in England might have been different if the book had appeared here earlier.

Popper left Vienna in 1937 and spent the war years in New Zealand. It was there that he wrote, in English, the two-volume work that first made him really famous in the English-speaking world, *The Open Society and its Enemies*. This is a massive and powerfully argued statement of the case for democracy and against totalitarianism – and also against the chief *philosophical* opponents of democracy, above all Plato and Marx. A smaller book, *The Poverty of Historicism*, dealing with the methods of the theoretical social sciences, was originally published as a series of articles at the same time as *The Open Society*, and can be seen as a pendant to that book. In the same way the latest volume of Popper's to be published, *Conjectures and Refutations*, can be seen as a pendant to his first and seminal work, *The Logic of Scientific Discovery*. Since 1945 Popper has been a British subject, and has been on the staff of the London School of Economics, from which he recently retired as Professor of Logic and Scientific Method.

Sir Karl, I know from our previous conversations that you regard being a philosopher as something that needs apologizing for. Why?

POPPER: Yes, I cannot say that I am proud of being called a philosopher.

MAGEE: It's an odd thing to say. Why do you say it?

POPPER: In the long history of philosophy there are many more philosophical arguments of which I feel ashamed than philosophical arguments of which I am proud.

MAGEE: But obviously you think that being a philosopher is at least worth while, even if it's nothing to be proud of.

POPPER: I think I can offer an excuse – something like an apology for the existence of philosophy, or a reason why there is a need for thinking about philosophy.

MAGEE: And what would it be?

POPPER: It is that everybody *has* some philosophy: we all, you, and I, and everybody. Whether or not we know it, we all take a great number of things for granted. These uncritical assumptions are often of a philosophical character. Sometimes they are true; but more often these philosophies of ours are mistaken. Whether we are right or wrong can be found out only by a critical examination of these philosophies which we take uncritically for granted. This critical examination is, I suggest, the task of philosophy, and the reason for its existence.

MAGEE: What would you give as a contemporary example of an uncritical philosophical creed that's in need of critical examination?

POPPER: A very influential philosophy of the kind I have in mind is the view that when something 'bad' happens in society, something we dislike, such as war, poverty, unemployment, then it must be the result of some bad intention, some sinister design: somebody has done it 'on purpose'; and, of course, somebody profits from it. I have called this philosophical assumption the conspiracy theory of society. It can be criticized; and I think it can be shown that it is mistaken: there are many things that happen in society which are unintended and unforeseen consequences of our actions.

The conspiracy theory of society is one of those many uncritical philosophies which create a need for a critical investigation. They constitute, I think, an excuse for being a philosopher. These mistaken philosophies are influential, and somebody ought to discuss them and criticize them.

MAGEE: Can you give some other examples?

POPPER: Lots. A very pernicious philosophy can be formulated in the words: 'A man's opinions are always determined by his economic or political interests.' Very often this is applied only to one's opponent, in the following form: 'If *you* do not hold the same view as *I*, you must be dominated by some sinister economic motives.' What is so bad about this kind of philosophy is that its acceptance makes serious discussion impossible. And it leads to a deterioration of interest in finding out the truth about things. For in place of the problem: 'What is the truth about this matter?', people merely ask: 'What are your motives?' And this is obviously a question of little significance.

A similar philosophy, also pernicious, and at present immensely influential, can be formulated as follows: 'Rational discussion is possible only between people who agree on fundamentals.' Those who accept this will also hold that rational discussion of fundamental problems is impossible. This philosophy is sometimes defended by the assertion: 'Only if we accept, to begin with, a far-reaching common framework of assumptions can we hope to reach agreement in a rational discussion.' This philosophy sounds quite plausible and reasonable, but it has terrible consequences. For it tears mankind asunder into groups – culture groups – between which there can be no discussion, but only war. This is not only a bad philosophy but, I think, a false philosophy – one which can be refuted, though not one which I can refute in a few minutes. But its existence and its tremendous influence, is, I think, one of the excuses for being a philosopher.

MAGEE: So your thesis is this: we are all practising philosophers in the sense that we all hold philosophical theories and act on them. But usually we are not aware that what we are doing is uncritically accepting the truth of a theory.

POPPER: Yes.

MAGEE: And some of these theories are true, you say, while others are not only false but harmful. And you say the real task for philosophy is to examine critically our often unconscious philosophical prejudices and to correct them where correction is needed.

POPPER: Exactly. Incidentally, I do not think that the need to correct what *professional philosophers* say would be a sufficient excuse for philosophy to exist.

MAGEE: That's the exact opposite of Moore's view. He once said that the world itself did not present him with problems that made him want to philosophize – that he had only been made a philosopher by the unacceptable things said by other philosophers.

POPPER: I think this leads to something like philosophic inbreeding. It would make a specialism of philosophy, after the model of modern science. Now I think that a strong case can be made against this all too fashionable specialization in the sciences; and the case against specialization in philosophy is even stronger.

MAGEE: You mention modern science – I gather you had some training in it, didn't you?

POPPER: Yes. I did start my studies in the fields of mathematics and physics and my first teaching appointment was as a secondary school teacher in these subjects. But I was never a specialist, and I always worked on what interested me most. In physics I was only an amateur, never a professional. A thesis which I wrote to qualify as a teacher in mathematics was on the axioms of geometry, and I later worked on the axiomatization of probability theory.

MAGEE: Was that the centre of your field of research?

POPPER: This is difficult to say. I might say, perhaps, that my research was centred on the methods of science, especially of modern physics; or to use a more fashionable term, the philosophy of science. But then, there are many other things that interest me.

MAGEE: What were the central ideas of your first book, *The Logic of Scientific Discovery*?

POPPER: The central idea was, I think, that in view of Einstein's new theory of gravitation all earlier accounts of the working of science and of the nature of scientific knowledge were mistaken.

MAGEE: How?

POPPER: The view generally held was that science, or scientific knowledge, was a peculiarly secure or a very *certain* kind of knowledge; also, that it was the result of observation and experiment. Observation and experiment led us to frame a hypothesis. When this was checked, and tested, again and again, it became accepted as an established or proved scientific theory. This was, in brief, the accepted view. I saw that it had become untenable, because of Einstein's challenge to Newton's theory – the most successful and important theory ever advanced and accepted.

MAGEE: What makes you give Newton's theory that unique status?

POPPER: Newton made us understand for the first time something about the universe in which we live. And for the first time we had good reason to think that we had a theory that was true. For Newton's theory allowed us to make the most detailed predictions of new kinds of effects – such as deviations from Kepler's laws – and these predictions stood up to the most searching tests. The greatest success of the theory was, of course, the discovery of the planet Neptune: this turned the threat of a defeat into a victory.

MAGEE: Can you go into that a little more?

POPPER: The observations of the planet Uranus showed some slight discrepancies with the predictions derived from Newton's theory. Then Adams in England and Leverrier in France pointed out that these apparent discrepancies could be explained on the assumption that there was an as yet unobserved outer planet. Both calculated the position of this unknown planet, and it was promptly discovered by Galle in Berlin. I think that this was the most startling and convincing success of any human intellectual achievement ever; although it must be admitted that similar successful predictions have since then become not infrequent. At any rate, after this great success, few people doubted that Newton's theory was true. The usual view was that it had been established by induction based on observations. But now Einstein appeared with a competing theory. Opinions about the merits of this new theory differed widely; and they still differ: some physicists still cling to Newton's theory, for a variety of reasons.

MAGEE: Which do you favour?

POPPER: I think that Einstein's theory is superior to Newton's; but this is really not my main point.

MAGEE: Which is . . .?

POPPER: It is that all the observational evidence which may be claimed to support Newton's theory may also be claimed to support Einstein's very different theory. This shows, decisively, that we were simply mistaken when we thought that Newton's theory could be said to be established, or inductively proved, on the basis of the evidence. It further showed that *no* theory can be claimed to be inductively established. For there could be no more impressive agreement between theory and observational evidence than we had in the case of Newton's theory. If even this could not inductively establish the theory, then clearly nothing whatever could.

MAGEE: Is that why you abandoned the theory of induction?

POPPER: Yes. Fundamentally, the logical situation is extremely simple. No number of observations of white swans can establish the theory that all swans are white: the first observation of a black swan can refute it. The observational support of Newton's theory was of course much more impressive, because of the very subtle measurements which the theory predicted in great detail. But the first real discrepancy can refute it.

MAGEE: And of course such a discrepancy did occur – something to do with the planet Mercury, unless I'm mistaken.

POPPER: Yes, but this discrepancy was extremely small, and might possibly be explained (as pointed out by Dicke) within Newton's theory. My point is not so much that Newton's theory has been refuted or that it has been definitely superseded by Einstein's theory; my point is, rather, that since Einstein offered his competing theory, we know that even the greatest predictive success, even the severest tests, cannot establish a theory inductively. Now this means a decisive change in our view of science; it means that we were mistaken about scientific knowledge; that scientific theories always remained hypothetical; that it was always possible, even for the best established scientific theory, to be superseded by a better one. All we could say was that the better one would have to contain any successful and well-tested predecessor as an approximation. In this way it would also explain why its predecessor had been successful.

MAGEE: Can you sum up, then, the new view of science which you arrived at?

POPPER: First, no scientific theory may ever be regarded as definitely established or proved. Secondly, there was something fundamentally wrong in the view that scientific certainty (or probability) increases with the number of repeated observations or experiments. Rather, the part played by observation and experiment is merely that of *tests*. These tests are the more important the more *severe* they are.

For example, the discovery of Neptune had been an extremely severe test. Nevertheless it did not establish Newton's theory. All this led me to describe scientific tests of a theory as attempted *refutations* of that theory. A theory was successful as long as it stood up to tests – as long as it resisted our attempts to refute it. And if it was refuted, there arose the need for a new explanatory theory which had to explain both the successes *and* the ill-successes of its predecessor-theory.

MAGEE: What happens if we can't find a satisfactory successor to the refuted predecessor-theory?

POPPER: Then we would, of course, continue to use the old refuted theory until a better theory was found; but we should use it with the knowledge that there was something wrong with it. There would be an open problem, and we should know in advance the minimum conditions which a new theory would have to meet in order to be regarded as an interesting solution to this open problem.

MAGEE: And of course it's with the logic of problem-solving that you made your great breakaway from traditional empirical philosophy. Can I now recapitulate up to this point? From Bacon onwards the orthodox view of the way knowledge advances was something like this. Scientists accumulate data by observation and experiment until they've got so much that certain general features begin to emerge. They frame hypotheses based on these general features. Then they try to confirm the hypotheses by further observation and experiment. In cases where their attempts are successful the hypothesis is established as a law – and lo, another Secret of Nature has been unlocked. This alleged process of arriving at laws by generalization from observed instances is what's known as induction. Now your view of the matter was totally different. You proclaimed the startling doctrine that there is no such thing as induction. The notion does not, you said, describe what scientists actually do, nor is it the rationale of what they do.

POPPER: Yes, my view was and is different. According to my view, animals and men are born with a great store of instinctive knowledge – of ways of reacting to situations, of expectations. The new-born child expects to be fed and to be cared for. Its expectation, its inborn conjectural knowledge, may be disappointed. In this case it may die, unless it manages to solve its problems somehow. The fact that our inborn knowledge may be disappointed shows that even this inborn knowledge is merely conjectural. Moreover, according to my view, we do not learn by observation, or by association, but by trying to solve problems. A problem arises whenever our conjectures or our expectations fail. We try to solve our problems by modifying our conjectures. These new tentative conjectures are our trial balloons – our trial solutions. The solution, the new behaviour, the new conjecture, the new theory, may work; or it may fail. Thus we learn by trial and error; or more precisely, by tentative solutions and by their elimination if they prove erroneous. As H. S. Jennings showed in 1910, this method is used even by the amoeba.

MAGEE: But – as you yourself have pointed out somewhere – it's not entirely the same when used by an amoeba and when used by Einstein.

POPPER: You are quite right: there is a most important difference. It is this. On the pre-scientific level we hate the very idea that we may be mistaken. So we cling dogmatically to our conjectures, as long as possible. On the scientific level, we systematically search for our mistakes, for our errors. This is the great thing: we are consciously critical in order to detect our errors. Thus on the pre-scientific level, we are often ourselves destroyed, eliminated, with our false theories; we perish with our false theories. On the scientific level, we systematically try to eliminate our false theories – we try to let our false theories die in our stead. This is the *critical method of error elimination*. It is the method of science. It presupposes that we can look at our theories critically – as something outside ourselves. They are not any longer our subjective beliefs – they are our objective conjectures.

Thus the general picture of science is: we choose some interesting problem. We propose a bold theory as a tentative solution. We try our very best to criticize the theory; and this means that we try to refute it. If we succeed in our refutation, then we try to produce a new theory, which we shall again criticize; and so on. In this way, even if we do not succeed in producing a satisfactory theory, we shall have learned a great deal: we shall have learned something about the problem. We shall know where its difficulties lie. The whole procedure can be summed up by the words: bold conjectures, controlled by severe criticism which includes severe tests. And criticism, and tests, are attempted refutations.

MAGEE: And it's only as a second stage that observation and experiment come in?

POPPER: According to my view, observation and experiment are essentially *ways of testing our theories*. They may thus be regarded as belonging to the critical discussion of the theories.

MAGEE: From your point of view it follows that we never really know anything – that there are only differing degrees of uncertainty . . .

POPPER: There are various senses of the word 'knowledge' and 'certainty'. There is a very strict sense of 'I know' which can be described in this way: 'I know' means, 'I believe, *and* I have *sufficient reason* for believing; that is, it is impossible that I am mistaken.' You are right when you suggest that in *this* sense we never know: there *always* is a possibility of a mistake. But I think this is trivial and unimportant. What is important is the distinction between *knowledge in the subjective sense* and *knowledge in the objective sense*.

MAGEE: Perhaps you'd better explain that distinction.

POPPER: Knowledge in the subjective sense consists of dispositions to act in certain ways, or to believe certain things, or to say certain things. *My* knowledge consists of *my* dispositions, *your* knowledge consists of *your* dispositions. Knowledge in the objective sense consists of spoken or written or printed statements – statements, or theories, which occur in certain contexts, for example in scientific journals. Newton's theory or Einstein's theory are examples of knowledge in the objective sense. Newton's dispositions to write down his theory, or to discuss it, are examples of knowledge in the subjective or personal sense. The moment he formulated his ideas in words, and wrote them down, there was also knowledge in the objective sense. Both kinds of knowledge are uncertain or conjectural or hypothetical.

MAGEE: But is there really all that crucial a difference in logical status between the knowledge I have in my head and the same knowledge written down?

POPPER: Yes. Putting our ideas into words, or better, writing them down, makes an important difference. For in this way they become criticizable. Before this, they were part of ourselves. We may have had doubts. But we could not criticize them in the way in which we criticize a linguistically formulated proposition or, better still, a written report. Thus there is at least one important sense of 'knowledge' – the sense of 'linguistically formulated theories submitted to criticism'. It is what I call 'knowledge in the objective sense'. Scientific knowledge belongs to it. It is this knowledge which is stored in our libraries rather than in our heads.

MAGEE: And you regard the knowledge stored in our libraries as more important than the knowledge stored in our heads.

POPPER: Much more important, from every point of view, even from the highly subjective point of view of our own personal enjoyment of knowledge. For what we enjoy is the theory itself. Assume that you or I produce a new idea, which is a very enjoyable experience; then there is its objective relationship to the objective old ideas, and to the problems which we solve by our new ideas; and this relationship forms an essential part of the enjoyment. And of course we should never have made a discovery without first grasping some of the existing objective theories, and of the objective problem situation – or in other words, without studying scientific books or journals; and all that means knowledge in the objective sense. Also, an important part of our enjoyment consists just in the fact that we make a 'contribution to knowledge', as a famous phrase goes. We are like workers who help in the building of an edifice, like workers building a cathedral. It does make a difference to our enjoyment that our contribution is one to the *growth* of knowledge in the objective sense.

MAGEE: I want to return to the question of certainty and uncertainty. Am I right in saying that when you talk of the growth of knowledge what you really mean is the growth only of systems of hypotheses or conjectures – though no doubt of well-criticized and severely tested conjectures?

POPPER: Yes. All our theories are conjectures.

MAGEE: And the growth comes about *as a result of* criticism?

POPPER: Through severe and imaginative criticism which helps us to uncover new problems, and through bold and imaginative guesses which help us to put forth new and revolutionary theories as tentative solutions of these problems.

MAGEE: But if we never actually *know* anything, what are the grounds of our criticism? On what grounds do we accept some hypotheses and reject others?

POPPER: The grounds are provided by our critical discussion of the various competing theories. In these discussions we try to evaluate the theories from the point of view of their truth or falsity. Or more precisely, we try to compare them by asking which of them appears to come nearest to the truth.

MAGEE: But if there's no certainty, no knowledge, what do you mean by 'the truth'?

POPPER: Correspondence to the facts. We know what it means for the theory to correspond to the facts even if you can't decide whether it *does* correspond to the facts or not.

MAGEE: For what you call nearness or approximation to the truth you use the term 'verisimilitude', don't you?

POPPER: Yes. What we try to do in our discussion is to find out which of our competing theories has the greatest verisimilitude. Our discussions sometimes contain good reasons for preferring some of the competing theories to others from this point of view. But it is at best only a *preference* for a theory which we can in this way rationally defend. And if somebody produces another theory tomorrow, then the situation of competition between the theories may change, and with it our preferences.

MAGEE: Which is why you have said that we can never justify a belief that a certain theory is true; though we can sometimes justify a preference for one theory over another.

POPPER: Precisely. Philosophers have usually tried to justify a theory, or our belief in a theory. This cannot be done; but if we are lucky we can justify a preference; for example I have shown why we can justify a preference for Einstein's theory of gravitation, even if we disregard the evidence of the motion of Mercury.

MAGEE: Is it irrelevant at this point to ask how?

POPPER: First, we can show that for every problem which can be solved by Newton's theory a solution can be obtained from Einstein's theory which is at least of the same degree of precision. This can be expressed by saying that the informative content or the empirical content of Einstein's theory is at least as great as that of Newton's. Then we can go further and show that the content of Einstein's theory exceeds that of Newton's because it allows us to raise and solve problems about the emission and propagation of light in gravitational fields which go beyond the power of Newton's theory. I have shown that this greater empirical content of Einstein's theory means that it is *better testable* than Newton's theory, and therefore better corroborable. And ultimately we can show that it is in fact better corroborated, even if we omit the case of Mercury. But since our critical comparison was made from the point of view of a better or worse approximation to the truth, we can sum up the result as indicating that Einstein's theory appears to be at present a better approximation to truth than Newton's.

MAGEE: When you say 'at present' I take it you mean 'in the light of the present state of the discussion'?

POPPER: Yes.

MAGEE: Doesn't this idea of 'the present state of the discussion' introduce an element of relativism?

POPPER: No. It does introduce an historical element; but not an element of relativism. Every unambiguously formulated proposition or theory is either true or false: there is no third possibility. But one false theory may be nearer to the truth than another. Also, one true theory may contain more truth than another: its 'truth content', as I call it, may be greater.

MAGEE: Example?

POPPER: Let us assume that it is now three minutes to twelve; then the statement that it is now five minutes to twelve is simply false; but it is nearer to the truth than either the statement that it is ten minutes to twelve or that it is ten minutes past twelve. Also, the false statement that it is now five minutes to twelve has a greater truth content than a vague true statement like 'the time is now between eleven and one o'clock'. That is, a larger class of true statements follows from it.

MAGEE: How is it that you've been chiefly concerned all your life with science and scientific knowledge rather than other sorts of knowledge?

POPPER: I was impressed by the great scientists, and by the revolutionary character of their theories. Besides, science is merely common sense writ large. It is part of common sense to be critical. It is part of common sense to submit our common-sense views to criticism; and science is, simply, the result of this criticism.

MAGEE: Now you've raised the question: 'What is science?' And your proposed method of demarcation between science and non-science constitutes one of your most important contributions to philosophy.

POPPER: I propose to say that a theory belongs to empirical science if we can say what kind of event we should accept as a refutation. Or in other words, a theory belongs to science if it is in principle refutable. A theory which cannot clash with any possible or conceivable event is, according to this view, outside science.

MAGEE: Let's be quite clear about this – you don't say that what is outside science is necessarily untrue. Still less meaningless.

POPPER: No. We cannot identify science with truth, for we think that both Newton's and Einstein's theories belong to science, but they cannot both be true, and they may well both be false. But they are both testable, which means that if they do *not* stand up to tests, they are refuted. Thus I take testability, or refutability, as a criterion of scientific character.

MAGEE: The members of the Vienna Circle, in fact all logical positivists, asserted that any statement outside science was literally meaningless, literally nonsense. You never went along with that.

POPPER: No, I never did. In my view a statement which is not refutable does not belong to empirical science; but this does not make it meaningless. Many of our scientific theories have developed out of non-testable pre-scientific theories. One can trace the history of Newton's theory right back to Anaximander and Hesiod, and the ancient theory of atomism was untestable until about 1905. In fact, most scientific theories emerged from prescientific story-telling. I should think it misleading to call these stories 'meaningless' . . . But it seems that my criticism of the positivist philosophies of meaninglessness has been fairly widely accepted.

MAGEE: In fact you've never concerned yourself much with questions of meaning at all, have you? Nor have you regarded language itself as all-important. This is all the more remarkable in a time and place where most philosophy tends to be linguistic in one way or another. What makes you take the approach you do?

POPPER: I do not think that you have got my approach correctly. It is true that I am not interested in the problem of meaninglessness; also, I am bored by discussions about the meaning of words. And it is also true that the people who sometimes call themselves philosophers of language or linguistic philosophers are interested in these problems of meaning which just do not interest me. But if you suggest that I do not regard language as important, then this is quite incorrect. Only remember what I said about objective knowledge. I think that there is nothing as important as language: I have a theory according to which it is language which makes us human, and that human consciousness – the consciousness of self – is a result of language. I am not interested in philosophizing about the meaning of words, partly because I think that even animals can learn the meaning of words. But human language begins with the *descriptive use of sentences*: or to put it in a less dry manner; it begins with story-telling.

MAGEE: I hadn't got you wrong, in fact, though I may have expressed myself badly. What I wanted to bring out was that you are not interested in analysis of the meaning of words. Can you explain why?

POPPER: Yes. Worrying about words and their meanings is one of the oldest pastimes in philosophy. Plato repeatedly mentions that the Sophist Prodicus was interested in distinguishing the different meanings of words; and the need for this distinction has therefore been called (by Svend Ranulf) the 'Principle of Prodicus'. This principle was new and important in 420 B.C., but by now some of us have perhaps learned this lesson. There are more interesting problems, even in this field.

MAGEE: Such as?

POPPER: To realize that words are to be used in order to formulate theories, and that any special interest in words and their meanings, and especially in definitions, leads to empty verbalism. I have proclaimed the emptiness of definitions for thirty years and I have refuted the superstition that if we want to be precise we have to define our terms. I tried to combat the influence of this superstition especially in the field of social and political philosophy; but to no effect. Political philosophers continue to write pages and pages comparing definitions. For example a book on Totalitarianism was published recently in which about fourteen definitions of 'totalitarianism' were compared and contrasted, among them also one attributed to me, although in a footnote I was censured 'because Popper never clearly defines totalitarianism'. The author failed to notice that I had argued, in the very book he quotes, against the empty verbalism which results from seeking precision in definitions.

MAGEE: People who know nothing about your work might be forgiven for supposing that your political philosophy has little to do with your philosophy of science. But in fact what you've done is, at bottom, to extend your view of the natural sciences to the social sciences – isn't that so? In other words your philosophy in these two apparently different fields is all of a piece.

POPPER: You may perhaps say that there are a number of common ideas. For example, in politics and elsewhere, we always make mistakes, but we can try to learn from our mistakes. The readiness to learn from our mistakes, and to look out for them, I call the rational attitude. It is always opposed to authoritarianism. In the field of politics the method of learning from your mistakes is a method based upon free criticism and discussion of the actions taken by the government.

MAGEE: And you have based your definition of democracy on this, rather than on the notion of rule by the majority.

POPPER: I don't want to define democracy at all. Moreover, the majority does not rule: whatever party may win the elections, neither you nor I rule. But I should explain that I distinguish two kinds of government. Of one kind, we can get rid without bloodshed; of the other we cannot get rid without bloodshed, and perhaps not at all. I propose to call the first kind democracy and the second tyranny. But nothing depends on words. What is important, however, is this: if a country possesses institutions which make it possible to change the government without violence, and a group of people try to use violence because they did not succeed without it, then whatever they may think or intend, their action is an attempt to establish a government that is upheld by violence and cannot be got rid of without violence, or in other words, they are attempting to establish a tyranny. Although this is obvious, people usually do not think so far as this.

MAGEE: Why has so much of your political philosophy taken the form of an attack on Utopianism?

POPPER: There is a lot in our social life which is cruel, ugly, stupid, and unjust: there is always much room for improvement. People have always dreamt of a better world, and some of these dreams have inspired social reforms. But, as I have shown in my *Open Society*, dreams of a perfect society are dangerous. The Puritans hoped to establish a perfect society, and so did Robespierre. What they achieved was not heaven on earth but the hell of a violent tyranny.

MAGEE: Some of your neglected discoveries in political philosophy have been rediscovered independently by others. For instance Djilas, after being one of the leading figures in the Communist world, put forward in his now-classic *The New Class* ideas which you published long before him in *The Open Society*. And again his latest book *The Unperfect Society* unpacks at length the sentence: 'It is my belief that society cannot be perfect.' He now thinks that the idea that society can be perfect is the basic mistake made by Communists.

POPPER: I think you are right about Djilas: he has arrived through long years of suffering and imprisonment at some views which others arrived at through critical thinking. Somehow I find his results more impressive and valuable.

MAGEE: But we are now seeing a marked revival among the intelligent young in precisely those writers and doctrines you attacked: Hegel, Marx, psychoanalysis, Existentialism. What is your explanation of this?

POPPER: There has always been a tendency to look out for the philosopher's stone – for some recipe for all our ills. The present situation is hardly new – except for a sad decline in the rationality of discussion. It is partly due to impatience and partly due to a feeling that there has been too much talk and that it has led to nothing. So it is no longer fashionable to argue with one's opponent. One does not try any longer to find out what is wrong in one's opponent's argument. One accepts some impressive theory wholesale. This is an understandable tendency, but a sad one if it becomes the characteristic mark of young intellectuals. It shows a decline of intellectual standards and of intellectual responsibility. An example of the thoughtlessness of this kind of anti-rationalism is the present vogue of anarchism. Surely, we should oppose the growth of bureaucracy, and the growth of the power of the state. But it is incomprehensible to me that the same people who must realize that, on the international level, anarchy means atomic war, can believe that we can have anarchy on the national level without getting involved in atomic war.

MAGEE: Although you haven't published a book for some years you've been producing a steady flow of articles, papers, lectures, and so on. What have been some of your more recent concerns?

POPPER: I have been working on many subjects: on the theory of what I call the 'Third World', by which I mean the objective world of the products of the human mind. It comprises objective knowledge – the world of scientific problems, theories, and discussions – but also the world of objective works of art. Another and connected direction of my interest is the theory of evolution; and a link between these two fields is the theory of human language, particularly from a biological point of view. This has further led me to some thought on the problem of the relation between body and mind.

MAGEE: That's a welter of problems. What are you working on literally now?

POPPER: I am working on a reply to my critics.

MAGEE: For the forthcoming volume devoted to your work in the Library of Living Philosophers?

POPPER: Yes.

5
Conversation with Geoffrey Warnock

The Philosophies of Moore and Austin

MAGEE: So far the subject matter of this book on contemporary British philosophy has had, perhaps surprisingly, a decidedly international flavour. We've seen how the modern movement began with a breakaway from German Idealism, and, much later, how A. J. Ayer imported logical positivism into Britain from Vienna. Of the other individuals to whose work we've devoted whole discussions, both Wittgenstein and Popper were born and grew up in Vienna – though neither was ever a member of the Vienna Circle, nor a logical positivist. And Russell, of course, is a world figure. So it is only now, for the first time, that we turn to a restrictedly British tradition, in the work of G. E. Moore and J. L. Austin – philosophers whom one would scarcely hear mentioned if one studied philosophy in most places outside the English-speaking world. They are, I should say, the two most important philosophers of whom this is true – and their influence has been much greater than it suggests: to give only one illustration, Moore had a decisive influence on Russell, who wrote in *My Philosophical Development*: 'It was towards the end of 1898 that Moore and I rebelled against both Kant and Hegel. Moore led the way, but I followed closely in his footsteps.'

Moore was born in 1873, the year after Russell, and died in 1958. He published four books: *Principia Ethica* when he was 30 years old, then *Ethics* in 1912, *Philosophical Studies* in 1922, and *Some Main Problems of Philosophy* in 1953. However, it was not through his books that he exerted most of his influence but through personal contact in teaching and conversation, discussion, seminars, lectures. This was even more outstandingly true of J. L. Austin, who published no books at all. Austin, who was born in 1911 and died in 1960, has probably been the most influential presence in Oxford since the

Second World War as far as philosophy is concerned. Since his death three volumes have appeared: *Philosophical Papers*, edited by Geoffrey Warnock and J. O. Urmson, *How to Do Things with Words*, edited by Urmson, and *Sense and Sensibilia*, reconstructed from lecture notes by Geoffrey Warnock.

I think for clarity's sake, Mr Warnock, we should discuss Moore and Austin separately. But before we do, are there any important features they have in common?

WARNOCK: Yes, I'm sure they did have a good deal in common. For one thing they were both, clearly, exceptionally clever men, and no doubt much of their authority among their contemporaries was due simply to their exceptional intellectual gifts. But that goes without saying.

MAGEE: Were they exceptional in this respect even among philosophers of reputation?

WARNOCK: Certainly – among philosophers each of them was simply an outstandingly clever man. But it's perhaps more worth saying that they had a great deal in common temperamentally. They both liked philosophy to be, and insisted that philosophy should be, as plain as possible, as clear as possible in expression. They liked extreme exactness and explicitness of argument. And both had an extreme distaste, I think, for eloquence, rhetoric, looseness, and rapidity in philosophical writing. In these ways, temperamentally, they had a great deal in common. And then another point that is a very important one, I think, and to which I am sure a good deal of their influence is attributable, is that they were both exceptionally impressive men – people you couldn't but take notice of, who clearly were not in any way to be disregarded or treated lightly – both rather formidable men, and simply by the force of their personalities making a considerable impression, quite apart from the merits or content of what they actually said.

MAGEE: Let's start by considering Moore. His first work was in ethics – and we have it on Keynes's authority that it influenced a whole generation of younger men at Cambridge. Also of course the Bloomsbury Group were constantly paying lip service to it, in fact treating it as a sort of Bible. Why did it so influence these people?

WARNOCK: Well, it's not very easy to say; and in fact I find the whole phenomenon here, I must say, slightly comical as well as perplexing. After all, the people who say they were – and no doubt actually were – influenced by this book were so different from Moore in many ways; and the book itself is in a way so dry, so intensely academic, that it's at first sight hard to see why it should have been so influential on such people. Of course most of the people we're talking about here knew Moore personally – were exposed, so to speak, to that powerful personality; and no doubt they received his book with sympathy partly for that reason. But there is also the conclusion Moore reaches as to what is ultimately of value in the world, namely certain states of consciousness associated with personal relations and the enjoyment of beautiful objects – which certainly has a good sort of Bloomsbury ring to it. And then there is his Intuitionism – I mean the rejection of any sort of authority in morals, indeed the denial, really, that there is any room for argument, at any rate at the basis of moral judgment. Moral judgment was, on Moore's showing, very much a matter ultimately of personal, direct intuition, and I suppose this might have been found sympathetic by that group of persons as well.

There is one point that I think ought to be mentioned, and which is very often forgotten – namely that there are important aspects of *Principia Ethica* which were conspicuously neglected by this group of its admirers, doctrines which they didn't at all take over from Moore. What I'm thinking of here is that Moore's actual recommendations as to conduct in *Principia Ethica* come out as absolutely conventional. He had the idea that the moral rightness or wrongness of actions really depended exclusively on their consequences; he took the view that the consequences of any action inevitably stretch into an infinitely remote future; and this led him to the conclusion that it is actually impossible for us ever to be sure whether an action is morally right or not. Though he thought there was in principle an answer to this question in terms of the consequences of the action, he also held that the answer was something which we could never know, or never be sure that we had got right. So that his recommendations for conduct reduced to the proposition that we should probably do best if we simply followed, quite exceptionlessly and rigorously, the time-honoured moral conventions of the society in which we lived. We couldn't possibly be justified, he thought, in making any exception to conventional morals, because we could never be sure enough that we were right in doing so.

MAGEE: It's obvious from the way you put it that you are critical of this view. How good do you think Moore's work in ethics actually was?

D

WARNOCK: Well, it's been, I suppose, certainly as influential as any of his other work, but I'm bound to say that, in my own view, Moore is rather far from his best in this particular field. I personally find *Principia Ethica* rather a disagreeable book; there is something rather painfully arrogant in its manner. The way, for example, that he writes off Mill and a number of other earlier moral philosophers is really excessively sweeping and condemnatory, in a rather unpleasing way. And then the most philosophically celebrated section of the book – the discussion right at the beginning about the so-called Naturalistic Fallacy, about goodness as a simple non-natural quality – in my view this is simply philosophically not very good. There are all sorts of objections to what Moore says that are really quite readily visible to the eye of the first-year undergraduate; it may not be easy to say what's right on those questions, but it's not hard to see that what Moore says won't really do. The argument isn't anything like so penetrating as his work in other fields.

MAGEE: In what fields do you think he did his best work, then?

WARNOCK: I think there can be no doubt that his best work was done in the theory of knowledge and philosophical logic.

MAGEE: His most famous paper was *A Defence of Common Sense* – Wittgenstein and many others thought it his best piece of work – yet there are conflicting views about what he was trying to do in it. What do you think he was trying to do?

WARNOCK: Yes, there's been a lot of argument about how Moore's *Defence of Common Sense* should be read. He presents himself at the outset as simply stating a large number of very simple-looking propositions, as to which he wishes to insist that we all know them to be true absolutely for certain; and we all know, he also says, exactly what they mean – they are not in any way ambiguous or obscure. These truths together are presented as encapsulating what he calls the common-sense view of the world; and what he says he is doing is simply insisting, in the first instance at any rate, that all these propositions are absolutely certainly true. Now some philosophers have thought that that couldn't really be what Moore meant to do. They didn't believe that other philosophers could really have *denied* these simple propositions, and accordingly couldn't believe that Moore just meant to re-assert them. It seemed to them, I think, that it could scarcely be of any serious interest to produce a great string of truisms and just insist that they are true, and they thought Moore *must* be doing something other than this; so that there did arise, at quite an early stage, a rather more sophisticated interpretation of what Moore was up to, which represented him as really aiming at a defence of common forms of speech. The suggestion was made that many philosophers who have said extraordinary things have in saying them been subtly repudiating or attacking, not so much ordinary beliefs, as ordinary forms of speech; and it was suggested that Moore's real aim was in some way to vindicate or defend the propriety or adequacy of ordinary ways of speaking. But it seems to me that this involves reading into what Moore says a great deal that isn't by any means explicitly there; it implies, indeed, that Moore was radically mistaken as to the significance of his own work. For Moore himself would certainly have disavowed any particular interest in forms of speech. He himself certainly wrote for preference in very plain orthodox English, but I think he thought that how you expressed propositions didn't matter all that much – what was important was whether your propositions, however expressed, were true or not. And I believe he did really want to maintain vehemently – and not, incidentally, pointlessly – that the propositions which he put forward as constituting the common-sense view of the world were true propositions and known for certain to be true.

MAGEE: Can you give some examples of propositions which he thought were indubitably true yet which he took other philosophers to be subtly denying?

WARNOCK: Well, he said he knew absolutely for certain that he had a body, that there were in his physical environment other physical objects like desks and chairs, and that there were a great many other people who also had bodies and who had experiences of the same general sort as his own. He knew that he'd lived for some years previously on the surface of this planet, that the planet had existed for thousands of years before he was born, and that lots of other people had lived for thousands of years before he was born; and I think he also claimed to know for certain that the world and some of its inhabitants would go on existing after his own death. Things of that sort – which, surely, we do all suppose that we know.

MAGEE: I take it that among what he was implicitly denying were philosopher's statements to the effect that, say, time and space are forms of human consciousness.

WARNOCK: More extremely than that, some philosophers had come out with the curious-looking proposition that time was unreal, or

that space was unreal; or had regarded it as open to doubt whether
there really are material objects; or open to doubt whether there
really are minds other than one's own. That kind of thing. Moore
was arguing against – or perhaps, at this stage, simply *opposing* – a
whole sceptical tradition in philosophy, and also, I suppose, an
idealist tradition which represented the world as in many respects
quite other than one would ordinarily suppose it to be.

MAGEE: Did he ever ask himself why some philosophers said these
extraordinary things?

WARNOCK: I don't believe he did really, no. He didn't, I think, ever
get quite so far as that. He was simply amazed, apparently, by the
things that other philosophers said, and looked to see whether they
had actually stated any explicit and adequate arguments for the
things that they said; but when he came to the conclusion, as he did,
that philosophers had the curious habit of stating in their philosophical works all sorts of things which, according to him, they and
everybody else knew for certain to be untrue, I think he just rather
stuck at that point. He said: 'This is absolutely amazing; it's astonishing that people should do this.' But I don't think he had any
particular hypothesis as to why this should come about in philosophy
– why philosophy should seem so *peculiarly* liable to that sort of
oddity. Wittgenstein had views about that, but I don't think Moore
had.

MAGEE: From what you've said so far I think it would be difficult
for anyone to realize what was so original about Moore. What was
it?

WARNOCK: His originality was a product of his quite remarkable
independence of mind. He was able to operate – I think this is true
of Austin as well – as it were quite outside the orthodox conventions
of his day, to look at the whole subject from a quite detached and
independent point of view, from which the way that philosophers
went on struck him as absolutely astonishing. And he introduced a
quite fresh, novel way of looking at the subject, which he was able to
achieve and sustain largely because of the unshakeably independent
strength of his own convictions. In this he was quite unusual, I think.
Philosophers tend very much to take up the subject in the state in
which they find it, and to swim contentedly along in the way the
stream is going – which conspicuously Moore was able not to do.

MAGEE: If we know certain propositions to be true with absolute certitude, what more can we hope to get out of analysing them? What is the *point* of analysis in such cases?

WARNOCK: This brings up the other main theme of Moore's *Defence of Common Sense*. He insisted first of all that there are all these things that we know for certain to be true, and that further-more, in a sense, we know exactly what they mean. He then went on to say that, nevertheless, their *analysis* is deeply in doubt. And your question was, what was the object of analysis in Moore's view?

MAGEE: Yes. If we know the propositions to be true —

WARNOCK: And know what they mean —

MAGEE: Yes, and know what they mean – what is there for analysis to give us?

WARNOCK: Yes. This is a rather complicated question, I think, because Moore not only produced a great many, and a great variety of, specimens of analyses, but also discussed the nature of analysis itself a great many times, so that it's difficult to give any useful short answer to the question. I think one could say, though, that the interest in analysis in Moore's view was at any rate very,·very often essentially epistemological. I think he thought that if we could, so to speak, take some complex concept or some complex proposition to pieces and set out its constituents in a more explicit way, showing clearly the way in which they fitted together, then we would get light on what the *grounds* of propositions were. (Of course one is speaking metaphori-cally there, but the metaphor is implicit in the term 'analysis' itself.) We would be in a better position to say not only (what he thought indubitable) that we know for certain that they are true, but we'd be able to say something about *how* we know them to be true, or what it is that we know in knowing them to be true. This was certainly one result that analysis was supposed to yield.

MAGEE: What is an example of analysis as Moore understood it?

WARNOCK: When discussing the nature of analysis he was apt to produce, as a rather over-simple specimen of what analysis was, the proposition that a brother is a male sibling – where you have one notion to begin with, the notion of a brother, and that is, so to speak, decomposed into two, the more general notion of a sibling, with the further distinguishing feature of being a *male* sibling. But no doubt that's a bit too simple to be very illuminating; it's hard to see how *that* analysis could be philosophically profitable. I think more interesting, and more relevant to what I was saying a moment ago about the purpose of analysis, is what he did with propositions about ordinary material objects, objects of perception. Moore was always convinced that the analysis of propositions of this sort must bring in the very puzzling items which he called sense-data. If I said, for instance, of some object that this is a hand, he was quite sure that this proposition was really about, and in its analysed form would be seen to be about, a sense-datum that I have, and the problem was exactly how in the analysis the relation between the sense-datum and the hand should be spelled out. I think this – the fact that in analysing propositions of this sort he thought one must bring in sense-data – brings out the epistemological flavour of Moore's analyses. For in his view the question how sense-data are related to objects is exactly the question how we know propositions of this sort to be true.

MAGEE: Was it propositions about our knowledge of the world that primarily concerned him?

WARNOCK: Primarily, yes. I think he was prepared to turn the analytic batteries on any sort of proposition that seemed to him in need of the treatment, but certainly very, very often he was talking about perfectly ordinary propositions about familiar objects like hands and inkstands and tables and chairs, and was chiefly concerned with *how* we know them to be true.

MAGEE: Wasn't his view that the task of philosophy is to give a general account of how things are the same as that held by the Idealists he had broken away from?

WARNOCK: Yes, it was. I don't believe he ever did differ from his predecessors at that point. He took the view, as one very well might, that traditional metaphysicians, including the Idealists of the immediately preceding period, had wished to give some sort of general account of the universe and its contents, and Moore certainly – officially, so to speak – always said that this is indeed the ultimate object of philosophy: to give a general account of the universe and what it contains. Of course, in practice what Moore did came out looking very different, but the official object in view was the same.

MAGEE: So one might say they shared the same programme.

WARNOCK: Yes, he didn't ever say that philosophy should be radically differently conceived in that way.

MAGEE: You've mentioned the influence of his work in ethics. What was the influence on others of the work in philosophical logic and theory of knowledge which we've just been discussing?

WARNOCK: I think one could sub-divide the answer to that under a number of distinct headings. First, I'm sure that his way of doing philosophy – the extreme plainness and care and clarity, the taste for small steps and small points – was very influential. Predominantly, people came to adopt this cool, cautious manner of philosophical argument. Then, secondly, his example led many philosophers to think that philosophy is *entirely* analysis – that the philosopher does not, so to speak, assert propositions on his own account, but *only* analyses propositions asserted by others. Moore himself didn't say this, but others did; and Moore's *practice* seemed to support their view. But I think, in fact, his actual defence of common sense was very important too – I mean his insistence that there are vastly many things which as a matter of fact we all know for certain to be true, and that there must be something seriously wrong if philosophers seem to be denying or questioning these. Before Moore it had been very common for philosophers to suppose that somehow it was their professional business to go around questioning or denying what everybody else felt absolutely sure about. And Moore insisted very powerfully indeed that this was often just nonsense – that there are so many things which are really paradigms of knowledge and certainty, and by a sane philosophy must simply be accepted as such. This, I think, has since Moore become a very generally held view, at any rate among English-speaking philosophers. Such philosophers – I think I'm right in saying – would be very much disposed to agree with Moore that there are vastly many things which as a matter of fact we know absolutely for certain about ourselves and the world; and that it would really be a kind of non-sense to fall into treating these as doubtful or false. And this has been very important, I think, in changing the way philosophers look at what they're doing. The philosopher Prichard, for instance, had a kind of fanatical regard for deductive argument – very respectable in itself, but he was frequently prepared to follow a deductive argument to absolutely amazing and often absurd conclusions. He has some-where a little argument, for instance, which finishes up with the proposition that we never see anything move. Now that's the kind of thing that I think, post-Moore, has become very much more difficult to swallow. Moore would have said, and taught others to say: 'Look, something must have gone wrong; we know for certain that we very often see things move, and if you've got an argument that leads to the contrary conclusion there must be something wrong with it.' And I think this is an important change of angle among philosophers, which is largely attributable to Moore's influence at this point.

MAGEE: But isn't it of enormous value to have a few people around who question what the rest of us take absolutely for granted?

WARNOCK: Well, in a way I would agree with that, certainly. No doubt it is a besetting sin of human nature, and one thing that philosophy ought to check, to be unwarrantably confident in the convictions one holds. But I think what was really valuable in Moore's idea was that you have to have some fixed points somewhere. If you're going to raise the question what we know for certain, or even the question what knowledge itself is, there has to be something that you're prepared to hold on to, otherwise you're utterly at sea. I think Moore would have been inclined to say that, if the proposition that I've got shoes on my feet at this moment is not a proposition that I know for certain to be true, then I simply have no idea what knowledge is supposed to be; I don't know what it is that we're trying to define or scrutinize, if this isn't an example of it. And I think this is an important point. I mean, if you question absolutely everything – if you regard *every* suggested instance of knowing as perhaps not an instance of that at all – then, so to speak, all the guide-lines go, and we no longer have any way of testing whether we're talking sense or not. In a way, we literally don't know what we're talking about.

MAGEE: So you're saying that although it's logically possible to question everything – just as it's logically possible to be a solipsist – it's, in the same way, an unworkable position.

WARNOCK: Yes, I think so. You just get into a position in which there you are, treating everything as open to question; and in a sense this is a possible position, but an intrinsically hopeless and rather uninteresting one.

MAGEE: Where was Moore's influence most felt?

WARNOCK: He has had a considerable influence in the United States, for example, not only through his writings but also through the work of, for instance, Norman Malcolm and Morris Lazerowitz – both American philosophers who knew Moore well in Cambridge. And then, of course, Moore himself also taught in America for some years during the war. But among British philosophers he was – as it may be relevant to say at this point – certainly one of the philosophers most respected by Austin.

MAGEE: Was his influence on Austin specific?

WARNOCK: Well, as I mentioned before, there are marked similarities between Austin's manner of doing philosophy and Moore's; they had in common the taste for plainness, exactness, care, small points and small steps, and nothing grandiose or over-ambitious. But it would be very difficult to say to what extent Austin may have acquired this style of doing philosophy from Moore, or how far his own natural style may simply have coincided with Moore's. I really don't know what the answer to that would be. It may simply have been a case of temperamental affinity rather than of actual influence.

MAGEE: But it was an affinity Austin was aware of?

WARNOCK: Oh, certainly. He is on record as actually saying at one point 'Moore's my man' – certainly meaning by that that this was what he liked, the way he liked to see the subject done.

MAGEE: And meaning also, presumably, that he didn't like seeing it done in Russell's way.

WARNOCK: I think, on that occasion, yes – the relevant contrast was with Russell, whom Austin regarded, I think understandably, as altogether too fluent and rapid. He thought of Russell – not of course in his earlier, strictly logical writings, but in his later philosophy – as dealing with huge problems at a very high speed, and writing that beautifully smooth, swiftly flowing prose in which, Austin certainly thought, crucial points and distinctions were constantly whizzing by too quick for the eye to catch. He always very much distrusted that way of operating, I think.

MAGEE: Austin has been dead for ten years now. Has the time come when one can give a reasonably confident assessment of his contribution to philosophy?

WARNOCK: I think one could say certainly that what is most conspicuously alive in current discussions in philosophy is his work in the philosophy of language. This was the field in which he did, in fact, his largest continuous and systematic (though unfortunately unfinished) piece of work, in the book called *How to Do Things with Words*. Although many of his papers, and *Sense and Sensibilia*, are still discussed, it does seem to me to be in the philosophy of language that continuing interest is most clear at the moment.

MAGEE: What was he trying to do?

WARNOCK: In the philosophy of language in particular? I think one could say that what he essentially wanted to get away from in the philosophy of language was what he regarded as excessive abstraction – the tendency to look at language as an isolated phenomenon simply in itself, so to speak, in abstraction from the wider context in which things are said. In some ways here verging on – though not, I believe, influenced by – some ideas of Wittgenstein's, he wanted language to be put back into the context of human behaviour. He thought one should start from a consideration of talking as simply something that people *do* in particular situations.

MAGEE: Speech as an act, in other words.

WARNOCK: Yes: his, I suppose, most widely known and adopted technical term in the subject is precisely the notion of a 'speech act'. He always insisted that this is where one ought to begin – with the notion of something being *done* by somebody in a certain situation, characteristically involving other persons to whom he was speaking, and so on. The higher flights of the subject should be regarded as more or less sophisticated abstractions that one might get on to later, but at any rate one should begin with the concrete phenomenon of something being done in a certain way.

MAGEE: I take it he was rejecting the way philosophers have traditionally considered propositions and arguments in isolation from their practical context?

WARNOCK: Yes, he regarded that as always a possible cause of trouble. If you, so to speak, took simply the *words*, out of the context in which they occurred, and gazed at them on their own, he thought – fully justifiably in my view – that you were going to overlook a great deal that was crucially important in language and communication; if you concentrated too much on the words alone, in abstraction from the rest of the situation in which they occurred.

MAGEE: His minute, meticulous analysis of small points at a slow pace can easily seem to people – indeed seems to some philosophers – pedantic, scholastic and boring. But I take it you would defend it against such charges?

WARNOCK: Well, one couldn't deny, I suppose, that this way of approaching a philosophical problem could actually be sometimes boring and unproductive; but then, is there any way of doing philosophy that *can't* be? If one is invited to take more than usual care over details, its being boring or otherwise can only depend on whether the details to which one's invited to attend do or do not turn out to be illuminating; and of course sometimes they don't. This, however, was a question which Austin never liked to raise; he always objected, I mean, to raising the question *in advance* whether what you were doing was really important and interesting. He was inclined to say: 'We don't know *yet* whether this is going to turn out to be important and interesting or not. Let's just keep going for a bit and then see whether we are getting anywhere.' But of course it is perfectly possible in some subjects that in turning one's eye to Austinian minutiae you really aren't getting anywhere; this is certainly possible, nor would Austin have dreamed of denying it. He wasn't peddling a panacea for all philosophical ills.

MAGEE: Didn't he take the highly unusual view that philosophy could be – perhaps even ought to be – a group activity?

WARNOCK: Yes, he said this from time to time and I'm quite sure meant it very seriously. This connects, I think, with his belief that the only serious aim in philosophy ought to be to get things really settled; and he very much wanted to get away from the idea that philosophy was in any way a kind of literary pursuit in which the individual operates strictly as an individual performer – he thought that to see philosophy in that way was to import, into what ought to be in a sense a scientific subject, essentially literary values which he thought quite out of place and disastrous. Yes, he would have liked to try out the idea of a team of persons working in an organized way on small points – though perhaps, collectively, on a large problem – combining their results, criticizing each other's work, and really coming up with some agreed, solid conclusions at the end.

MAGEE: Can you give an example of the kind of thing such a group might be doing?

WARNOCK: Well, I think he thought of it as, partly, just a matter of getting the benefits of mutual criticism and suggestions in advance of producing your work rather than afterwards, which seems to be the more usual style. But also I think he had in mind the way in which, for some purposes, the natural sciences operate; he would have liked large problems to be broken down into limited areas, and these, so to speak, farmed out in an organized way to individual operators. For example, there were his so-called 'Saturday mornings', weekly meetings held in Oxford during term under Austin's chairmanship (to put it over-formally); here, at an early stage, the notion of a *rule* came under consideration, a notion which figures importantly in all sorts of fields – mathematics for instance and philosophy of language, and of course ethics as well – in all these fields philosophers talk a lot about rules. Well, on that occasion Austin decided, characteristically enough, that they'd better look at actual rules in some detail; he divided out among those present particular kinds of rules – rules of bridge, rules of cricket, rules of evidence, that kind of thing – and gave a particular field to each person to study in detail, and then see what they came up with. It was a kind – one kind – of scientific ideal that he had, I think; you divide a big problem into limited tasks, and assign a group or team of people to work on them in a systematic way.

MAGEE: Doesn't his view of philosophy – his desire to get things settled, his impatience with having permanently open-ended questions, and so on – make it a suicidal subject, by which I mean one which eliminates itself?

WARNOCK: Yes, I think that's true in a way, though the suicide is perhaps not very imminent. But I think perhaps one needs to make a distinction here. It has been said, with reason I think, that Wittgenstein represented philosophy as a suicidal subject, but this was not in the same way as Austin did (so far as either did). People say this of Wittgenstein for the reason that philosophical problems, according to him, arose out of certain kinds of unclarity, conceptual fogs and stresses and strains, and that the outcome of philosophical argument, as Wittgenstein represented it, would be simply the dissolution of these things, in a sense leaving nothing behind. But I don't think Austin meant anything quite like that. I think he thought that the most one could say of philosophy in general was that it consisted of a great mass of unclear issues of all sorts and shapes and sizes, and that one thing one could hope for, in the way of philosophical advance, was that bits of this great confused mass should from time to time detach themselves, so to speak, and set up on their own. In this way he thought that logic, for instance, had started life as a more or less confused part of philosophy, and had then become detached and set up on its own, with its own procedures, criteria, standards and so on. Psychology similarly had become in due course an independent discipline, distinguished from philosophy, and one might say that linguistics by now has also made good a very flourishing independence. He certainly thought that this was not in any way a bad thing, but should be seen rather as the natural way things went – the clearer one became about what one was discussing and how questions of a certain sort might be settled, the more there would be a tendency for those questions, so to speak, to float away from the residual gaseous mass of philosophy and be recognized as a discipline in their own right.

MAGEE: What continuing influence does this work have?

WARNOCK: Well, I mentioned already that certain of his contributions, particularly to the philosophy of language, seemed to be well established as of continuing interest and importance – as well as several other papers of his on individual subjects. What I think you don't find, for one reason or another, is people actually doing the subject in the way in which Austin occasionally explicitly recommended that it should be done. The specific tactic of attacking philosophical problems through a very detailed examination of the vocabulary that ordinarily goes with them, which is something that he did himself and explicitly recommended, is something that in fact not many practitioners seem much inclined to adopt. Whether that's a good thing or a bad thing, I don't know, but certainly one doesn't see much philosophy actually being done in that way.

MAGEE: So his way of doing philosophy may not have much of a future, you think?

WARNOCK: I think it's very hard to tell. When one remembers the (certainly to my taste) extreme freshness and originality, and in a way excitingness, of this kind of work I cannot but think that it must appeal to people in the future who may at the moment not have come across it at all, and in that way it may well come back. But certainly at the moment there isn't anybody who springs to mind as explicitly doing the subject in this particular way. Older habits die hard.

MAGEE: Even so, wouldn't it be true to say that although nobody's doing the subject his way, nearly everyone who does philosophy professionally in Britain has learnt a good deal from him?

WARNOCK: That's certainly true. If you distinguish between the arguments he used, the doctrines he put forward, and the particular manner in which he thought one should work, the latter, as I say, may seem not to have caught on much; but the importance of the various theses he put forward, and the arguments he used, is undeniable, I think. A great many philosophers would have to admit, whether reluctantly or otherwise, to having learned a great deal from his writings, even if they haven't adopted the manner of them.

MAGEE: Why do you think the influence of Austin – and Moore too, for that matter – has been so small outside the Anglo-Saxon world?

WARNOCK: Well, it's certainly true that it has. I'm inevitably rather guessing about this, because philosophy outside the English-speaking world is a field in which I'm not particularly well informed; but I'd be inclined to say that philosophers, at any rate in Continental Europe, have traditionally been looked to for what one might call comment on the human predicament – taking moral standpoints, and very often political standpoints; they've been expected to be casting a sage-like look over the present state of the world's political and moral goings-on, and for that matter its literary and artistic goings-on. Whereas both Austin and Moore regarded philosophy very much as an academic discipline, a subject with its own problems and its own standards, capable of proceeding quite independently, in a sense, of what was going on in the world at large. Both would have thought it in a way quite inappropriate for a philosopher as such to weigh in on political problems, or moral problems, which conspicuously they didn't do; and I think this would seem acutely disappointing to somebody with what one might call the Continental image of what a philosopher should be like.

MAGEE: Doesn't it also have something to do with the fact that both of them happened to be men who exerted their chief influence not by writing but by personal contact?

WARNOCK: Yes, that may be true too. I think, of both Austin and Moore, one gets not at all a weak, but certainly a diminished, impression from just reading their writings. In each case it was the impression that they made as persons which was also immensely important, and that comes through only to some extent, I think, in the written word.

MAGEE: In my opinion Moore is much the more considerable figure of the two. Would you agree with that?

WARNOCK: Well, I'm not detached enough historically – or perhaps in any other way either – to be a good judge of that, but I can see that what you suggest may be what one might call the verdict of history in due course. Of course one has to remember here that, whereas Moore lived to be well over eighty, Austin died before he was fifty, so that the sheer amount of work that he'd done and the amount of time which his influence had had to operate in was very, very much less. Obviously it is an important as well as deeply to be deplored fact that Austin's time in which to work turned out to be so tragically short. But as it is, as the record stands, there is at any rate simply a lot more of Moore. It's probably true too that Moore will be judged historically to have made more difference, but that's at least partly because of the historical context in which he began to work; philosophy was much dottier and more extraordinary when Moore hit the scene than when Austin did – there was more difference to be made, so to speak, and partly for that reason I suppose Moore did actually make more difference.

6
Conversation with Gilbert Ryle

MAGEE: The first clear public statement of the view of philosophy that has come to be known as Linguistic Philosophy or Linguistic Analysis was made by the young Gilbert Ryle in 1931 at the end of his paper on 'Systematically Misleading Expressions': 'There is, after all, a sense in which we can properly inquire and even say "what it really means to say so and so". For we can ask what is the real form of the fact recorded when this is concealed or disguised and not duly exhibited by the expression in question. And we can often succeed in stating this fact in a new form of words which does exhibit what the other failed to exhibit. And I am for the present inclined to believe that this is what philosophical analysis is, and that this is the sole and whole function of philosophy.'

In spite of this prophetic pronouncement, and some well known papers, Ryle was a late developer as philosophers go. He was in his fiftieth year in 1949 when his first book was published, *The Concept of Mind*. Since then he has published *Dilemmas* in 1954 and *Plato's Progress* in 1966. Although recently retired from his chair at Oxford he remains, as he has been for nearly a quarter of a century, the Editor of *Mind*, the leading journal of philosophy in Britain. And for years he had the reputation of being the chief king-maker when it came to academic appointments in philosophy, not just at Oxford but in universities all over the country.

His latest book, *Plato's Progress*, is a reappraisal of the chronology of Plato's dialogues. The book before that, *Dilemmas*, is an investigation into some paradoxes in informal logic. But the book which is instantly associated with his name by most people remains *The Concept of Mind*. Perhaps only twenty-something years after its publication it would be misleading to describe it as one of the best known works of philosophy in the English language – though it is. It is also one of the small handful that the serious student of the subject simply must read. If I may summarize its central thesis, it's something like this. We tend to think of a person as consisting of a body and a mind, but it's a complete mistake to think of the mind as if it were an *entity* that exists and performs actions and has experiences and a history, in the way the body exists and performs actions and has experiences and a history. 'Mind' isn't a name for that kind of thing at all: it's simply a generic term for certain categories of behaviour, performance, disposition, occurrence, and so on. There is no non-material entity that *has* or *does* these things. Still less, therefore, is any such entity invisibly operating the body from inside, like a ghost in a machine. Least of all does it sit in there enjoying secret access to a flow of private, non-bodily experiences of its own.

This thesis, which is worked out in some detail and many aspects, has been the subject of hot debate ever since it was published.

Professor Ryle, has anything in all this spate of discussion and criticism caused you to modify *The Concept of Mind* in any important respect?

RYLE: I'm boastful enough to think and to say that the general theme of the book is dead right. But, of course, I committed some howlers in the writing of the book, and there are certain pages of the book which I can't now bear to read because it reminds me of how stupid or hasty I was in those days. I'll just mention one or two of them. These particular ones don't worry me very much now, but I certainly wouldn't write them again. First of all, there was a place where I was talking about motives, that is to say, about what it is for a person to act from this, that or the other motive. Now what I said positively about motives certainly won't do, though there were some negative things in what I said which I'm sure are right. I had in mind some views about motives which, for example, Sir David Ross had published in a book. He obviously thought that having a motive was a retrospectable or introspectable experience, some sort of an internal prod or a jab that goes off just before I do something – e.g. from hunger, or amusement, or lust, or something of the sort. As against this jab theory of motives the things that I said I think were perfectly right. But the things I put up in its place certainly won't do. For example, I seemed somehow to commit myself to the view that anything that a person does from a motive must be *in character*, in the sense that anybody would have expected him from previous knowledge of him to act in that way, and that may or may not be true in any particular case, but certainly isn't necessarily true. So there's a good deal of revision for me to do of that particular stretch when I get to heaven or the other place. I shan't try before. Then there's another chapter about Imagination where also the negative things that I was saying were dead right, and a lot of people who've gunned for me on that score have been and remain dead wrong. On the other hand, there's a positive part of the story which I didn't capture and haven't captured yet. But here I don't feel so very guilty, because nobody else that I have seen, who has chanced his arm on this particular thorny topic, has made very much more headway than I did. So on this one I'm going to say that I don't greatly mind having left a huge gap here. Somebody's going to fill the gap some day – I don't expect it'll be me – but whatever filling of the gap is produced it isn't going to do much damage to the central theme of the book, or even to the negative theme of this chapter. I can think of a good number of incidental things occupying a paragraph or two which I wish I hadn't written but I'm not going to bother you with those. They are incidental things, and if you like to cross them out as pathological misprints that's good enough.

MAGEE: So the two topics whose treatment in the book you would substantially change if you were writing it today are Motive and Imagination?

RYLE: Yes, if by 'changes' you mean 'cancellations'. There are plenty of things in those two bits that I want to cancel. There are other places where there's an enormous amount to be added. For example, there's a chapter – I'm glad to say I've forgotten which chapter – towards the end of the book, where I'm talking about the intellect, and about things like thinking, deliberating, etc. Here the things that I do say don't give me a guilty conscience, but the things that I don't say are so numerous and so huge that, in fact, I'm now spending a good part of my time thinking what there is to be said on these topics which I hadn't got to say in those days. But this won't in the main be a major cancellation, but an addition, filling up a hole, a very big hole in the book.

MAGEE: There seems to me another way in which what the book doesn't say constitutes a defect. May I put this to you? It seems to me that the book simply ignores well-known theories with which its own thesis is incompatible. For instance there are only two or three passing references to Freud, and if anything they're rather favourable, yet your thesis is completely incompatible with any kind of analytic psychology. Oughtn't you to have acknowledged that, and justified it, argued it out?

RYLE: Well, here I don't feel very penitent. I'd never studied any psychology, and I felt as unwilling to stick my neck out on technical questions of psychology as I feel unwilling to stick my neck out over technical questions of, oh, for example, radar astronomy, or chemistry. I don't know the ground so I don't want to step on it. I think, from memory, that I said only one thing about Freud – I remember describing him as psychology's one man of genius, which I still think to be true. But I didn't want to go into his or any other sorts of theories chiefly for the reason that I don't think amateurs ought to talk as if they were professionals.

MAGEE: Talking of not dealing with aspects of the subject of which you have no knowledge, particularly the scientific ones: Bertrand Russell wrote a review of the book, which one has to say was pretty hostile, in which he took you to task precisely for this. He said it was pointless to write about matters like sensation and perception if you weren't thoroughly familiar with what neurologists, opticians, psychologists and other empirical observers had said about them; in short that there was no point in doing this kind of philosophy at all if you didn't know a lot of science. Obviously you don't think that, or you wouldn't have written the book. What's your answer to this kind of criticism?

RYLE: It's a pretty familiar kind of criticism. I think one certainly ought to be careful, to repeat a previous metaphor, not to step on ground where one isn't at home. It doesn't seem to me that one is *not* at home in the field of perception. Inevitably one's very much at home in the field of perception, given that one is all the time, all the day, looking at things, examining things, ransacking drawers for things, talking to people about the view, misjudging the distances and speeds of cars, and so on. One has a great deal of familiarity with everyday facts about perception and misperception, non-perception, and so on. But this isn't what Russell was talking about. Russell thought one ought to know a lot about, say, the rods and cones in the eye, and I don't pretend to know anything about them, and, if I may speak a bit rudely, I don't want to.

MAGEE: But the intelligent layman who doesn't know much philosophy may genuinely wonder how it is that you can deal with perceptual questions if you don't know about the rods and cones in the eye. How would you explain yourself to such a person?

RYLE: I'm a little bit tempted to use this analogy, though perhaps I tend to use analogies rather too much. Supposing I'm walking along the cliffs and I see a notice which says 'Danger'. If I'm very ignorant indeed I may think that the notice is telling me of the presence of some wild animal, or something of the sort. But if I've got ordinary intelligence I know that the notice is simply warning me that there is some hazard to look out for – it doesn't specify what. The particular hazard that it's warning me against may be that of falling over the edge of the cliff where the cliff has broken away. This involves the notion of tumbling, and this I expect involves the notion of falling towards the centre of the earth at a rate of acceleration of whatever it may be. But to suppose that I had to have a Galileo-type knowledge of things falling at this rate of acceleration towards the centre of the earth, in order to stop and turn back when I see a danger notice, this seems to me absurd. Similarly I don't need to know things that I don't in fact know about rods and cones in order to know things about, e.g. overlooking misprints, which is an optical thing that I often do; or misjudging the speeds of approaching cars, which is another optical thing that I rather often do; or misrecognizing people's faces, which is an optical thing that I very seldom do, and so on. The facts of perception that I was occupied with are facts about which I know and you know pretty well everything we need to know.

MAGEE: You're rearranging the geography of already familiar facts and already familiar concepts?

RYLE: Certainly.

MAGEE: You don't in fact, do you, put your thesis in the context of a general theory at all – though if you did I suppose it would have to be a behaviourist theory.

RYLE: I'm going to say 'blast any words that end in "-ist" or "-ism" ' from the start. They always interfere with any serious discussion of any subject. But certainly, if you want a general thesis, it is that there are around people, of whom I myself happen to be one; these people have a great number of different attributes, and they differ from one another in a great number of ways. Some people, e.g. the very newly-born, are infants, and no one is yet going to say that they are clever or stupid, or that they remember or forget anything, and so on. A little bit later these descriptions do begin to apply, and so do a number of other ones, about their muscular abilities, strengths, etc. In a way this is all totally familiar. But I'm saying that in order to describe a person, whether an infant or a grown-up, whether a lunatic or a sane man, you don't need to – in fact you'd much better not – talk in terms of a couple of entities mysteriously laced together in the way in which Descartes and the Cartesians right up to the 1970s have required us to do.

MAGEE: But I agree with Russell that if I sit quite still here and con-jure up a mental picture of a horse something different happens inside me from what happens when I conjure up a picture of a hippopotamus. First of all I would assert that it is an event. Both are events. Second, I have a direct private access to them that nobody else has. And third, there's not the slightest reason why either of them should be manifested in perceptible behaviour of any kind.

RYLE: What we have here is a perfectly special, but quite little point about imagining, that is, for example, seeing things in the mind's eye, about which I said a lot in the chapter on Imagination. I think it's a very special *little* subject. We wouldn't deny a person this, that, or the other quality of wits or character if we heard that he was very bad at seeing things in his mind's eye – as a lot of people are, indeed as most persons of my age are, compared with what they were like when they were much younger. But now take the important point. You said that something different happens when you see in your mind's eye a hippopotamus from what you see in your mind's eye when you see the other thing, whatever it was – oh yes, a horse. I perfectly agree. But similarly, if you're scribbling on the blotting paper during a committee meeting, something very different is happening if you scribble a picture of a hippopotamus on the blotting paper from what is happening if you scribble a picture of a horse on the blotting paper. For example, if I ask you, pointing to one, 'What is that meant to be?', you'll say without hesitation 'A horse.' Or if I point to the other, you'll say without hesitation 'A hippopotamus.' If I now ask 'How do you know?' surely you're not going to say that you have scanned something in your mysterious 'insides'? What you'll say, quite rightly, is 'Well, who drew the damn thing?' I carry the parallel through as far as I can. But there comes the point where I can't carry it, because my positive account of seeing things in the mind's eye, as I say, has got a big hole in it. But this is a fairly unimportant hole. The sort of mind, i.e. the sort of wits and character a person has got, has got very little to do with the things that he does see, or fails to see, in his mind's eye. His exercises of his qualities of wits and character only very incidentally take the shape of his visualizing things or hearing 'voices', say, in his mind's ear.

MAGEE: But there remains the point that you have direct, indepen-dent access to my drawing of the horse and the hippopotamus – and therefore you don't have to ask me, you can see them for yourself – whereas you do have to ask me what I'm seeing in my mind's eye, and you have no independent check on the answer I give you.

RYLE: Certainly, certainly.

MAGEE: So there are uncheckable private events going on inside me.

RYLE: Oh, and there are heaps of other secrets that you can keep if you want to keep them secret. For example, supposing you want to keep secret the fact that you stole a half-crown from the newspaper-seller's tray. I can see very good reasons why you should want to keep this secret. But supposing you do keep it secret and nobody saw you steal the half-crown, and no machine was taking a picture of it, or anything, then that is your secret. Too bad. No way of breaking your secret.

MAGEE: If psychologists are right about dreams and we all dream for a great deal of every night then each of us spends several hours out of the twenty-four seeing a whole lot of things in his mind's eye. How does your thesis accommodate dreams?

RYLE: I don't know that I'm going to bother much about them. Let me first say that not all dreams are in terms of visual imagery. A person who's been blind from birth has no visual imagery and his dreams are therefore not visual. I daresay they are auditory instead. I just don't know. But is it worthwhile bothering about what sort of account one is going to give of dreams? They are very peripheral things. You don't judge – though Freud may – *you* don't judge the sort of person a person is by the sorts of dreams that he reports when he is talking about his dreams. Dreaming is a very subsidiary part of his life, though it may be revealing. His dream-telling also can, as we all know, be a very great bore. The total life that he lives with the wits, character, equipment, history that he has, does not, thank Heaven, *reduce* to the visualizings and the dreamings into which he now and again drifts. We know a huge lot about Napoleon's mind – that is, about Napoleon. I don't suppose anything much is known about his nightmares or his reveries – or needs to be known. But still, if you like to say that I haven't given a full and clear account either of dreaming or of seeing things in the mind's eye I'm perfectly happy to say: 'No, indeed I haven't.' But the unhandy adjective 'mental' does not *mean* 'of the stuff daydreams and dreams are made of'.

MAGEE: One aspect of the book that some people emotionally disliked – which is not at all the same thing as rationally objecting to it – was what seemed to them your denial of an inner life. There's a much-quoted sentence on page 155: 'The sorts of things that I can find out about myself are the same as the sorts of things that I can find out about other people, and the methods of finding them out are much the same.' Were you denying an inner life to the extent you've been accused of doing?

RYLE: I think I was wanting to deny that one of the things that people would label a part of one's 'inner life' has anything specially 'inner' in it. Another thing I was wanting to deny is that there is anything specially important about the things that one does succeed in keeping 'inner'. To take the latter point first, which ties on with what I was saying before: there are plenty of things which I could blab but don't. Not in this case because there is any point in keeping it secret, but because there is no point in bothering you with it. I remember, for example, walking across Dartmoor on a cold wet day with a party of undergraduates, one of whom was enjoying the walk like anything; and every single object that he noticed he drew my attention to. He'd say 'There's a sheep,' and a little while later, 'And there's another sheep.' And 'There are some pebbles.' Now the other undergraduates didn't do this, though they saw the same sheep and the same pebbles as he did. We can say he was letting things out which they were keeping in, and therefore that their 'inner life' was richer than his, because he took the lid off and they didn't. If this is what you want, let's say that there's a good deal of inner life in all of us and much more in some people than in others. For a variety of sorts of things it doesn't matter if it's blabbed or unblabbed. If by 'inner' you just mean 'unblabbed', then I wish much more was kept 'inner' than is – especially on country buses.

MAGEE: But a lot of philosophers with whom you have so much else in common – Wittgenstein is the obvious example – thought that we have a great deal going on inside us concerning morals, religion, the arts, and perhaps other things, which is incommunicable in words and yet of the highest importance. Do you deny that?

RYLE: What I want to do is to throw a brick at you for saying 'inside'.

MAGEE: Okay, sorry.

RYLE: Now let's take one of the arts about which I can only talk like an outsider, namely music. Take a person who is musical – and let's suppose that he even sometimes composes music. Whether he composes or not, if he hasn't got an instrument like a fiddle or a piano around, and if he doesn't want to disturb his company, then he may indeed go over some piece of music that he is composing, or someone else has composed, in his head, and be quite annoyed if anybody interrupts him. He is enjoying it. Or if there isn't any company around then he may hum it, so that if there had been anybody around they'd have heard it; and again he gets annoyed if this is interrupted. There is a sense of 'inner' or 'inside' in which you can say that when he isn't humming it aloud or playing it on the fiddle but only going over it in his head, this is 'inside'. If he is good at this, blessings on him. But this makes no difference to the question whether he is a musician of this, that or the other sort – whether he's the sort of musician who can compose things, whether his taste is good or bad, etc. The 'insideness' of the non-humming of the non-hummer is of no more interest to me than the 'outsideness' of the humming if he is a hummer. Save for the point which I mentioned at the start, that there is a philosopher's question about what it is to see things in the mind's eye, what it is to hear things in the mind's ear, of which the positive account escapes me. But I don't think that this is very important; it is, so to speak, a philosopher's interesting crux, but not a key one. Mozart is not disqualified from having been a fine composer by the fact – if it is a fact – that he sometimes hummed his notes aloud while composing. Why on earth *should* he have done it in his head – or, inside, if you like? What's the advantage?

MAGEE: You write a great deal about categories and category mistakes in *The Concept of Mind* but you never say what you mean by a category. I don't myself think it's an important shortcoming – if indeed it's a shortcoming at all – but can you say now what you mean by a category?

RYLE: Ah yes, I think so. I don't quite agree that this isn't important. In a way it's a lead-in to one of the most important things that the book contains, or I think that any philosophical book contains. Let's consider two sorts of mistakes – of course there are plenty more – two sorts of mistakes, one of which is philosophically of no particular interest and the other I think of very great interest. (1) If you mistake, as you well might do, a rabbit for a hare or a hare for a rabbit, there you've got two creatures that belong in fact to different species of quadruped, and they look rather alike – so you may easily think that what is a rabbit is in fact a hare, or vice versa. Or if you are writing some words down you may easily write down a set of letters thinking that this is the way to spell, say, the word 'habitude' and what you've written down is a misspelling of the word 'habitude'. Here is another mistake, a wrong spelling for a right spelling. (2) But there's a totally different sort of mistake. Take first of all – this is not as yet interesting – a child who comes up to my notice-board on the cliff and he sees 'Danger – keep away.' He asks innocently: 'What sort of animal is a danger?' Or more likely he'll pronounce it: 'What sort of an animal is a dangger? Is it rather like a kangaroo?' What sort of explanation do you give? You don't give the sort of explanation you give of the difference between a hare and a rabbit. You don't say that a danger isn't an animal but a fish, or isn't an animal but a bird. You give quite a different sort of explanation. You say 'Oh no, a danger is a situation where the probability of something harmful happening is relatively high. So that there may be a danger of falling, as here over the cliff; or there may be a danger of picking up influenza; or there may be a danger of being misunderstood when you are making a public speech; etc.' There is something that the rabbit and the hare both are – quadruped, animal, creature, etc. There isn't anything that a risk and a rabbit both are – or that a collision and a hypotenuse both are. Drawing attention to *this* sort of difference, the difference between a danger and, e.g. a creature or a happening, this I would say is explaining that the terms belong to quite different categories, and not to two different species of one genus or two different members of one family. Part of what I was trying to do in the book, and I think it's also part of what all philosophers are always trying to do, is to show that certain radical mistakes about, e.g. people's intellects or their imaginations or whatnot are not mistakes of putting things into the wrong pigeon-hole in the right desk, but of trying to put a thing into a pigeon-hole in a certain desk when it doesn't want to go into that desk at all. It's not that sort of thing.

MAGEE: So you think that concern with mistakes of this kind is fundamental to what philosophy is about?

RYLE: Certainly.

MAGEE: And in other spheres besides those in which you yourself happen to be working?

RYLE: Yes, certainly.

MAGEE: Can I go back to *The Concept of Mind* and take up a new point? Although I was young when I first read it I was, even so, startled to find you attributing the 'ghost in the machine' model to Descartes, because even such pre-Cartesian literature as I'd become familiar with in my schooldays – the Old and New Testaments, for instance, and some of the plays of Shakespeare – are pervaded with it. Why did you?

RYLE: I attributed it to Descartes because I think it got into philosophy and pseudo-scientific thought from Descartes in a way in which it hadn't got there from the other sources. So that, if you like, I gave him the *philosophical* credit or discredit, and I still think as a matter of fact that that's where it belongs. Of course, as Stuart Hampshire pointed out, you can find some things to that effect in Plato's *Phaedo* and there are some in the medieval philosophers, and there are some in common-sense talk and there are some in the tragedians and so on. It's been hanging around for donkey's years. No one could think Descartes invented this mistake. The point was he put nice firm edges and labels on to it so that there it was, a doctrine or a dogma from his time. Descartes said, in effect, what Shakespeare and the Bible didn't, that my mind is one substance and my body is another substance. They sometimes talked *as if* this were the case. Descartes said that it *was* the case.

MAGEE: Usually, as J. O. Urmson says about you in *The Encyclopaedia of Philosophy*, your writing 'avoids, rather than lacks, any historical discussion. There is the very minimum of reference to even recent learned controversy, and the great philosophers are rarely given even a casual mention.' Is this deliberate?

RYLE: Yes. There's a bit of back history there. When I was a young undergraduate philosopher and a young don philosopher, the intellectual atmosphere at Oxford was very stuffy. Most of my elder colleagues were so obsessed with writing articles or giving lectures on the great and glorious dead that one couldn't start, or anyhow maintain, a discussion about anything without the subject being changed before long to 'Which dialogue did Plato say that in and did he really mean it?' and 'Could the Greek be interpreted in another way?' and so on. So that I as deliberately minimized the amount of historical reference in *The Concept of Mind* as I minimized the number of footnotes, which, for quite a different reason, seemed also to me at that time to be a bane on philosophical literature. I'm not at all hostile to philosophical scholarship. Indeed, for good or ill, I've made lots and lots of my own shots at it elsewhere. But mixing the drinks is always a bad thing. In *The Concept of Mind* I wanted to raise and discuss an issue without side issues cropping up as to whether Kant had or had not improved on Hume in this or that respect, or whether Duns Scotus had been more original than Ockham on this or that point, or whether the text of so and so should have read in this way or in that way. Nice enough questions, but not ones that I wanted to discuss. It's a great thing to move in one direction at a time rather than two.

MAGEE: A most distinctive feature of the book is its style: novelistic rather than academic, trenchant, very aggressive, yet full of colourful images and metaphors; it's brilliant in an almost literal way – it's hard and it shines. It's commonly been said to be part of the texture of the thought and the argument in a way that's unusual for a philosopher. As Austin once said, the style is Ryle. Have you taken conscious pains to keep your writing non-technical? And have you been consciously influenced by any specific non-philosophical writers?

RYLE: In answer to the second question, I think you could probably find echoes of Oscar Wilde, and perhaps even more, of Saki, here and there. I did find them very refreshing at times when I found some other people a bit stodgy.

MAGEE: What about the other barrel to my question? Is your non-technicality deliberate?

RYLE: Oh that's deliberate, yes. This is one of the things that is sometimes meant by the very misleading phrase 'ordinary language', which in general I'm not interested in. I think in most subjects there is great utility in a carefully worked-out and from time to time pruned technical vocabulary, whether in archaeology or in chemistry or in matters connected with rowing, or whatever it may be. But, in philosophy – outside the field of strict formal logic – while I don't want to say that technical terms never do any good, it is my experience that having done what good they've got to do – usually in the first three or four years of their life – they then begin to do harm. I do think that a philosopher's arguments, when couched in technical terms, tend either to elude one or in fact to go agley. It's much easier to catch a philosopher out, including oneself, if he is not talking in technical terms with which you are unfamiliar, and the most important thing about a philosopher's arguments is that it should be as easy as possible for other people, and especially for himself, to catch him out if he can be caught out.

MAGEE: Let's leave *The Concept of Mind* now. You said near the beginning of this discussion that you're still actively engaged in the philosophy of mind, and in particular on questions of thinking. Can you say something about what you're doing?

RYLE: Yes. Naturally if I had got anything complete, then I'd say 'Read my typescript when it leaves my secretary's hands,' but we aren't in that happy position. Yes, my interest at the moment centres around the notion of thinking – not the very dull notion which philosophers talk much too much about, that of a person believing this or that, though we do use the verb 'to think' as a paraphrase of the verb 'to believe' in English, unfortunately. No, what interests me, to put it crudely, is what on earth is 'Le Penseur' doing sitting on his rock with his chin in his hand and very few clothes on which makes us want to say 'Yes, Rodin really does make him look like a person who is wrapped in thought.' We aren't often wrapped in thought quite as much as 'Le Penseur' is, but still we all know what it is like to be thinking about something, puzzled, baffled, trying to work things out; making or, more often, failing to make headway, going round in circles, etc. But if you try and describe what this activity, or more likely this family of activities, is, you get into very great difficulties. I'll just illustrate one little difficulty. Let's suppose – and now you have to ignore questions of chronology – let's suppose that Pythagoras was sitting in his study, or, if you like, on a rock outside, with his chin in his hand, trying to find the proof of the theorem that the square on the hypotenuse of a right-angled triangle is equal to the sum of the squares on the other two sides, or whatever the theorem was; and let's suppose that as there is no one else around he is not bothering to bottle up the things that he's going through, so he's muttering . . . for example, 'The square on this side plus the square on that side would not equal the square on this third side,' or something of the sort; and then he says, 'Oh damn, that gets me nowhere'; and so on. So there he is, muttering away; he's still baffled; and not yet getting anywhere in particular. Now let's suppose that his little son, if he had a son, joins him there. He hears his father muttering, and being a mimic he echoes what he hears his father saying. For full measure, there's also a parrot there, or if you like a tape recorder, or both. The parrot too mimics what Pythagoras is muttering, and the tape recorder takes it down to play back later on. So there are four things, or creatures, all producing Greek sentences in which the Greek equivalents of phrases like 'right-angle' and words like 'hypotenuse', etc., keep on cropping up. We certainly don't want to say that the tape recorder is thinking out a proof, or trying to think out a proof of Pythagoras's theorem. We certainly don't want to say it of the parrot either, because obviously the parrot is simply parrotting. (The tape recorder isn't even doing that.) Of the boy, if he's past a certain age, we want to say that he's mimicking his Dad, but it's a bit more than parrotting, because some of the words in it mean something to him. He's not trying to solve a geometrical problem, but still it isn't just noises for him, as it had been for the parrot. So, what is Pythagoras himself doing that none of the others is doing?

To say that he's trying to think out what arguments would establish the truth of the theorem is perfectly true, but only repeats the question. We hanker to say that besides the noises, the words, phrases, etc. that he produces, and which the boy, the bird and the gadget mimic or reproduce, there's *something else* that Pythagoras is doing *as well* – namely – and now we produce vague phrases like 'trying to solve the problem'. But notice my phrase 'we hanker to say that he's doing *something else as well*'. It is this 'something else as well' that is the source of the whole trouble, because if we stop Pythagoras from muttering, e.g. by giving him aphasia for a minute or two, he's going to stop thinking about his geometrical problem. So his thinking isn't *something else* that he's doing *as well* as muttering the things that he mutters, and he isn't merely muttering either, which is what his son is doing, and what the parrot is doing, and what the tape recorder will play back. So the question is how to describe the thinking that he certainly is doing (1) without taking seriously the tempting statement that 'inside' him he's doing something else as well as mutter, and (2) also without reducing what he's doing to mere muttering. This is a familiar case of a perfectly general philosophers'-type problem, how to account for something without either (1) reducing that something to what it isn't, or (2) multiplying it – duplicating it with just a ghost of itself. The problem is how to avoid what Peter Medawar has called 'nothing-buttery' on the one side and what Descartes, if he'd been sensible, would have called 'aswellism' on the other. I don't know if that answers your question at all.

MAGEE: It does. But it makes me want to ask another. Suppose Mrs Pythagoras came out to the rock because it was a nice day, and suppose she brought her knitting. She might say to her husband, 'Oh for God's sake can't you stop that endless muttering? I can't concentrate on my pattern with all that muttering going on.' So Mr Pythagoras carries on with solving his problem but without doing any more muttering. It's perfectly conceivable that he might stop muttering without stopping thinking.

RYLE: Certainly, certainly. But what he's going on doing 'in his head', if anything, will be, so to speak, some '*As If*' muttering, or something like it. But maybe he prefers – and this is a good way of doing it too – to take out his fountain-pen from his pocket, and a bit of paper, and without disturbing his wife, put down Greek words, phrases and sentences, dots and lines on the paper – crossing most of them out, of course, because they won't do, and then putting things in between the lines, and then copying it out again – what you and I do when we're thinking something out on paper. All that wouldn't disturb his wife's knitting at all. But this wouldn't raise the question of seeing things in his mind's eye, or hearing things in his mind's ear.

MAGEE: But aren't you making an upside-down version of the mistake you've spent so much of your life combatting? You're now suggesting that even if he's not doing any actual muttering he's bound to go on doing some ghostly muttering.

RYLE: Ah, but even if, what may not be the case, he does do some 'As-If' muttering in his head, I don't think this is ghostly. Whatever the right account may be of seeing things in the mind's eye, or of 'As-If' muttering things, so to speak, on the mind's tongue, I don't think it produces an any more ghostly story than, as I think I hinted in the book, does the difference between one person who is asleep, and another person who is pretending to be asleep. There's a very important difference between the two, since the person who's pretending to be asleep has to be awake. But if you ask what his pretending to be asleep consists in, this doesn't require you to mention anything ghostly or 'inner'. How could something 'inner' contribute to his pretence? It would take his mind off his acting. Roughly he just deliberately *doesn't*, for the duration of the pretence, act, look or sound like waking people act, look and sound. There isn't '*something else*' that he does '*as well*', e.g. a bit of '*inner* drowsing' or 'ghostly snoring'. He is just abstaining – carefully and even artistically abstaining – from acting as wakeful people act. Well, I think the same sort of story, though it won't quite do as it stands, is that Pythagoras, if he's, so to speak, muttering on the tip of his mind's tongue, is rather like the person who isn't asleep, but is pretending to be asleep; the same *sort* of story will do, I hope, and it doesn't involve any ghostly '*something else as well*'.

MAGEE: Are you in a position to say what sort of product is likely to come out of your current thinking about thinking? Will it be another book?

RYLE: It depends whether I get anywhere. I've got now a hat and a cap and a scarf and a mackintosh, and one or two other things. The big thing I haven't got is the peg on which to hang them. So that if you want to know whether there's going to be a book I'm going to say it depends on whether the peg turns up.

7
Conversation with Peter Strawson

MAGEE: Some of the philosophers we've discussed in these conversations – for instance Russell and Ayer – are already widely known to the educated public. They've produced a good deal of journalism, they've appeared often on television and radio; even some of their books on philosophy are readily accessible to the layman and appear in paperback editions under popular imprints. But others, like Wittgenstein and Austin, have had little or nothing to do with journalism or the mass media, and their philosophical books are too technical, rigorous and detailed to be read by many laymen. It's obvious how philosophers of this second kind may be scarcely known even by name outside academic circles and yet be of front-rank importance in philosophy, both for the intrinsic quality of their work and for their influence on other philosophers. This is true even to this day of Austin; and I think, as yet, one can say it's true of P. F. Strawson. He's the youngest of the philosophers we've considered so far – ten years younger than Ayer and twenty years younger than Gilbert Ryle, whose Chair he recently succeeded to at Oxford University. He first attracted the attention of the philosophical world with a paper he published in *Mind* in 1950 called 'On Referring', in which he made some criticism of Russell's Theory of Definite Descriptions from which the theory has never entirely recovered. Since then he has published three books – *Introduction to Logical Theory* in 1952, *Individuals* in 1959 and *The Bounds of Sense* in 1966. *Individuals* is sub-titled 'An Essay in Descriptive Metaphysics', and that phrase 'descriptive metaphysics' has acquired considerable influence. *The Bounds of Sense* is sub-titled 'An Essay on Kant's Critique of Pure Reason' – and I must say I can't imagine its being intelligible to, or even readable by, someone who hasn't read Kant's book first.

But let's begin at the beginning. I'd like to start, Professor Strawson, at the time when you first became active as a professional philosopher, in the immediately post-war Oxford when Austin was very much the dominant figure, or at any rate the most exciting to young philosophers like yourself. Am I right in thinking that – in keeping with the temper of that time – you began by doing close, detailed work on one or two concepts in philosophical logic, such as entailment – and of course referring?

STRAWSON: Yes. The first thing I published, in fact, was an article on entailment. I tried to resolve certain apparent paradoxes which come along with, or seem to come along with, the notion of one proposition logically entailing, or logically following, from another. The attempt, incidentally, was quite unsuccessful.

MAGEE: How strong an influence did Austin have on you at that stage of your career?

STRAWSON: Well I was greatly influenced and impressed by Austin and, of course, and for partly similar reasons, by Ryle. There was something in common to their methods at that time, though the style was very different. They both gave careful attention to what could, or couldn't, be naturally or non-absurdly *said*; and also to the *circumstances* in which we could or couldn't naturally say such and such a thing. And this method, for reasons which seemed obvious enough once they were pointed out, was a very fruitful source of philosophical data.

MAGEE: To a very young man as you were at that time, where was the excitement in this sort of detailed analysis? On the face of it, it might seem to have been dry and without much general application.

STRAWSON: No, not a bit, not a bit. The reasons why the thing was exciting were really two. On the one hand, in the face of this refined examination of actual linguistic practice, a lot of traditional philosophical theorizing began to look extraordinarily crude, like an assemblage of huge, crude mistakes. And it was, of course, extremely exhilarating to see these huge and imposing edifices of thought just crumbling away, or tumbling down, to the tune of this fairly modest sort of piping. And then, on the other hand, there was something else, something more positive: the sense of discovery, the discovery of the fine, rich, subtle texture of our actual thinking, of our actual conceptual and linguistic equipment.

MAGEE: Did you see this at first as exclusively an analytic, or at any rate critical, enterprise? Or were you from the beginning aware of some need for – or at least possibility of – construction?

STRAWSON: I suppose there's always some risk of falsifying things in retrospection. But roughly speaking I'd be inclined to draw a distinction between what I thought at first about philosophy of logic and philosophy of language on the one hand, and traditional problems in metaphysics and theory of knowledge on the other hand. In the philosophy of logic, and of language in general, I did think that it wasn't simply a matter of dispelling illusions: there were genuine theoretical problems to be solved, a certain amount of theoretical construction was necessary, the data had to be systematically ordered. But in the other sphere, the sphere of traditional theory of knowledge and metaphysics, I did conceive the task rather as destructive: not that of solving real problems, but of exposing problems which were spurious; not that of building theories, but blowing up bad and unnecessary theories.

MAGEE: Can you give an instance of the kind of work you were doing?

STRAWSON: I mentioned the article on entailment. I also did quite a lot of work on referring and on the notion of logical form. All these seemed to me to involve necessarily something like theory-construction. On the other hand, when one turned to problems in the theory of knowledge, the nature of perception, memory, imagination, free-will and determinism and so on, one had the feeling that the use of this new technique would really dissolve the problems, they'd just vanish away . . .

MAGEE: Bliss was it in that dawn to be alive!

STRAWSON: It was.

MAGEE: Of course the most famous of your articles at that time was the one in which you criticized Russell's Theory of Descriptions. Seven years after you attacked Russell he attacked you, in a belated counterblast which also appeared in *Mind*. I thought then, and still think, that his reply was excessively personal and intemperate. You were still young and he was a world figure – did it damage your confidence in any way?

STRAWSON: Not in the very least. What matters in philosophical criticism isn't the age or the distinction of the critic but the quality of his arguments; and the quality of Russell's arguments, on that particular occasion, wasn't, in fact, high. I would say he weakened his position rather than mine.

MAGEE: He never came to see the strength of your criticisms of his position, did he, not even years later?

STRAWSON: Apparently not; but then nor did he, apparently, see its real weaknesses either; for it had some.

MAGEE: Can you say now what you think those weaknesses were?

STRAWSON: Certain of the notions I employed, like that of presupposition, were certainly inadequately clarified, and indeed mistakenly presented, at the time. It is rather technical; but that is one of the things I would mention now as a weakness. I think I could give a better account now.

MAGEE: A moment ago you said something I ought to have taken you up on and didn't: you reeled off a list of classical problems in philosophy, such as free will, determinism, entailment, and so on, and said you used to think that all these problems could be solved —

STRAWSON: No, I distinguished between those of the entailment type, which I thought involved theory-construction, and those – of which I mentioned freedom *versus* determinism as an example – which called rather for dissolution.

MAGEE: All right. But when did you come to feel that these problems simply couldn't be dissolved?

STRAWSON: Well, I still think they can be *dealt with*, they can be *solved*. What I no longer think is that they can just be made to disappear by careful attention to our actual linguistic practice. But when did I come to picture them differently? I think that came rather later on, *after* I'd done a fair amount of work on logic, when I began to move on to the sort of problems I considered in *Individuals*.

MAGEE: Perhaps we'll leave that question till later, when we come to talk about *Individuals*. Going back to your dispute with Russell: it seems to me you were disputing with him on the same ground, in a sense. I don't know whether I'm wrong about this, but it does seem to me that in your *Introduction to Logical Theory* you were trying to do something not totally dissimilar from what he was doing – in fact this is a very interesting question to put to you: What exactly were you trying to do in that book?

STRAWSON: Well now, first, I don't think it would really do to say that what I was doing in *Introduction to Logical Theory* was similar to what Russell was doing in his logical work. He was, after all, a great logical innovator and his aim was to ground mathematics securely on formal logic. Now I had, and I have, virtually nothing of his originality and power as a formal logician, and I certainly have nothing at all of his competence in, or concern with, mathematics. So to compare us in that respect would be, I think, a little absurd, if I may say so – like comparing a great architect with an under-foreman.

MAGEE: Well I did mean – to do me a justice – that in the Theory of Definite Descriptions Russell was setting off constructions in an idealized language (which he had, of course, himself created) against propositions in ordinary language, and that this was also central to what you were doing in *Introduction to Logical Theory*.

STRAWSON: Right, right, there's something there certainly. So what was I trying to do in *Introduction to Logical Theory*? Well, partly it was intended to serve, like many another book, as an introduction to formal logic, but it was intended to do this with a certain difference. The point is, I suppose, that any system of formal or symbolic logic has a peculiar relation to the natural languages that we ordinarily speak. We have on the one hand the system, which presents, as it were, an idealized picture of deducibility relations which hold between statements or propositions, whatever they may be about, and which hold in virtue of certain very general structural features. Now you can introduce a student to such a system, and he can quickly master the system and work in it, but he may do this without thinking very much about how the system he's mastered is related to the language he ordinarily speaks; how it's related to the things he ordinarily says. A great part of what I was wanting to do was to raise questions precisely about this relation, the relation between the idealized system on the one hand and ordinary discourse on the other, and to suggest answers to those questions. And in the process I hope, and indeed think, that some light was shed both on the functioning of language in general and on the nature of formal logic itself.

MAGEE: So you were, after all – sorry to be insistent – concerned to set off one kind of language against another. Why?

STRAWSON: Not simply to set them off, but to set them off in such a way as to show each as illuminating the other, rather than to put them in any kind of opposition.

MAGEE: Can you give some indication of what form this illumination takes, what kind of thing it shows?

STRAWSON: Well, remember how Wittgenstein once said that one could say that there was really only one logical constant, and that was what all propositions, by their very nature, had in common; and that was the general propositional form. And then elsewhere he said that the general propositional form was: 'This is how things are.' Now what you have in these very obscure remarks of his, these oracular remarks of his, it seems to me, is the thought that the whole of formal logic, as we have it, is in principle excogitatable by pure reflection on the nature of the general propositional form, on the general idea of a statement, true or false, about how things are in the world. And I think there's something right and something true about that, that it does say something important about the nature of formal logic as a kind of abstract theory of the proposition. On the other hand, just reflecting on the general nature of the proposition, on the general idea of a statement, true or false, about how things are in the world, isn't going to take account of all the needs, even all the very general needs, of informative communication. So whatever abstract structure you excogitate on these lines is bound to be, precisely, *abstract*, to leave out aspects of the matter which you really need to take into consideration if you're going to get a realistic general picture.

MAGEE: Was there any direct line of development between your work up to this point and your next book, *Individuals*?

STRAWSON: Yes, there was a line of development certainly. Anybody concerned with logic and with general features of language must be concerned with a certain basic operation of speech or thought, the basic operation of predication. That is to say, you pick out, or refer to, some item and you say or you think something about it. Now, of course, you can say or think something about items of any sort whatever, you can say or think something about a number, a virtue, a momentary sense-impression or feeling, a dog, a poem, a person, a building and so on. But it's fairly natural to start wondering whether any of these types of item are in some way more basic subjects of predication than others. And, what's more, it's fairly natural too, if you do raise this question, to be attracted to a certain traditional, and indeed, if I'm not mistaken, Aristotelian, answer to the question. That is that the basic objects of reference or the basic subjects of predication are spatio-temporal individuals of a pretty substantial sort, such as the individual man or horse, as Aristotle said, or the individual car or building, as one might add. And I came to think that this answer is right. But the question is, of course, why it's right, and what is the significance of its being right. And these are the questions, or some of them, that I found myself trying to answer in *Individuals*.

MAGEE: I can only put your own questions back to you. Why is it right? And what is the significance of its being right?

STRAWSON: That is to say, what's the position in *Individuals*? Well I think I'd better begin by saying that there is in philosophy a traditional distinction between particulars and universals, or, roughly speaking, between those objects of thought which have spatio-temporal position and those which like, say, general qualities or numbers, don't. Now particulars, of course, are of various kinds; we have substantial material objects, people, particular events or processes, particular sense-impressions or experiences or mental occurrences, phenomena like shadows and so on. And I argued in *Individuals* that two kinds of particulars were the basic kinds in our whole conceptual scheme. The two kinds were material bodies and persons, the latter being thought of as essentially, though not only, corporeal beings. And in arguing this, I was arguing against a whole tradition, the whole tradition of classical British empiricism, which makes particular sense-impressions the basic particulars. The arguments I used were of various kinds, but they turned quite largely on the concepts of identity and identification. They were, you might say, a mixture of logical and epistemological arguments, they related to the conditions of the possibility of doing various things that we do in discourse, and conditions of knowledge, and so on. Well now – that was what I did in the first part of the book; I argued that a certain class of particulars are basic among particulars at large, at least in our scheme of thought. Then in the second part of the book I tried to do something else. I tried to explain the association between two pairs of ideas, the ontological ideas of particular and universal on the one hand and the logical ideas of subject and predicate on the other. And this, of course, is where the matter of reference and predication comes in. Now if I even partly succeeded in this – that is, in showing that certain particulars were basic among particulars at large, in showing that particulars in general were the basic objects of reference, the basic subjects of predication, and in explaining in both cases why this was so – then it seemed to me I should have gone some way towards explaining the most general structural features of our conceptual scheme, of the way we think about the world.

MAGEE: You write a good deal about the framework within which particulars are ordered, and you assert that it's a spatio-temporal framework. Am I right in saying that you regard it as existing independently of our experience?

STRAWSON: Oh! What exactly am I being committed to? I certainly don't think that to talk about space or time is to talk about anything other than spatial and temporal relations between particular items and events.

MAGEE: But is it conceivable that they might be in these relations to each other independently of our experience?

STRAWSON: Oh, yes, the existence of the relations I certainly would hold to be independent of experience. What I was rejecting just now was the notion of absolute space and time.

MAGEE: What you've now said puts you in opposition not only to the British empiricist tradition but also, to some extent, to the Kantian tradition.

STRAWSON: Yes, I am to some extent in opposition to the Kantian view.

MAGEE: Despite the fact that what you were dealing with were Kantian problems, in many ways?

STRAWSON: That was so, though it was not really quite my intention at the time. It became clear to me rather as I went on. There are really two ways in which I became aware of asking Kantian questions and using Kantian procedures in the book. I tried, as I said, to give an account of some general structural features of our conceptual scheme as it actually is. But then of course the question naturally arises: Could it be different? Could there be an alternative, a different structure? And this really means, or I take it to mean: Could we make sense of the idea of an alternative structure? This is really a rather Kantian question, and I played with it a bit in *Individuals*. I considered for example the fantasy of a purely auditory world without material bodies, and I asked how far we could reproduce our conceptual structure in these extremely exiguous terms.

Or again I considered the Leibnizian theory of Monads, the theory, you remember, which tries ultimately to dispense with spatio-temporal objects of reference altogether, while at the same time preserving individual centres of consciousness or quasi-consciousness as the ultimate subjects of predication; and I argued that the scheme was really incoherent. But I didn't really press the question of possible alternatives very far in this book. But there was another way in which I became aware of Kantian elements in *Individuals*; and this was when I found myself using the technique of arguing from the conditions of the possibility of making certain distinctions or achieving certain results. For example the conditions of the possibility of distinguishing between oneself and one's states of consciousness on the one hand, and what wasn't oneself or a state of consciousness of oneself on the other; or again the conditions of the possibility of identifying certain items. Now these are Kantian types of argument, and this phrase, 'the conditions of the possibility of' is an extremely Kantian phrase. So though I didn't set out with a consciously Kantian aim, I did thus find myself, as it were, asking Kantian questions and using Kantian techniques.

MAGEE: Was it the fact that you found yourself asking Kantian questions, and using Kantian techniques, that led you on to the specific study of Kant which produced your next book, *The Bounds of Sense*?

STRAWSON: Partly that, and partly because, ever since I was an undergraduate, I've been fascinated and perplexed, as everybody who knows it must be, by *The Critique of Pure Reason*.

MAGEE: I'm sorry to keep asking you to summarize your own books. It must be an infuriating request. My only excuse is that you're very good at summarizing other people's! Anyway let me plunge in a third time and ask you to summarize what it was you were trying to do in *The Bounds of Sense*.

STRAWSON: You might say that what I was trying to do there was to perform the intellectual equivalent of a surgical operation on the body of a great philosopher's greatest work. Of course that involved a risk that one needn't name. *The Critique of Pure Reason* is a very complex work with many interconnected doctrines in it, but there is I think a central distinction we can draw. There is in the work a body of doctrine about the necessary general structure of experience; and this really means, as I said before, a body of doctrine about the limits of what we can make truly intelligible to ourselves as a possible structure for our own experience. Now this body of doctrine, though not acceptable in all respects, is in its general outline and in many substantial points, I think, correct. But it's surrounded by, and in Kant's own view it's dependent on, another, second body of doctrine, probably that by which he's best known. And this is the doctrine that the nature of things as they really are, or as they are in themselves, is necessarily completely unknown to us – that the world as we know it, including our ordinary selves, is mere appearance, and that experience as we enjoy it has a certain necessary structure indeed, but only because that structure is imposed by us on the matter of experience which reaches us from this necessarily unknown source of things as they are in themselves. Now all this second body of doctrine I take to be a kind of nonsense, though it has a certain appealingly dramatic and exciting quality, like most metaphysical nonsense. So I conceived my task to be that of extracting as it were the kernel of truth and sense – that's to say, the first body of doctrine – from the surrounding shell of falsehood and nonsense – that's to say, the second body of doctrine. Actually this image of a kernel and a shell surrounding it isn't really as good as my first image of a surgical operation, for a shell isn't really connected with a kernel, it just surrounds it and protects it. But Kant of course conceived of this second body of doctrine as intimately and, indeed, vitally connected with the first body of doctrine; so these connections had to be severed, and I had to show they could be harmlessly severed, without killing the patient; and in order to do that I had to make clear exactly what these connections were supposed to be. So there was this double task of expounding, amending and defending what was defensible on the one hand and explaining its apparent dependence on what one wanted to discard in such a way as to show that one could carry through the task of separation. Of course that isn't the whole story, but perhaps it's the essence of the story. As for the connection with *Individuals*, to come back to that, well one obvious connection – apart from what I've already mentioned – is, I suppose, that the actual structure of our conceptual scheme, as described in *Individuals*, turns out really to have rather a lot in common with the necessary structure as revealed in *The Bounds of Sense*.

MAGEE: I was about to say, rather irreverently, that when I read *The Bounds of Sense* it seemed to me that one of the things you'd succeeded in extracting from *The Critique of Pure Reason* was your own previous book. But I suppose unavoidably there has to be an element of that in the enterprise.

STRAWSON: Unavoidably there's an element of that, though of

course in dealing with *The Critique of Pure Reason* I had also to deal with aspects of the matter which didn't really much come to the fore in *Individuals*.

MAGEE: Having read the two books in straight succession I find that they merge in my mind to constitute one big, single position. But I take it it's not unacceptable to you that they should be seen in that way?

STRAWSON: No, not at all.

MAGEE: Right at the beginning of them – at the beginning of *Individuals* – you make a distinction between what you call 'descriptive metaphysics' and what you call 'revisionary metaphysics'.

STRAWSON: Yes.

MAGEE: Can you say what this distinction is – and why you are so sceptical about revisionary metaphysics?

STRAWSON: Well I think I describe descriptive metaphysics as the attempt to reveal the overall structure of our conceptual scheme, of our way of thinking about ourselves and the world as it actually is. Revisionary metaphysics I described as the dreaming up of possible alternative structures. Why am I sceptical about it? Well, in a way, I think the answer is implicit in what has gone before. If there are limits to what we can intelligibly conceive of as a possible structure of experience, then there are such limits, and anything which contravenes them is bound to be – however plausible, dramatic and exciting it appears – a kind of nonsense.

MAGEE: Perhaps the commonest general criticism of your work – and it connects with what we're talking about now – is that it is inherently conservative: that you're content to describe our conceptual scheme as it is without making any attempt to improve it. What is your answer to that criticism?

STRAWSON: Well now, improvements in our apparatus of thought come, of course, and they come from advances in this or that specialism; and they're things that take effect, they have consequences; and I think there's nothing inherently conservative, in a sense that implies resistance to such changes, in anything that I've done. Nor is there, indeed, any implied resistance to innovation or change in philosophical techniques, in philosophical method. After all, Wittgenstein, who was a philosophical innovator if anyone was, was also the man who said 'Philosophy leaves everything as it is.' So I don't think there's any conservatism in either of those senses in what I've done. On the other hand, if it is conservative to resist essentially ineffective philosophical dreaming, constructions of the kind I've just described, then I'm all for conservatism. It's true that the conservatism I disavow may get muddled up in people's minds with the conservatism I acknowledge; and this may happen because people get over-excited about the imagined implications of advance in some special-ized field; and then you get metaphysics in the bad sense. It seems to me the real implications of conceptual innovation in some specialized field come out in the difference those innovations make within the specialized field and sometimes perhaps in the field of social life at large; and perhaps therefore in ethics. But ethics is something I've not very much ventured into.

MAGEE: When I was an undergraduate at Oxford, metaphysics was a dirty word – to refer to a man as a metaphysician was to dismiss him with contempt. Yet now – and I think this is largely owing to you – the word has become respectable again: a lot of people describe themselves, as you do, as being engaged in metaphysics. How radical a change does this represent in what philosophers are actually doing?

STRAWSON: I doubt very much whether the verbal change is owing to me. As for the extent of the real change, I am not sure that it's really been so very radical. The word 'metaphysics' seems to me a bit like the word 'politics': it's used pejoratively at certain times to refer to the more regrettable manifestations of an essential civilized activity. When the word 'metaphysics' was an anti-word, as I agree it was, the word 'analysis' at the same time was rather a pro-word, and I'm half inclined to say that respectable metaphysics is just analysis *en gros* and analysis is metaphysics *en détail*, as it were. But that isn't quite right, I realize. You can do effective analytical work in a particular conceptual area while taking an enormous amount for granted about the relations between what's in the area and what's outside it. It's when you feel the pull of connections which run from one area to another, it's when you feel a sense of the interdependence of the whole structure, it's then, I suppose, that you're being con-sciously metaphysical; and I don't think you can move in quite the same way then, partly because the connections you're then concerned with don't display themselves in quite the same way in our ordinary talk. Still, I've drifted a bit from your question. I think the answer to it is that there has been some shift in the direction of generality, but that it might be quite easy to exaggerate that shift by taking one's own experience as typical —

MAGEE: — and that under the surface of many of these general or constructive concerns a great deal of traditional analysis is going on, and has to go on.

STRAWSON: Oh absolutely must go on. This is the test in detail of what you're doing.

MAGEE: Nevertheless, when analysis was, as you've just said, a good word —

STRAWSON: It still is.

MAGEE: — still is indeed. But at one time it was common for philosophers to say that the proper task of philosophy was analysis and only analysis. Don't you think the time is now past when that view is tenable?

STRAWSON: Yes, I think it probably is. Unless of course you construe analysis broadly enough to cover the whole field of the legitimate activity, as might be done; I mean, certainly the *title*, 'analytical philosophy', is one under which most of us conduct our operations, however large-scale they are in intention.

MAGEE: You sound as if you don't think there is really all that much difference between analysis and synthesis, or between analysis and construction.

STRAWSON: Well there is the fact that I've mentioned, that once you get to feel the pull of these larger connections and the sense of the interdependence of the whole structure, you can't quite get the results you want by the method of attention to the way words work in ordinary discourse alone, the method which we practised with, I think, much success and certainly much amusement in the immediate post-war period. You have to use rather different methods.

MAGEE: Can we move to your present work? It's some years since your last book appeared: what are you engaged in now?

STRAWSON: Well I've continued to work in philosophical logic, as I do all the time, an absorbing thing; and the philosophy of language generally. But, rather specifically, I've become interested in the newly systematic study of grammar; and by this I don't mean just the problems of providing a systematic grammar for a particular language, though those are interesting enough, but in the more general idea of supplying general explanatory foundations for grammar at large. Or, if you like, or as it's sometimes put, in explaining the common human capacity to master the grammar of whatever language the individual's initially exposed to. It seems to me that if truly explanatory foundations are to be provided for grammar, one thing that has to be done, not of course the only thing, but one thing, is to close the present explanation gap that I think there is between what you might call semantico-logical features on the one hand and formal syntactic features on the other, to make the links between these two kinds of thing perspicuous. Now there's one purely schematic way of picturing the way in which this might be done: that would be to imagine a type of language described solely in terms of certain types of semantic elements and certain types of semantically significant combinations of those elements; to imagine such a language-type and then to deduce from this description what the *essential* requirements of any syntax, of any set of formal arrangements for a language of this type would be; and then to illustrate how these requirements could be variously realized, variously met, in different formal arrangements, in different actual formal arrangements. So what we would have, in accordance with this scheme, would be, on the one hand, the idea of, as it were, an abstract essential grammar for the type of language imagined, and, on the other hand, the idea of variant contingent realizations of the essential grammar. Now what you'd get from doing something of this sort would of course be only a model; but it might be a model for the facts. Indeed if it's the case that the basic categories for the organization of human experience are not widely different throughout the species, and if it's also the case (as I think it must be if the first thing is true) that the basic logico-semantic types of element and combination in human language aren't too widely different either, if these things are so, then one's inclined to say that some such pattern of general explanation, which would close the gap I spoke of, must be theoretically possible – that's what I'm inclined to think. But of course I'm no sort of specialist here – I may be absolutely wrong about this, I may be making some huge mistake. Anyway I think it will be clear what the connection is between this interest and my previous work. Anyone who's interested both in language and in general structural features of human thinking will surely find it natural enough to think about grammar, which is, if anything is, structured, however bizarrely and capriciously it may seem to be structured in particular cases, in particular languages.

MAGEE: What you say makes one think immediately of Chomsky. Are you now labouring in the same vineyard as him?

STRAWSON: I wouldn't say exactly in the same vineyard. He's a linguist, which I'm not. He is interested in providing what he calls a descriptively adequate grammar for English, that's to say, a systematic grammar for English. He's also of course interested – and this is where the point of contact comes if there is one – he's interested in providing a general linguistic theory in the absence of which the provision of a descriptively adequate grammar for a particular language wouldn't be, he says, explanatory. Now the provision of the general linguistic theory would be the provision of a theory in a set of terms which would, as it were, help to explain the picking out of a particular grammar for a language from the rather exiguous data to which anybody who learns the language is exposed. And this is a point at which what I've been describing and his concerns might come together. On the other hand, at least from what he's written up to now, it seems that he's rather cool towards the idea of a semantic basis for syntax; rather cool, therefore, to the idea that the general or universal features to which you might seek to relate the particular grammars, the working out of the particular grammars, should be conceived in semantico-logical terms. He wants rather, I think, to think of them in formal syntactic terms. Now this may not be as big a difference as it seems; because of course when I was talking earlier about this notion, I said that *one* of the things that needed to be done was to close the explanation gap between semantico-logical features on the one hand and syntactical features on the other. And of course this would be at most *one* of the things. It may very well be the case that, even granted that you could carry out this programme, there are nevertheless also certain universal tendencies to construct languages, to frame grammars, in respects which are, as far as my part of the programme is concerned, left open, in one way rather than another, so there could very well be formal universal features of syntax, which wouldn't be my concern. I feel very rash really, to talk like this at all, because I know so little about linguistics; but it seems to me not impossible that the sort of concerns that he has and the sort of programme I wildly and rashly sketch might be complementary.

MAGEE: In any case you've made it clear that this is 'work in progress', and may not reach the destination you hope.

STRAWSON: Right. It might not. What I am positive about is that it would be a source of the sort of questions and problems that philosophers are characteristically interested in.

MAGEE: Well, can I now recapitulate – and do please interrupt me if

I go wrong. When one looks back over the ground you've covered up to this point in your life you can be seen to have been following a single route even though you yourself may not have been aware of it at the time. You started by doing detailed work on such concepts in philosophical logic as entailment, truth, reference, naming, describing – and that culminated in your first book *Introduction to Logical Theory*. Then, from dealing with reference and predication it was a natural step to concern yourself with what it is we predicate *of*, and refer *to* – what *are* the basic particulars in our conceptual scheme? This brought you to the position set out in your second book, *Individuals*. But by this time you had come to realize that the problems you were concerned with were to a considerable extent Kantian – and that led you to the study of Kant which produced your third book, *The Bounds of Sense*. Now, being by this time involved in the systematic study of our whole articulated conceptual scheme – and given the philosophical tradition in which you grew up – it was again a natural step to get involved in an also systematic study of the relationship between our conceptual scheme and language – in other words linguistics. And this is the field in which you're working at this moment.

STRAWSON: Yes, I think that's right.

8
Discussion among Karl Popper, Peter Strawson and Geoffrey Warnock

The Philosophy of Russell: II

MAGEE: To the end of his life Russell was hostile to what has become known as 'Oxford philosophy'. This umbrella term covers a number of different activities, but what they all have in common is a primary concern with language. They rest on the view that philosophical problems are largely, or wholly, conceptual muddles into which we have been misled by an insufficiently aware use of the language in which we think, and describe the world, and communicate with each other – with the corollary that our philosophical ills can best be diagnosed, and cured, by linguistic analysis. Russell held that to regard philosophy's subject-matter as linguistic was frivolous. And he never understood how anyone could do it. He himself had not even considered philosophical questions of language until his mid-forties, by which time he had done virtually all his most important work. He explains in *My Philosophical Development* (p. 14):

> I had thought of language as transparent – that is to say, as a medium which could be employed without paying attention to it. As regards syntax, the inadequacy of this view was forced upon me by the contradictions arising in mathematical logic. As regards vocabulary, linguistic problems arose for me in investigating the extent to which a behaviouristic account of knowledge is possible. For these two reasons, I was led to place much more emphasis than I had previously done on the linguistic aspects of epistemology. But I have never been able to feel any sympathy with those who treat language as an autonomous province. The essential thing about language is that it has meaning – i.e. that it is related to

something other than itself, which is, in general, non-linguistic.

From this standpoint he goes on later in the book to launch attacks on, among other people, two of the participants in our present discussion, Peter Strawson and Geoffrey Warnock. The others include the Wittgenstein of *Philosophical Investigations*, and indeed the whole school of philosophy that centred on that book. He finds their work, he says (p. 216), 'completely unintelligible. Its positive doctrines seem to me trivial and its negative doctrines unfounded. I have not found in Wittgenstein's *Philosophical Investigations* anything that seems to me interesting and I do not understand why a whole school finds important wisdom in its pages.' Of that school he also says (p. 215): 'I have been unable, in spite of serious efforts, to see any validity in their criticisms of me.' The absoluteness of these dismissals is typical of Russell's utterances on the subject. Of the critical discussion of his own work in J. O. Urmson's book *Philosophical Analysis* he writes (pp. 215–216): 'I find myself totally unable to see any cogency whatever in the arguments that Mr Urmson advances.' And of Strawson's criticism of his Theory of Descriptions he says (p. 238): 'I am totally unable to see any validity whatever in any of Mr Strawson's arguments,' – almost the same words, in fact. He praises the personal abilities of these men, but can see no point in what they are doing.

Mr Warnock, how is it possible that someone phenomenally intelligent, like Russell, could fail to see the point when every bright undergraduate sees the point?

WARNOCK: I think this is extremely curious and interesting. Because, as you say, what we have here is not just an ordinary case of philosophical disagreement – of one philosopher dissenting from what another says. As Russell repeatedly says, his position is that he can see absolutely nothing in what these people are saying, no point in any of it, no validity in any of their criticisms. And this does take some explaining. It is, for instance, quite different from the way in which he talked about the logical positivists. Here he disagreed with some things that they said, but clearly regarded them as perfectly respectable figures with whom he was prepared to have an argument; whereas the later work of Wittgenstein, and most, I suppose, of postwar philosophy in Oxford, he seemed to be prepared to write off as just completely unintelligible nonsense. I could suggest, I think, up to a point anyway, why there was such animus in this very comprehensive rejection of certain kinds of philosophy. I think it goes something like this: Russell says repeatedly, and says in this connection, that the general aim of philosophy is to achieve *understanding of the world*. And I think there were certain assumptions he made about how this was to be done. I think he took it for granted that to understand the world a philosopher must invent a *theory* of some kind; and that such a theory would consist partly of philosophical doctrines which might be very unexpected and surprising to the ordinary citizen, and would also involve a technical philosophical terminology. This was because Russell thought that a great deal that is commonly taken for granted by the non-philosophical world is simply mistaken, and can be shown to be mistaken either by philosophical argument or by scientific evidence; and then he believed that natural languages are in pretty hopeless case – imprecise, unclear, and even, he thought, in a sense incorporating mistaken philosophical doctrines. (He said more than once that ordinary language incorporates what he called the metaphysics of the Stone Age.) That being so, I think he assumed that a philosophical theory devised in the attempt to achieve understanding of the world must contain novel and possibly startling philosophical doctrines and must be couched in a specially invented technical terminology. Now what I think occurred in the thirties and thereafter was that a very large number of philosophers came to look at this in an entirely different way. Partly – primarily, I suppose, under the influence of G. E. Moore – they came to believe that the ordinary beliefs that the ordinary man entertains about the world are not to be dismissed as massively mistaken in the way that Russell was inclined to suppose they must be; and perhaps more importantly, they came to think that, while it's perfectly correct to say that the natural languages we ordinarily speak are in certain respects unclear, imprecise and potentially very misleading, the right way to achieve a better understanding here is not to replace natural languages with a different kind of technical terminology, but simply to understand, better, natural languages themselves – in such a way that one won't be misled. And the effect of that was that philosophers like Wittgenstein in his later writings, and after the war conspicuously J. L. Austin and many others, didn't devise, and in a sense lost interest in the construction of, philosophical theories in any way that Russell would have recognized. And this looked to him, I think, simply like abandoning all serious interest in the subject. He couldn't think what people could be doing, if they weren't doing the kind of theory-construction in which understanding seemed to him to consist. But not only did he not see the point of Wittgenstein's later work: I am bound to say I don't think he very seriously tried to. It looked very unfamiliar to him; and although there is a general theory about the nature of philosophical problems which Wittgenstein subscribed to, and in terms of which his work is at any rate immediately intelligible, whether or not you agree with it, Russell didn't, I think, even try to see what this underlying view of Wittgenstein's could be. He simply saw the results as extremely unfamiliar, not even trying to do what he thought a philosopher must try to do, and he reacted with a kind of contemptuous bafflement.

MAGEE: I think it would be useful for me to bear out what you say with a couple of quotations from Russell. At one point in *My Philosophical Development* he says (p. 241):

> This brings me to a fundamental divergence between myself and many philosophers with whom Mr Strawson appears to be in general agreement. They are persuaded that common speech is good enough, not only for daily life, but also for philosophy. I, on the contrary, am persuaded that common speech is full of vagueness and inaccuracy, and that any attempt to be precise and accurate requires modification of common speech both as regards vocabulary and as regards syntax. Everybody admits that physics and chemistry and medicine each require a language which is not that of everyday life. I fail to see why philosophy, alone, should be forbidden to make a similar approach towards precision and accuracy.

And elsewhere in the book (p. 230) he says:

> Although I feel strongly about the importance of analysis, this is not the most serious of my objections to the new philosophy. The most serious of my objections is that the new philosophy seems to me to have abandoned, without necessity, that grave and important task which philosophy throughout the ages has hitherto pursued. Philosophers from Thales onwards have tried to understand the world. Most of them have been unduly optimistic as regards their own successes. But even when they have failed, they have supplied material to their successors and an incentive to new effort. I cannot feel that the new philosophy is carrying on this tradition.

WARNOCK: The strange thing is that Russell seems never seriously to have considered the possibility that there might be a quite different way of trying to achieve understanding in philosophy from his own. He compares, I think, rather unfavourably in this connection with his contemporary Moore, who also found Wittgenstein (understandably enough) a very perplexing phenomenon, but Moore certainly took immense pains to attend to what Wittgenstein was saying, to try to see what was behind this way of approaching philosophical problems. Moore, in fact, convinced himself that Wittgenstein really had got on to something extremely important, which he would have liked to understand better – which is quite different from the very rapid dismissiveness with which Russell reacted here. I think one can understand Russell's reaction, but it's not very easy to defend it.

MAGEE: Sir Karl, you also have been a critic of Oxford philosophy. Do you share any of Russell's grounds for criticism?

POPPER: Yes I do. I fully agree with these passages from Russell which you have read out, and I think they have to be interpreted quite differently. I think that Russell was always interested in human problems; but he realized that our knowledge of the world (and our so-called mastery of the powers of nature) was one of the greatest of human problems. Thus he was right, I think, when he complained about philosophers whose interest in the world, and especially in the physical world, in the universe, was flagging. One cannot understand human problems if one neglects their general background: this, I think, is Russell's view, especially in the last passage you read out. As to the preceding passage where he speaks about language – about 'common speech' – I do not think this is quite so important. Throughout he's defending the need for, and the interest in, a philosophy of science. I think that both passages have practically the same meaning: that a philosopher who has no interest in science isn't a philosopher. This is, briefly, what he says. I don't think there's anything particularly difficult here to find out – about what Russell thought, or why and how Russell thought so. There's no doubt that in the various works which he attacks in these passages there's no indication of any interest in the great problems in which he was interested; certainly not in science. In fact it was part of Russell's view, not only of a philosopher but of any fully responsible man, that his interests must not be too narrow. I do not agree that he thought a philosopher should construct philosophical theories. What he wanted of them was that they should have problems: that they should have genuine philosophical problems and not only second-hand problems (as he would have regarded problems connected with language). Well, this whole affair of language philosophy has, of course, a background. Why did philosophers become so interested in language? Very largely because some of them had discovered the need for a criticism of language. It's a very interesting development. Up to a certain point all linguistic philosophers, including Wittgenstein, were highly critical of language. Then we can see a sudden switch-over: suddenly linguistic philosophers are no longer critical of language, but are only interested in the usages of language as it is, without trying to criticize it. Some even appeal to common speech as a kind of authority. This sudden switch-over led Russell to the remark that, after all, common speech is not perfect. I do not think that these remarks of Russell's are particularly important. But I think this is Russell's position. It is a position I fully share.

WARNOCK: But could I just put a question to you about this? What seemed to me strange in some of the things Russell had to say about, say, the later work of Wittgenstein is not so much that he didn't find it particularly interesting or disagreed with it, as that he says repeatedly: 'I can see no point in this at all. I can't understand in the least how a philosopher can go on in this way.' This does surprise me because there is at least a way – not perfectly simple, but at any rate a way – of understanding why Wittgenstein thought it appropriate to go on in this way, and Russell never seems to have given much attention to this.

POPPER: I very much sympathize with Russell. I don't like to attack anybody, and I hesitate to support Russell when he attacks Wittgenstein, but I sympathize with Russell's feelings. Wittgenstein very fittingly compares a certain type of philosopher with a fly in a bottle, going on and on, buzzing about. And he says it is the task of his philosophy to show the fly the way out of the bottle. But I think it is Wittgenstein himself who is in the bottle and never finds his way out of it; and I certainly don't think he has shown anybody else the way out. This is what I feel when I hear you say, 'Wittgenstein thought it appropriate to go on in this way': he did not even *think* it appropriate! I may perhaps concede that one could go on buzzing in this way for, let us say, a week or two, but to spend one's life on it! I should find it terribly boring.

STRAWSON: Well this is where I would like to dissent. I entirely agree with Popper that it has been characteristic of Oxford philosophers at large, as it was of Moore, whom Russell treated with respect, to show very little interest in, and probably to possess very little knowledge of, natural science. I think this has been true of us all, and it is, I surely must concede, a limitation. However, that it leaves us with nothing very serious to talk about does seem to me false, as well as being damaging if true. Because, after all, it seems to me that ordinary people employing ordinary language – and the emphasis on language isn't always essential here – ordinary people employing the ordinary conceptual resources of mankind have at their disposal not a crude, rough-and-ready instrument, but an enormously sophisticated instrument, for thinking; and that it's an immensely and inexhaustibly interesting task to trace the various connections between the concepts which people handle in their ordinary life with no particular difficulty. There are enormously difficult and interesting problems about the *structure* of this whole conceptual scheme which ordinary people manage so easily in the ordinary course of events. The difficulty consists in saying what the structure *is*, in saying how the notions of perception, action, personal identity, ethics – all the ordinary notions which we handle quite easily – are related to each other. Their complexities, and the interest of this structure, seem to me quite inexhaustible, and have seemed inexhaustible, I should say, to many philosophers throughout the history of the subject. I think it is a limitation in Russell's sympathies that he was unable to extend to Wittgenstein, and perhaps to us, the kind of sympathy that he clearly felt for Moore, who as far as the evidence of his writings goes, appears to have been without specialized knowledge in natural science, or indeed much interest in it.

POPPER: As to Moore: first of all, Moore knew some mathematics. He didn't write about it because he didn't know enough, and he had no original ideas in the field. But he knew enough mathematics to understand quite a bit of what Russell was doing, and he even published some criticism of Russell's logic. That's one thing. The second thing is that Russell owed to Moore a kind of liberation: he owed to Moore the liberation from Hegelianism. And Russell was a man who didn't easily forget an intellectual debt. Incidentally, he was also very grateful to Wittgenstein for certain contributions which Wittgenstein in his earlier period had made to Russell's thought. And he was most concerned in a personal way about Wittgenstein – about what he regarded, almost, as Wittgenstein's intellectual suicide. But to answer another point which you made just now: you said that one mustn't be contemptuous of ordinary language because it is a subtle and wonderful instrument for thinking. I agree. But who has used this wonderful instrument in a more wonderful way than Russell? And was it not his use of this instrument, his masterly use of ordinary language in discussing difficult problems, that made ordinary-language philosophy possible? I think you owe to him at least the revival of the idea that one can philosophize in ordinary language. There was no philosopher contemporary with Russell who philosophized in ordinary language as he did. Certainly not Moore: for example, in *Principia Ethica* Moore is sometimes pretty far removed from ordinary language. I have in mind those passages where Moore distinguishes 'good' written in the ordinary way from 'Good' with a capital 'G'. This is certainly not what Russell would have done. I mean, Russell was very much more a man who could master ordinary language, and he could do with it things that

Moore could not do. And I think that what Russell felt was that philosophy – language philosophy – was about to decline into a new scholasticism: this is really what he felt.

WARNOCK: But would you not think that he was in rather a hurry to be certain that nothing was going to come out of it, that no enlightenment was going to result? I suppose this is really the question: does anything come of this or not?

POPPER: What has come out of it? Russell read the *Philosophical Investigations* without deriving any enlightenment from it. So did I, I must admit.

WARNOCK: You would have to say, I suppose – as perhaps Russell would – that people who read this work and believe themselves to be enlightened by it have been victims of some sort of illusion.

POPPER: Yes.

STRAWSON: But one must distinguish. I mean, Russell wasn't only attacking Wittgenstein. It may be that the Wittgensteinian formal conception at any rate – that the task of philosophers is to let us out of muddles – is a bit limited, but it doesn't follow that all of those whom Russell condemned had a similar conception. Many of them might have thought it perfectly possible to trace positively and interestingly the structural connections, the conceptual connections, throughout this network of ideas with which we manage our ordinary intercourse with each other and the world: not merely to get rid of our muddles, though that's a good thing too, but to give us insight, to give us a clear view – as Wittgenstein also said, so perhaps he didn't have quite such a negative picture – of our conceptual scheme.

POPPER: To this I can only say: I have spectacles, and I am cleaning my spectacles now. But spectacles have a *function*, and they function only when you put them on, to look through them *at the world*. It is the same with language. That is to say, one shouldn't waste one's life in spectacle-cleaning or in talking about language, or in trying to get a clear view of our language, or of 'our conceptual scheme'. The fundamental thing about human languages is that they can and should be used to describe something; and this something is, somehow, the world. To be constantly and almost exclusively interested in the medium – in spectacle-cleaning – is a result of a philosophical mistake. This philosophical mistake can quite easily be traced in Wittgenstein. Wittgenstein was originally impressed by the fact that the medium may impose limitations on us, or that it may actually deceive us, and he was also impressed, upon further analysis, by the fact that we can't really *do* anything about the medium. By a kind of recoil from his earlier views he then said that all we can really do is to list the various usages (of a word, for example), to try to see the differences, and to understand them – somehow. The real issue as I see it is different: do we have a philosophy of language which explains to us the functions of language, and which helps us to understand the significance of human language (which is more than a game)? Do you have a philosophy of language in this sense? I think I have. I don't know whether Russell had one, and I don't want to speak about myself. All I want to do here is to defend Russell's views as well as I can, for I think there's a very great deal in them. I suggest that behind this kind of preoccupation which he was trying to combat, there is fundamentally a mistaken philosophical doctrine, a mistaken epistemological doctrine. And I also suggest that if it goes on, it may well lead to a thing one can describe as scholasticism (though I wish not to be found wanting in respect for the distinguished schoolmen of the Middle Ages).

STRAWSON: You associated scholasticism earlier with the bad, boring and trivial. Now, of course, in any department of human intellectual activity there can be examples of work which are bad, boring and trivial, but I don't think one should judge a general field of human intellectual activity by such examples.

POPPER: You see, the history of man is a queer thing. It's a history of a succession of attacks of intellectual madness, of all sorts of strange intellectual fashions. I don't need to give many examples of revolts against reason (such as Existentialism), for we know how strongly certain fashions have taken hold, not only just in a comparatively small insular group, but in large parts of mankind. Russell saw these things in that light, and so do I.

MAGEE: I'd like to invite Geoffrey Warnock's comment on something Karl Popper has just said: namely, that at the time when he wrote the *Tractatus*, Wittgenstein was – as he later came to think – bewitched by a certain theory of language; that he became so concerned at the discovery that language might deceive us that he thought that, before we do anything else, we must get down to a study of the different ways in which it can deceive us; and that this became a conception of philosophy.

WARNOCK: Well, I think that is perfectly true. He came to think that he himself had at one time been led astray in a certain way, and perhaps rather incautiously extended this to a general diagnosis as to the way in which philosophical problems arise. But then what puzzles me in what Russell had to say about Wittgenstein's later work is not so much that he disagreed with it – because I can quite understand how he and Sir Karl Popper might very well disagree with it: it's the *incomprehension* he displays which seems to me so puzzling.

POPPER: Include me here too.

WARNOCK: Well, I don't think I could, you see: because if I say to you, 'What do you think of the *Philosophical Investigations*?' it is clear to me that you understand it and disagree with it and —

POPPER: Oh no! There just isn't anything definite enough for anybody to disagree with. That is the terrible thing. I mean, if you force me at gun – how does one say?

WARNOCK: Gun-point.

POPPER: Should you force me at gun-point to say what it is I disagree with in Wittgenstein's *Philosophical Investigations*, I would have to say: 'Oh – nothing . . .' Indeed, I only disagree with the *enterprise*. I cannot disagree with anything he says, because there is nothing one can disagree with. But I confess that I am bored by it – bored to tears.

WARNOCK: Ah, that's another matter. One might be bored, yes, but at least you could give a description of what the enterprise is. You can say, 'This is what the enterprise is and I don't think it's worth doing' – which is more sympathetic than Russell.

POPPER: How can one disagree with things which are so vague and so trivial? I do think the possibility of disagreeing with what a writer writes is of decisive importance. One could regard it almost as a criterion of whether it's worth reading. If a man writes only things with which one cannot possibly quarrel, and to which one can only say, 'Well – maybe – perhaps – well – maybe – maybe – maybe yes, maybe no,' then I should be inclined to say there isn't much point in an enterprise of this kind. That is how I see the issue.

MAGEE: Could I invite you, Mr Warnock, to answer your own question?

WARNOCK: Which one?

MAGEE: You've said two or even three times that it seems to you extraordinary that Russell totally failed to see any point, etc, etc. Well, why do you think he *totally* failed?

WARNOCK: I would be tempted to say simply that he didn't see, in these writings of which he was so critical, anything that he was accustomed to look for.

POPPER: That is certainly true: I agree. But why? Russell was accustomed to look for *arguments*.

STRAWSON: Oh no, that's not quite fair. Even if Wittgenstein was a bit parsimonious in actually explicit arguments, there are implicit ones. But I think I'd like to say something else about this. It's clear that Russell, and he acknowledges it himself, thought, apart from mathematics, that his major philosophical preoccupation was to link up the findings of natural science, especially physics, which he accepted, with a rather Hume-like empiricist picture of the actual *data* of our lives, of our experience – that's to say, sense-impressions, images of imagination, and images of memory. He wanted to accept natural science. He thought the data were of this order, and the whole of his metaphysics and epistemology outside of mathematics is really an attempt to link these together; and a good deal of theoretical construction has to be got through in order to do this. Now this is a particular conception of philosophy, a belief that philosophy had to face this particular problem; but it's by no means clear that this is correct. Many of the philosophers Russell criticizes would reject this initial picture of the problem of philosophy, and substitute what you might call an anthropocentric interest, starting from man in his world and in his relation to other people, not bothering with traditional philosophical scepticism because this didn't seem to them a real issue, but actually concerned, in (if you like) this anthropocentric way, with the structure of man's picture of his world. Now the theories and entities of natural science would have a place in this overall answer, and there's nothing necessarily *mesquin* or mean or limited or tiny about this enterprise. It can be as large-scale as you please, but it starts from a point which Russell wouldn't allow it to start from, and its interest is anthropocentric in a way in which Russell's interest was not.

POPPER: That's an interesting diagnosis. But I think I can refute the diagnosis. I think that my own approach is utterly different from the one you have just described. I'm not interested in sense-impressions or sense data: I'm a realist. I'm even a common sense sort of realist. My own ideas are far removed from what you describe as Russell's 'initial picture of philosophy'. But I do agree with his views on Wittgenstein: Russell and I have talked about Wittgenstein and we agreed completely. So it can hardly be this particular picture of Russell's which explains why he found himself so unimpressed by Wittgenstein or (in your view) why he couldn't make head or tail of what Wittgenstein tried to say.

STRAWSON: My diagnosis wasn't meant specifically to be an explanation of Russell's inability to take Wittgenstein. There are, after all, other philosophers than Wittgenstein engaged in the task who come under the general Russell ban. I know you, Sir Karl, are a realist and I'm with you there. I can understand anybody being bored by and repelled by Wittgenstein, who is a very, very peculiar person, though I think a genius. But would you really want to repudiate also the entire Oxford style, the entire Oxford school?

POPPER: I don't repudiate anybody, and there are very good philosophers in Oxford. As to the linguistic school, some day, perhaps, something may come out of it: something interesting. My own attitude towards this school is that I don't read its publications any longer. I do other things. And, of course, I'm not read by them either. So it doesn't really matter. The relationship is kind of mutual.

STRAWSON: I must correct you on that point. You are read by us.

POPPER: I don't think so; anyway, it seems that ours is a kind of broadened mutual admiration society.

MAGEE: Can I move this discussion on to some other aspects of Russell's work? Sir Karl has been saying that Russell thought almost all philosophical problems of importance arose outside philosophy: in science, in mathematics, and so on.

POPPER: Or in ethics, or religion.

MAGEE: Indeed. But is it possible to ask you if you can summarize the importance of Russell's contribution to the philosophy of science?

POPPER: Summarize? A bit difficult, but I will try. Now, I think there is a very important thing which one can see from Russell's book *My Philosophical Development* and also from his *Autobiography*. It is that the young Russell set out with a fantastically optimistic philosophical hope. He hoped that he would be able to show that we possess absolutely certain knowledge, founded on bedrock. And that we have not only a little, but quite a lot of it; not only in mathematics, but also in physics, and possibly beyond. It is also quite clear that after a terrific effort to show this, and after coming nearer to success than anybody before him, he had to face defeat. He turned into a sceptic. This is the history of Bertrand Russell, and it is a great tragedy. The great life of a great man who set out to find, not only truth, but certainty, and who was honest enough to admit to himself that he didn't succeed in finding certainty. This, really, is his history. He tried to find certainty especially in mathematics, and that was the field of his great effort. As you will remember, one of the first books he wrote was *The Principles of Mathematics*. It is, I believe, one of the greatest and most astonishing books ever written. Its history is hard to credit. He had no serious philosophy of mathematics before he went, in July 1900, to a Congress in Paris where he met Peano, by whom he was greatly impressed. He got Peano to give him all his writings. He read them, all of them, in August; this alone was a fantastic effort. (I should break down if I attempted such a thing.) In September he wrote an original paper on the logic of relations which was published in Peano's journal. In October he started writing *The Principles of Mathematics*, and by 31 December he had completed the first draft of this great work. Four parts of it were published (three years later) almost exactly as they were first written, while three parts (one, two and seven) had to be rewritten. I do not think that anything quite like this has ever happened in the history of philosophy or of literature. The achievement of the book is without parallel. Russell rediscovered Frege's logic and theory of numbers, and he laid the foundation of arithmetic and analysis. He gave the first clear and simple definition of real numbers on this basis (an improvement on Cantor, Dedekind and Peano). And he not only gave a theory of geometry but a new approach to mechanics. It must have been a terrific experience, and a very happy one. Russell says that it was 'an intellectual honeymoon' such as he 'never experienced before or since'. I doubt whether anything like this has ever been experienced by anybody. It shows what a genius the young Russell was. But then the catastrophe came. A silly little difficulty arose. It was a trivial logical point, quite uninteresting in itself, and far less challenging than the many great problems he had already solved. But it turned out to be a very unpleasant difficulty: Russell was unable to get over it in any way that satisfied or convinced him. He was forced to attend very closely to the difficulty – a logical antinomy, or paradox, which he called 'the contradiction' in *The Principles*. And he found that the paradox invalidated not only his work but the work of all his predecessors. Now about this there is a passage in his book, *My Philosophical Development*.

MAGEE: Shall I read it out?

> When *The Principles of Mathematics* was finished, I settled down to a resolute attempt to find a solution of the paradoxes. I felt this as almost a personal challenge, and I would, if necessary, have spent the whole of the rest of my life in an attempt to meet it, but for two reasons I found this exceedingly disagreeable. In the first place, the whole problem struck me as trivial, and I hated having to concentrate attention upon something that did not seem intrinsically interesting. In the second place, try as I would, I could make no progress. Throughout 1903 and 1904, my work was almost wholly devoted to this matter, but without any vestige of success (p. 79).

POPPER: You see, the really interesting thing is he found the problem exceedingly disagreeable and trivial. Yet it marked not only the end of his intellectual honeymoon, but also the end of his high hopes, of his philosophical attempt to lay secure foundations for human knowledge. If one reads between the lines of his *Autobiography*, it was an absolutely tragic experience for him. It was no doubt this terrible disappointment which largely explains the strange experience which he describes in his *Autobiography* – his sudden disappointment with his first wife which led nine years later to a divorce. In his *Autobiography* he describes both experiences on the same page (vol. I, p. 147). Thus his *Autobiography* connects his sudden disappointment in his first love – that is, mathematics – with his sudden discovery that he no longer loved his wife. This shows, I think, that he felt frustrated to a degree which is quite incredible. Here was an absolutely trivial problem and he could not solve it!

I think we should perhaps briefly discuss one or the other form of a logical paradox. Take a piece of paper and write on one side, 'The statement on the other side of this paper is false,' and on the other side write: 'The statement on the other side of the paper is true.' You will find that the assumption that any of these statements is true leads to the conclusion that it is false, and vice versa. Now that's a trivial affair – there could be nothing very serious in this for a man who had solved such fantastically difficult and interesting problems as Russell had already done in this book. He had been the first to give a satisfactory theory of irrational numbers, a problem which had agitated mankind for 2,400 years. And he had given a really brilliant solution of the ancient problem of motion. Yet now he was faced with a silly thing like this, quite obviously an affair of elementary logic which he should have been able to solve easily. The frustration of his struggle, which went on for about ten years, almost destroyed the man. One can read this clearly between the lines of his *Autobiography*. It marks the great change in Russell from a hopeful optimist in philosophy to a man who becomes something like a sceptic. (Alan Wood has called him 'the passionate sceptic'.) Anyway, he ends up with a position utterly different from anything he set out to prove. *Principia Mathematica* is an attempt to rescue from the old programme what can be rescued. Nevertheless, this great work is a compromise – a compromise with scepticism. Although Russell never gave up the search for the foundations of human knowledge, he never again even tried to dig down to rock bottom. And he often changed his mind, trying candidly to discover and to correct his own mistakes. This, I think, is a kind of very rough and very superficial bird's eye view of the main development of Russell.

MAGEE: In *My Philosophical Development* Russell says (p. 74): 'The primary aim of *Principia Mathematica* was to show that all pure mathematics follows from purely logical premises and uses only concepts definable in logical terms.' In the course of this attempt he and Whitehead developed a very powerful and suggestive system of notation which was to have great influence on philosophy – not only on symbolic logic but on general philosophy, partly through Russell's own Theory of Descriptions. It's amusing to read later in *My Philosophical Development* (p. 83):

The Theory of Descriptions was first set forth in my article 'On Denoting' in *Mind*, 1905. This doctrine struck the then editor as so preposterous that he begged me to reconsider it and not to demand its publication as it stood. I, however, was persuaded of its soundness and refused to give way. It was afterwards generally accepted, and came to be thought my most important contribution to logic.

Russell believed that every meaningful assertion must be either true or false. If you take a sentence like 'The Queen of England is more than 30 years old,' this is true if the individual denoted by the definite description 'the Queen of England' is more than 30 years old, and false if she is not. But what happens if we substitute the name of another country for 'England': say, 'France'? This ought to give us a sentence of exactly the same logical type. Yet suddenly we no longer know whether to say that the statement we now have is true or false.

Obviously it can't be true to say that the Queen of France is more than 30 years old, because there isn't a Queen of France. On the other hand, to say that the statement, 'The Queen of France is more than 30 years old' is false would seem to imply that the statement, 'The Queen of France is not more than 30 years old' is true; and that causes us acute intellectual discomfort. The example is trivial; but obviously it's of the highest importance that in our thinking and speaking about the world we should be able to distinguish between these two different sorts of statement, which on the face of it look so alike, and yet logically are so very different. Otherwise it's only too easy to see how we might be seduced by our language, or our grammar, into very serious error. Russell's proposal was that we should transcribe all such sentences into a form that would make their logic manifest. And to help him to do this he used the logical notation of *Principia Mathematica*. Without resorting to symbols I think we can render his transcription in ordinary words, as: 'There exists something which is unique in being Queen of France and which is also more than 30 years old.' And now, he says, it is clear that we no longer need feel any intellectual discomfort in saying this is false. And the logic of every sentence of the form, 'The so-and-so is such-and-such,' becomes clear, says Russell, when it is transcribed in this way: 'There exists something which is unique in being so-and-so and which is also such-and-such.'

Once the theory had succeeded in establishing itself it became something of an orthodoxy for decades. But then it began to come under criticism. And the most notable critic of it was Peter Strawson. Professor Strawson, can you say something about what the theory's shortcomings were?

STRAWSON: Perhaps first I might get at the shortcomings better by underlining its virtues a bit more fully. You see, it's perfectly correct to point out that phrases of the form 'the so-and-so', and sentences containing such phrases, may be perfectly significant, even though there's nothing the phrases apply to. Indeed their significance, in fact, is guaranteed simply by the significance of their parts. As long as you observe the grammatical restrictions and certain semantical restrictions in putting the parts together, you're bound to have a significant phrase. So far the theory is all right, and again it's perfectly reasonable to try to give, for any sentence of this kind, a full and explicit statement of the conditions under which such a sentence is used to say something true; and it's perfectly reasonable to regard such a statement as a contribution to the semantic theory of those phrases, and indeed of the language that contains them. I think one ought to add here that this matter of stating the truth conditions wasn't quite so simple as Russell's early versions of the Theory of Descriptions suggested. For example, if a wife says to her husband at the end of the day, 'The baby has been sick today,' although she no doubt thinks her baby is unique, it's exceedingly unlikely that she thinks it's unique in being a baby. So the simple form of paraphrase suggested won't do quite, but one may suppose that a suitable supplementation could be found to overcome that difficulty. There remains the question of what's wrong with a theory which has such virtues, and I think the real objection to it consists in this matter of the claim of an equivalence of meaning between the type of sentence to be explained, and the full statement of truth conditions in terms of a uniquely existential assertion which enters into the supposed analysis. And it does seem to me that anyone who's seriously interested in language as a means of communication between human beings must find that claim of equivalence of meaning somewhat insensitive and, as it were, flattening. Of course, it's perfectly true that we do sometimes make assertions of this form – explicit assertions of unique existence. But also very, very often, and relevantly, we do something rather different. We assume, that is, in our partners in a communication situation, in a speech situation, we assume in them knowledge of individual items, particular individuals, as being unique in certain respects: we assume this knowledge and we use various linguistic forms or devices to draw on, to invoke, this knowledge in the course of saying what we have to say. And these devices are of various kinds and include 'the so-and-so' phrases. But now, as far as these phrases are concerned, it's precisely this feature of them that the Theory of Descriptions diverts attention away from. A serious semantic theory of the language ought, among other things, to stress this feature of these phrases; and what the Theory of Descriptions does is to divert attention away from this feature by equating them in meaning to explicit assertions of unique existence. And indeed there isn't only this general complaint one has to make, but as soon as you apply the form of expansion to particular cases you see something of the absurdity – let alone the inadequacy for the purposes of semantic theory – that results. Take my example of 'the baby has been sick today'. Obviously this doesn't mean the same as: 'There is something which is unique in being a baby, and which has also been sick today.' If you try to supplement it in a *generally* acceptable way, it seems very hard not to come up with something like this: '*There is something which is unique in being both a baby and what I might reasonably take you to expect me to mean when I use the expression "the baby", and which has also been sick today.*' This form of paraphrase gives the game away, besides being intrinsically unattractive, in that it clearly points to the possibility of giving a semantic explanation which would make the paraphrase itself superfluous. So that's the sort of objection I would have to accepting the theory as an adequate account, for the purposes of semantic theory, of these phrases.

POPPER: I don't really understand. I should say that a mother's report such as 'The baby has been sick today' is a comparatively unimportant example. Nevertheless, I should say even in this case one can see that Russell is right, for if there are two babies in the family – say twins – then the phrase 'the baby' would hardly be appropriate. That is to say, 'the baby' in this case means 'the *one* baby which is our baby', and if there are two babies which are our babies, it wouldn't work. So the mother who uses the phrase does think that the baby is unique in being the one baby (of her family). But apart from that, I think it is obvious that in cases of colloquial use such as 'the baby has been sick today', our standards of articulating what we want to say are low. There is no need in these cases to be explicit, to explain things beyond a certain point, simply because so much can be taken as understood. What Russell was after were contexts in which not so much is to be taken as understood, and this is why I am not quite convinced by your example. Apart from this, we must not forget that Russell's fundamental problem here arose in mathematics: in connection with his analysis of mathematical reasoning. The 'the' was important in such contexts as '*the* solution of the equation $x+2=5$'. Linear equations have only *one* solution. Otherwise the phrase 'the solution' cannot be applied. If we have quadratic equations with two solutions, we can't say 'the solution', but we can say 'the solutions', and there is, of course, a Russellian description which applies to a unique pair, or to a unique triplet. Individual uniqueness is therefore not really essential. It would be possible, for example, for the mother to say, 'The twins have been sick today,' and obviously the meaning wouldn't be very different from the meaning: 'The baby has been sick today.' Although nobody would refer to the twins as unique in every sense, they are unique as the twins of this particular family. So I am not quite clear what is at stake. Also the following worries me. 'Meaning' is a terribly vague term. I wonder whether one couldn't defend the view that two obviously equivalent sentences – let us say 'Today is the 13th, a day of misfortune' and the other, 'The 13th – oh, the day of misfortune – *that's* what it is today!' – have not really the same meaning. If you think of any two equivalent statements which are differently formulated, though the difference is slight, you might always distinguish slight differences of 'meaning'. But this sense of 'meaning' was not, I think, Russell's sense at all. I think that what he was interested in was an analysis which replaced one statement by another which had the same meaning in so far as it was describing *the same state of affairs*, and which could be formulated in some standard language. The state of affairs, that's the decisive thing. If two sentences refer to the same state of affairs and describe the same state of affairs, and are thus logically equivalent, then this, I think, suffices for what Russell meant by equality of meaning. I don't really think he had any further intention in this respect.

STRAWSON: Yes. It is a question, isn't it, of *interest*, as you say. If you're interested in giving a full and accurate account of the semantics of a natural language, then I think, though you can learn from the Theory of Descriptions, you won't take it over without any criticism at all. You'll seek to modify it in a certain way, in the way I implicitly suggested. If, of course, on the other hand, you're concerned with something really rather different, how best, for example, we can find substitutes for these forms of words in the notation of *Principia Mathematica*, this clear and powerful notation, then indeed you might say the Theory of Descriptions gives the general form of a solution to that problem.

9
Conversation with Bernard Williams

Philosophy and Morals

MAGEE: Of the many possible ways of approaching the study of philosophy, three are the commonest: one through the history of the subject, one through the examination of particular philosophers, and one through an investigation of problems. Each has its merits, and so far in this book we have followed a combination of the first two; that is to say we have focused all our discussions on the work of individuals, and by considering them in a roughly chronological order we have thereby outlined the recent history of the subject. Now we move over to the third way. For the rest of the book we shall consider the current state of certain groups of problems, in other words certain areas of the subject, without confining ourselves to the work of any particular individual.

The first field we are going to consider in this way is moral philosophy, a subject which is felt by most of its leading practitioners to have fallen into a profoundly unsatisfactory state. To discuss its development over the period covered by this volume would be to devote all our space to explaining what it is that is unsatisfactory. We are not going to do this, but are going rather to consider the problems that have to be faced now, and the forms which some of the necessary new departures might take. Even so, the recent history of the subject is important as the background to our discussion. An admirably lucid, elegant and brief account of it exists in Geoffrey Warnock's *Contemporary Moral Philosophy*, and it will be extremely helpful if I quote here at length from Mr Warnock's summary of the contents of that book as set forth in his Introduction:

The aim of this essay is to provide a compendious survey of moral philosophy since about the beginning of the present century.

Fortunately, the tale that thus falls to be told is not in outline excessively complex, and can be seen as a quite intelligible sequence of distinguishable episodes. The major stages on the road are three in number. There is, first, Intuitionism, to be considered here as represented by G. E. Moore (*Principia Ethica*, 1903), H. A. Prichard (*Moral Obligation*, published posthumously in 1949) and W. D. Ross (*The Right and the Good*, 1930, and *Foundations of Ethics*, 1939). Second, in somewhat violent reaction to the undoubted shortcomings of that style of ethics, we have Emotivism; and here the chief spokesman is C. L. Stevenson (*Ethics and Language*, 1944). And third, as an amendment of and an advance from Emotivism, we shall consider what may be called, and often is called, Prescriptivism, whose most lucid, persuasive, and original exponent is R. M. Hare (*The Language of Morals*, 1952, and *Freedom and Reason*, 1963). . . . It is possible, and may be helpful, to sketch out in advance one short version of the way in which things seem to me to have gone wrong. Intuitionism, to begin with, emptied moral theory of all content by making the whole topic undiscussably *sui generis*. Fundamental moral terms were said simply to be indefinable, and fundamental moral judgments to be simply, transparently and not further explicably, self-evident. Moral truths were, it seemed, such that nothing could possibly be said about what they meant, what their grounds were, or even why they mattered at all. Now this, we may say, understandably provoked the emotivist to look quite elsewhere in search of something to be said. In effect he abandoned altogether the idea – the apparently barren idea – that moral utterances should be regarded as genuine judgments having (or even not having) statable meanings and discoverable grounds, and turned instead to the quite new topic of such utterances' *effects*. But thus, though for new reasons, the emotivist like his predecessor had nothing to say on what moral judgments are, or say, or mean; he was interested only, and somewhat crudely, in what they are *for*. Prescriptivism next contributed a meritorious distinction. We should consider, it was urged, not what is sought to be achieved *by* issuing a moral utterance, but rather what is actually done *in* issuing it – not what effect is aimed at, but what 'speech-act' is performed. This was all to the good. But this enquiry, it will be observed, still stopped short of considering what such utterances actually say, what they mean, what sort of grounds can be urged for or against them. And thus there remains out of view, or at least at the margin of attention, all that is of distinctively moral interest. . . .

When the leading practitioners of a subject feel that its most important content has been overlooked in this wholesale way we are probably on the threshold of some major new development.

One of the most distinguished philosophers now working in this field is Bernard Williams, a Professor of Philosophy at Cambridge. Professor Williams, can we start this discussion by making clear, as I have not yet tried to do, what sort of questions moral philosophers are concerned with?

WILLIAMS: They've been tremendously concerned with the status of moral beliefs or moral attitudes. They've been very concerned with the similarities and differences between moral views on the one hand and say scientific theories or scientific opinions or ordinary common sense empirical factual beliefs on the other. They've been concerned more, perhaps, with the differences between these than with any similarity they possess, though they've been interested in both. They've been concerned again with the similarities and the differences between moral opinions on the one hand and tastes or individual preferences on the other: exploring the ways in which, whatever view you take about the foundations of morality, a moral view isn't just the same sort of thing as a taste for spinach or a liking for this kind of music as against that. They've been very concerned, correspondingly, with the activity of giving reasons for moral judgments; and with what sort of business giving reasons for moral judgments is, and how far it is and isn't like giving reasons for factual opinions, scientific theories; or again, to take a different case, giving reasons for a legal judgment.

MAGEE: It seems to be generally agreed by moral philosophers – and I know you hold this view too – that until recently the subject was impoverished, and indeed almost fell into bankruptcy a generation or so ago. How did this happen?

WILLIAMS: There are two sorts of reasons for that. Some are reasons which are internal to the history of the subject in our culture and some are remarks about our culture and the whole role of philosophy in our culture, and perhaps it would be better to say something about the first sort – I mean, things that have happened in the history of philosophy – and we may or may not have a chance to follow up the other aspect of it. I think that one of the major reasons is that moral philosophy has got extremely interested in, indeed obsessed by, the distinction between fact and value. This is a distinction between, on the one hand, factual knowledge of which some people think a paradigm is scientific knowledge, and, on the other hand, moral and political opinions and so forth. It ties up with a rather obvious point, that people expect there to be a kind of professional public validity about scientific activities which it seems is lacked by moral and political opinions, and this comes out in everyday life, in the fact that the scientists of different cultures – as it might be, scientists belonging to a Marxist society on the one hand and to a capitalist society on the other – will get together and if they're allowed to stick to their science have no great difficulty in discussing the advances in quantum-mechanics or relativity or something of this kind. There seems to be here something entirely common between the two, or if there is a difficulty it is perhaps because the science has been itself polluted by ideological considerations. Such considerations can actually hold back its development, as in Soviet biology for instance; but apart from that, scientists just *qua* scientists will often recognize them as an alien incursion. All this time they may substantially disagree about social provisions, about what society ought to be up to, the role of individual freedom and other evaluative questions of this kind. This sort of situation is a model of the distinction between fact and value which has been so much emphasized.

Now one of the consequences and concomitants of this is the following, that moral philosophers have discussed what a moral position is, what a moral argument is, what a moral opinion is, at a very high level of abstraction: being interested in what a moral opinion is *as such*, what an evaluative opinion is *as such*, they have abstracted on the whole from the concrete detail of particular sorts of evaluative outlook; from the particular sorts of moral concepts that might be deployed by one group rather than another. They've been concerned with the enormously general level in which fact as such is opposed to value as such, and morality as such contrasted to law as such; and so on. Now at that level of abstraction you not only don't say anything very interesting about any particular moral questions; you tend to imply that there is nothing very interesting to say. What they tend to do, I think, is to illustrate these very general points by illustrations of an excessively banal kind – banal in the sense that everybody agrees about them, or in the sense that they are absolutely local, or morally trivial. Can I add one further remark about the boringness of moral philosophy: here I think there's a genuine disagreement of principle between moral philosophers. Suppose we're concerned with a philosophical question about knowledge. If a philosopher is interested in knowledge in general, or a particular sort of knowledge, for instance, perceptual knowledge, it will quite often be appropriate to take some fairly boring and uninteresting example: it'll be perfectly proper to discuss what it is to know some rather banal everyday matter of fact as opposed, for instance, to merely believing it; in perception to take some trivial case of perceiving a tomato, or something of this kind; the point being that the issues which precisely are the issues of knowledge as against belief, or the perceptual grounds of knowledge, can here be laid bare in a context which is uncluttered by other issues which perhaps are connected with some rather dramatic character of the subject matter. Now similarly many philosophers have thought that in moral philosophy it was better, in order to illustrate the nature of morality itself, to take a case which has no great complexity or emotional weight, or as it were, existential force attached to it: if we're talking about *ought* and *right* and *good* and those sorts of things, better – they had thought – to discuss some case which nobody is going to get very steamed up about, than to discuss the cases which, to take the opposite pole, have been the meat and drink of those philosophers who have been called existentialist philosophers in the European tradition, who have concentrated precisely on questions of betrayal, life and death. And the motivation which has led to the cultivation of the banal example is not dishonourable. One sees what it's about. It's an attempt to lay bare the intellectual issues, the structural conceptual issues, without what has been seen as the confusing force of emotional commitment, in which case people can take many different views, in which various interpretations and facts and so on come into it. But I think (and I think that quite a lot of philosophers would agree with me) that the motivation of this has been misguided. The basic reason for this is that the category of the serious and the trivial is itself a moral category, and that it is itself a moral criticism to say of somebody that he is regarding a serious issue as trivial or a trivial issue as serious; and therefore it's a selection of the processes of moral thought themselves to concentrate on the ones which no sane man would get too worked up about.

MAGEE: So you think we ought to start thinking about dramatic situations and moral conflicts?

WILLIAMS: Well, I wouldn't put it quite like that. I'd say not dramatic, necessarily, but serious – and when I say not necessarily dramatic it is because I think it is itself a rather profound ideological issue, both in personal life and in politics, as to how serious the dramatic is. It's a feature of some present rather romantic views of politics to equate the dramatic and the serious, but that's not necessarily a just equation.

MAGEE: I'd like to go back to the point where you were talking about fact and value. There's no doubt in my mind that this distinction goes deep in our culture – the notion that no amount of factual knowledge can ever entail a value judgment, or in other words that no argument can ever give you a value judgment in the conclusion unless you already had one in the premises – the doctrine, which comes from Hume, that you can't get an 'ought' from an 'is'. I take it from what you're now saying that you think this belief ought to be radically questioned?

WILLIAMS: I do think that there is something about the motivation and some of the central insights of the fact/value distinction which, as you rightly remark, is very deep in our culture and is of great intellectual importance – we've got to face up to that. The form it's taken, however, seems to me to have been unfortunate and to have distorted the whole nature of the debate. I think I mentioned a bit back that one of the things that philosophers in our recent tradition have been very interested in is the characterization of moral positions or moral outlooks as such —

MAGEE: When you say 'as such' you mean: 'What makes a moral outlook moral?'

WILLIAMS: Yes, certainly. Now the idea is – a not unreasonable one – that if you find sets of positions, outlooks, attitudes, decisions in different cultures, or on the part of different individuals, each of which outlooks you've got some licence to call moral though they disagree in their content, there must be something in common which makes them all *moral* outlooks, as opposed to some other sort of outlook. Because they disagree in their content, it's very tempting to say that what must be in common between them is something formal. So what moral philosophers have tended to say is that there's a certain form which is the form of moral thought; and some, though not all, have identified this with people having sets of principles – sets of principles which issue in judgments about what they ought to do. Then the substantial differences, which are the value differences, are represented as different contents in a similar framework of principles. The simplest model is of everyone's having a set of principles of the form: 'You always ought to do so and so in such and such circumstances.' And then people take this form and . . .

MAGEE: . . . and fill in the blanks differently.

WILLIAMS: Exactly. Now these are evaluative principles with 'oughts' in them, and because of your 'can't get an ought from an is' they are not deducible from pure statements of fact. This is the model which has been employed, or some variation of this, by many. Now this distracts attention from, regards as secondary, the enormous numbers of concepts which we ourselves use and other societies, and people in the past have always used, which have got an evaluative force of a certain kind – that is, their deployment has got something to say for or against acting in certain ways, or suggests an attitude for or against certain courses of action and persons and so on – which concepts are not simply choppable up into these, as it were, 'ought' and 'is' bits. Take an everyday concept, the concept of owing somebody something – I mean literal owing, money owing: you might almost say it's a question of fact – certainly the law regards it as a question of fact – as to whether A owes B some money. Question: how is 'he ought to pay it' related to 'he owes it' in that legal or institutional sense? Again, one that's caused a lot of controversy in moral philosophy is the relation between 'he promised' and 'he ought to do it' – 'he promised' looks like, give or take a bit, something more of the factual kind. What about terms of virtue and vice, to use old-fashioned words, I mean like 'cowardly', 'sentimental' (a rather ambivalent case), or 'treacherous'? These again are cases where it can hardly be simply chopped up —

MAGEE: — you can't unscramble the moral content from the descriptive —

WILLIAMS: — in any very obvious sense. Again, what about a notion like 'it's his job to'. Or the notion of professional etiquette. Again, let's take more exotic examples, examples from other cultures, examples like, for instance, the oriental conception of face, and the concept of losing face. This is a notion which obviously has very strong evaluative implications – governs what people do – but is deeply tied up with a network both of institutions and of interpretations of human behaviour.

MAGEE: But might it not be possible in all these cases to at least *logically* separate the moral force of these terms from their descriptive content? After all, there's even an old matchbox joke to the effect that dirt is merely matter in the wrong place.

WILLIAMS: This is, of course, what the fact/value theorists say: that these are, as they put it, mixed terms. Putting it very crudely, such terms are seen as a set of purely factual descriptive considerations running along on a trolley with a *pro* or *con* evaluative flag sticking out of them – a flag which has been attached by a prescriptive choice. But I think that this leaves out a number of important considerations.

It leaves out the important point that if it were not for the evaluative interest, if it were not for the kind of human interest that those concepts respond to, it's not that you'd have a different evaluative flag in it, you wouldn't have the concept at all. We have a good example of this with a concept which is not a moral concept at all, namely the concept of being poisonous. *Being poisonous* seems to be a descriptive concept, all right, but it's a concept which we have, under which we select certain things in nature as being poisonous or not, because it responds to certain interests – in this case the rather obvious interest of staying alive. In the case of the poisonous, we have certain natural facts, and a concept which serves to pick them out: a concept which is related to a certain interest, and which we would not have if it were not for that interest. In these other cases, of debts, promises, etc., we have as well as facts of nature, certain social or institutional facts, and also different sorts of interests; for besides individual attitudes to particular social facts, there are also the points that social institutions owe their existence to human interests, and that what interests members of the society have is itself conditioned by its institutions. Institutions are, notoriously, both effect and cause of human desires. Thus in those cases we are concerned with social or institutional facts, as well as natural ones, and with more complex sets of interests. But this does not mean that a social fact is not a fact. To draw lines between different sorts of facts, and again different sorts of interests, is often more illuminating than trying to draw it between fact and value. There's a contrast here: the important case is precisely not that in which there is another name for the same thing if you happen to be in favour of it. I mean the matchbox joke ones are the cases in which what one man calls fresh air is exactly the same thing as what the other man calls a draught: the difference of word just represents a simple difference of attitude. But the point about concepts like face or one's job or property or stealing or a debt, is that the deployment of these concepts is just intimately bound up with an entire set of institutions, and the proposal to remove it or try to get rid of its evaluative force is not a proposal for a kind of logical reform about what words we use to describe the world, nor, merely, how we commend what is there, but a proposal to change our entire view of our social relations. Similarly with assessments of human character: the things which given societies find it fit to pick out as characteristics of human beings, to praise, condemn, remark and so on, are tied up with the kind of expectations they have of human beings.

MAGEE: If it's the case that in many of these important concepts we can't separate factual from moral elements, how do we set about validating the use of some moral concepts as against others? Aren't we thrown back into some sort of subjectivist position?

WILLIAMS: This has been a recurrent question in the entire history of moral philosophy. I said earlier that I thought that people had discussed these issues in too impoverished a framework; and one aspect of that is that they have concentrated on issues of absolutely face-on, head-on evaluative disagreement. The model that I mentioned earlier – the confronting sets of evaluative principles of the same 'ought'-form with different content – precisely implies this kind of head-on conflict: 'I will this principle of action, you will this conflicting principle of action' – how do we ever choose between them? In the first place we need to soften this picture a bit if we're to get a realistic picture of what moral disagreement is. It is very important that at the *end* of this road, something of the head-on conflict, the thing which gives rise to the notions that all moral values are not quite as objective as people wanted, something of that remains; but I think there are several things to be said first. The first is that because, as I've suggested, moral concepts aren't as distinctively moral as all that, but are tied up with the sorts of concepts we use to describe human nature, the sorts of human characteristics we find interesting, important, significant and so forth, it means that the line between where you've got an evaluative disagreement and a factual disagreement is much less sharp than the other picture suggested, and one of the things about this is that there are presuppositions of using one set of values rather than another, and these can be explored by philosophy. For instance, let me just take one case. Some moral outlooks put an enormous premium on a characteristic called strength of will; and this notion is not unconnected, for example, with those genuinely moral questions about the fanatic, whether he should be admired for doing what he sincerely believes is right. These issues are related not just to other moral or evaluative questions but to a whole set of questions in philosophical psychology, in thoughts about what the self is, what the will is, what action is, which are to be explored at the philosophical and psychological level. So the first thing I want to say is that we can treat some evaluative disagreements not at the pure level of adjudicating the evaluative disagreement, but by pursuing those presuppositions which make sense of that set of values: views of human nature, of society, of what human beings are. And some of those may be found to be incoherent at the philosophical level. It may be that some moral views rest on a view of the will which is just philosophically or scientifically incoherent.

MAGEE: Obviously moral philosophy done in this way, or at this level, can't be done in a vacuum: you're going to get involved in psychological questions, anthropological questions, historical questions, institutional questions . . .

WILLIAMS: Certainly, and the idea that there is a department of philosophy which is entirely autonomous called Moral Philosophy would seem to me to be obviously wrong, and indeed falsified by all the interesting history of the subject.

MAGEE: Wouldn't it be a legitimate criticism, then, of many recent moral philosophers to say that they haven't concerned themselves sufficiently with the empirical aspects of what they're doing?

WILLIAMS: That I would say is true. I would add to that that they have, perhaps, in some cases, concerned themselves insufficiently with other aspects of philosophy. I mean reflective conceptual issues about social understanding, about psychological understanding – which are indeed properly, and are recognized to be, the business of philosophy, but have not been sufficiently integrated in recent work in moral philosophy (I think partly for the reasons I mentioned, namely the absolute obsession with the fact/value distinction and the confrontation of conflicting moral beliefs). Could I add one further remark just to illustrate your point here? There's another way in which this question about moral conflict and moral disagreement has been discussed too much in the abstract. One has to see that a lot of the so-called conflicts of moral outlook – that is, sets of thoughts which do conflict, in the sense that they would lead to different ways of going about things, different moral choices – are not actually realistic competitors in any one social scene. I mean the activity of taking on the thought-world of medieval heroism, or the thought-world of the oriental Samurai, is just not in any realistic sense an open option.

MAGEE: Only a madman would try.

WILLIAMS: Exactly. And of course it's a profound criticism of certain sorts both of art and of certain romantic political outlooks that they suffer from this. I think this is part, to take an appalling large scale example, of the peculiar madness of Nazism, that the pictures of the form of human life that went with it were free-floating, were rhetorical in relation to the economic realities, the social realities with which it had to deal. I think at a more innocuous level the pictures that some persons have of their activities in some demure British campus in a country town as bearing a strong resemblance to the activities of those in the bush in Cuba suffer from some mild unrealism of the same kind. And these are, I think, important points, because it's quite a deep sense in which a given outlook is not 'on' for people in a given historical situation. The recent analytical approach in moral philosophy tends to regard such considerations as mere contingencies, irrelevant to the logical structure of moral disagreement. But if moral disagreement and moral thought can, as I suggest, only properly be understood in terms of more *substantial* value-bearing concepts, and if these concepts stand on presuppositions about society and human nature, we should recognize that the possibilities of genuinely comprehensible conflicts of such outlooks are restricted to the range of social situations that they can jointly relate to. If you want to consider seriously such disagreements, I think you should consider situations in which different evaluative systems, thought-forms of this kind, are in real conflict. One evident case of this is in newly independent, let us say, African states, in which we get not only the conflict of the colonial outlook and some national outlook but, much more importantly now, the conflict between the modern Western utilitarian aspirations of a newly emerging government and the outlooks of a tribal society which are often very deeply entrenched in those societies.

MAGEE: There's always been, in fact, an intimate relationship between political theory and moral theory, hasn't there?

WILLIAMS: Yes, though the political aspect has been in the recent tradition excessively thin. But to mention one thing which has had a good deal of attention: moral philosophy is concerned, as it has been for a long time, with the critique and articulation of utilitarianism; by which I mean the aim of securing the greatest happiness of the greatest number within a framework of just distribution. And that is politically very relevant, because so much of our operations have a kind of hazy utilitarian outlook in mind. Of course, in our sort of society, with a lot of individualism, with an emphasis on consumer choice and so on, it's not surprising that utilitarianism is the sort of ideology which you fall back on as the common datum for our less ambitious political calculations. Now some problems of utilitarianism are theoretical problems that practically belong to economics. They are like problems about welfare economics, involving interpersonal comparisons of utility, and things of this kind. But there clearly are profound philosophical problems within the context of utilitarianism which are now becoming more and more pressing. Utilitarianism is all about the distribution of something called, ambitiously, happiness. Or less ambitiously, satisfaction. And these notions of happiness and satisfaction are clearly ones which are in fact in a state of great conceptual confusion. And we can see, from very justified modern discontents of various kinds, that they are, at the actually lived level, felt to be incoherent. The notions of happiness involved in this are just unanalysed, unsatisfactory, people have the feeling that something shallow is being passed off as something deeper, and so on. Here there is a form of moral enquiry, and moral philosophical enquiry, which is evidently relevant to political thought.

MAGEE: There's a common element in several of the things you've said up to this point in the discussion, namely that moral philosophers have got to get down to examining the actual categories in terms of which people conceive moral entities. What *are* the moral terms in which people think? Also it becomes important to distinguish between a conflict between two moral concepts within the same category system and a conflict between category systems. Does this mean that you're engaged in a kind of metaphysics, a metaphysic of morals?

WILLIAMS: The answer to that, I think, is ultimately yes. Can I make one previous remark – I think you've given a just description of something that we are necessarily engaged in when you speak of examining the moral categories within which people view the world. But there is a danger in this – the danger that it can turn into a kind of armchair sociology. Now philosophy must avoid the path of being an armchair sociology, or armchair anthropology. Although, as I've already implied, I think that the moral philosopher should be aware of sociological and historical realities, I also think that creative moral philosophy must work from, and on, what the philosopher himself really believes in. It seems to me that moral philosophy has got to have authenticity in this sense, that the concepts which anybody is pursuing have got to be concepts which are alive to him. He may be a success as a historical anthropologist, looking at the views of the Greeks, or something. That is an important and helpful activity. But onward-going moral philosophy must grow from concepts you yourself believe in. It's got to be in that sense a self-examination: examination of the concepts which you yourself find important for understanding individual life and society. Now of course those concepts will be concepts which as a social person the philosopher shares with many others. And so he will be examining the coherences and incoherences in a way of looking at the world which is both something common and also individual – in this sense, that it is something which he himself is committed to. Now when you refer to metaphysics: if it's true that ways of looking at the world which have these evaluative implications, both with regard to politics and to morals, do have implications about human nature and one's view of what are important and significant and coherently understandable human characteristics, then obviously they must have implications about what the role of man is in society's arrangements, and implications about the role of science, the status of scientific knowledge vis-à-vis other forms of understanding, and a range of problems which certainly are metaphysical. The religious interest, which has been a traditional concern in the past of Western moral philosophy but for obvious reasons is less so now, is an evident metaphysical dimension of moral philosophy in this sense.

MAGEE: Do you see only descriptive metaphysics as being allowable in morals, or may the metaphysics also be revisionary? In other words, should the moral philosopher confine himself to investigating those categories and category systems which are living for him and for the society of which he is a member, or may he legitimately try to change them?

WILLIAMS: Oh, well certainly the latter. My only qualification of the phrase 'try to change them' would be perhaps a modesty or scepticism about the impact on man's thought of the philosophical endeavours of any but the largest geniuses. If you mean by 'change them' change how everybody looks at the world, that clearly would be a somewhat ambitious activity, but if you mean give an honest statement of what he sees as imperfections in ways of looking at the world, trying to see some new basis, certainly yes. That is open. Indeed, revision is probably more open with the kinds of evaluative concepts to which we referred than with some others: it's arguable with regard to certain fairly general categories of thinking about the world in terms of things and their properties, space and time and so on, that the shifts in these are of a much more slow and partial kind. There's much in common between different societies in their way of looking at the world in these fundamental categories. How much is a matter of dispute, but there clearly is a great deal in common; and of course that there is much in common is the foundation of the fact side of the fact/value distinction, because it's only if that is true that there is such a thing as a common inter-societal factual understanding of the world at all. And the idea that there is a common world of fact between different societal groups, even over time, would be connected with that point. But the kinds of things which are particularly exposed at the evaluative end, such as views of what are important human characteristics; of how far there is a distinction between natural human characteristics and conventionally developed ones; of how far there is a distinction between non-moral skills or characteristics and morally relevant virtues or excellences; those sorts of categories both more readily admit of revision and, in my view, demand it. First of all, there isn't straightforwardly a shared common understanding on these matters, anyway, just to describe; and a purely descriptive metaphysics is going to find itself short of an agreed thing to describe, I think. And second, in so far as there is, it tends to suffer from two limitations. One is that if you just take it at the level on which we are all agreed, you'll often be frightfully superficial – I mean you'll just be echoing banalities, and even if there are some places in which it's important for philosophy to be echoing banalities this isn't one of them. Further, such agreement as we have is quite clearly historically conditioned. A lot of things that moral philosophers, even of the more unambitiously fact/value kind, take for granted as features of moral thought are historically traceable legacies of Christianity and Kant. The very distinction between moral characteristics like courage or conscientiousness on the one hand, and non-moral excellences like playing the violin very well or running fast, or something of this kind – this is a distinction which, although clear in extreme cases, is at its heart deeply problematical.

MAGEE: So is there no clear answer even to the question: 'What is a moral question?'

WILLIAMS: We can give sufficient for our purposes for a lot of questions. We can say various relevant things about what is a moral issue. But there is a very, very important and fruitful area of uncertainty on this very point. Because I think that it's not merely that we use the term 'moral' as against 'non-moral' in ways which are somewhat unclear and hazy at the edges, though that's also true. I think that we do it in response to a set of beliefs of an ultimately metaphysical and psychological kind which are deeply suspect. If you ask why is it that courage, let us say, is regarded, or conscientiousness, as a moral characteristic, whereas the other things I mentioned aren't, I think it's because people have inherited in some part from Kant, in some part from certain kinds of Christian views (certainly post-Greek Western views) certain beliefs about the will, and the relevance of the will to the development of certain kinds of approved excellence, which, as I've tried to suggest earlier, may themselves be deeply suspect. The Greeks didn't draw this distinction between the moral and the non-moral the way we do with regard to human characteristics. We also have distinctions between moral and non-moral in other connections – not about human characteristics only but between what's a moral question and not a moral question; and these further distinctions have highly evaluative implications. For instance, there is a real division in our society about whether there is such a thing as distinctively sexual morality. Some people clearly do think – perhaps statistically they'd still be a majority – that there is a distinctively sexual morality. In fact it's commonplace that when you read 'immoral' in the newspapers it often just means 'sexually lax' or something of this character. But of course it's perfectly possible, and it seems to me highly plausible, to suppose that there is no distinctively sexual morality. What there is, is the highly important truth that, sexual matters being what they are, they precipitate moral issues more frequently, and with grea er intensity, than many other matters – obviously, because they involve the personal dimensions of trust, betrayal, and so forth, if conducted at any serious level. And they are rooted in social and institutional matters of the first importance, such as the family. So obviously they're the locus of what are, as it were, in their own terms moral issues. But the question of whether sexual issues are *per se* moral issues seems to me itself a matter which involves the whole question of how you look at morality.

MAGEE: Given that the subject was so impoverished such a short time ago, and therefore that there's a lot now to do, what do you think moral philosophers ought to be chiefly concerning themselves with in the foreseeable future?

WILLIAMS: I do believe that you've got to pursue the issues which make most sense to yourself. Just trying to survey the subject in some sort of blandly equable way, giving due justice to all issues which people have found important, is deathly. So I can't in that sense answer for what everybody might find interesting. Another general qualification I've got to make is that there is a certain sense in which I personally don't know how to do the subject.

MAGEE: There's a rare thing for a professor of any subject to admit!

WILLIAMS: Perhaps. But there's a problem about finding a style, and that's not a shallow question. The problem of how to find a style in moral philosophy is actually one of the deepest questions about it. For how do you make it realistic without trying to turn into an amateur novelist or, again, an armchair anthropologist, as we mentioned earlier? Or if you stick to your last and don't try and do those possibly phoney things, how do you stop relapsing into the meticulous boredom which has sometimes surrounded the subject?

I've given what is easy in a discussion of this kind – large gestures of the sorts of things that ought to be pursued – but how do you combine a sense of wider issues with the concern for detail, and the respect for the fact and the particular, which is one of the great strengths of our philosophy, and which represents an honourable and very important commitment of our philosophy, which it would be insanity to throw away? I hope we'll find the answer to that. For what I regard as central problems, I'll mention two or three things, two of which we've already touched on. One – the realistic treatment of moral conflict in relation to things that might really be options for somebody. Second – what is extremely difficult – the critique of utilitarianism, and the notions of satisfaction and happiness. Third (a particular concern of mine): what are the demands of consistency and coherence in moral thought? A lot of people just take for granted that consistency in one's moral views is as obvious a requirement on them as it is on one's logic or science or history. But it's not clear to me that the notion of consistency is the same in morals. I think it was Strawson who once suggested that morality was the field in which there could be incompatible truths; and in fact this is honoured in much literature, though not in much moral philosophy. And the notion of tragedy is in some part the notion —

MAGEE: —'The conflict of right and right.'

WILLIAMS: Yes, the conflict indeed of right and right. And what moral philosophers have said about that has tended to be overly rationalistic or bland, or to lean too much to models drawn from some purely logical framework, and it seems to me that the notion of consistency – what it is both to be rational in one's moral thought, in the sense in which that is indeed a proper ideal of human activities, and to honour the existence of genuine and deep and, it may be, at the end of the line, irresoluble conflict – that seems to me to be one of the things that moral philosophy ought to be exploring.

10
Conversation with Ninian Smart

Philosophy and Religion

MAGEE: For most of its past, Western philosophy has been closely and intricately linked with religion. Yet now we've come to the tenth of this series of conversations on contemporary British philosophy, and religion has scarcely been mentioned at all. Behind this fact is a historic shift in Western civilization from being what one might call a religion-dominated culture to being a science-dominated culture. Even so – and as one would expect – there have always been philosophers who were vividly interested in religion. And, if anything, the philosophy of religion is now enjoying a revival. Among its best-known practitioners in this country is Ninian Smart, Professor of Religious Studies at Lancaster University. Both he and the department under him are particularly noted for the breadth of their interests, the detailed concern they give to other religions besides Christianity.

Professor Smart, I suspect quite a lot of people are not entirely sure what philosophy of religion is about. Could you simply start by saying what some of the main things are that people working in your field have been concerned with – shall we say, since the Second World War?

SMART: Yes, I think the period since the war has been an important one because the war itself was a kind of water-shed in philosophy. It's true that A. J. Ayer's *Language, Truth and Logic* was pre-war and many of the concerns with linguistic analysis already showed themselves before the war. But these trends became dominant in the post-war period. And not unnaturally philosophy of religion has been bound up considerably with these things – first of all, and most importantly, with the challenge, as one may call it, to religion presented by verificationism as in the style of A. J. Ayer. Probably the most important single work since the war in philosophy of religion was *New Essays in Philosophical Theology* edited by Antony Flew and Alasdair MacIntyre, which came out ten years after the war. It was a series of essays much concerned with the problem of analysis of religious language in the context of questions about verification and meaning. You have on the one hand somewhat stringent critics of religion, like Flew himself, who have argued that religious statements, or alleged statements, are meaningless because not falsifiable in terms of sense experience. And you've had others who have tried to fit the analysis of religious language into the framework provided by this kind of empiricism and this kind of linguistic tradition. Perhaps I can mention three sorts of responses on that side. One was Braithwaite's famous or, as some people would say, notorious lecture, *An Empiricist's View of the Nature of Religious Belief*, which attempted to see religious discourse mainly in terms of expressing an ethical commitment and also evoking it. Braithwaite looked upon religious beliefs, or religious stories in particular, as parables which expressed and evoked commitment to loving behaviour. But the beliefs and stories could not be taken as true, i.e. as describing a transcendent or supernatural realm. That might be described as chopping religious language to fit the empiricist framework. You had others who attempted to stretch empiricism somewhat. For instance John Wisdom's famous essay 'Gods' involved attempting to show that one could have different views of the world which couldn't be settled in a straight way by observation. And more sharply you get Hare's account (in *New Essays in Philosophical Theology*) of religious beliefs as being like 'bliks' or attitudes which cannot be overthrown by counter-evidence. Another form of what I've called stretched empiricism is the appeal to religious experience of some kind. One version of this is found in Ian Ramsey's book *Religious Language* where he operates within an empiricist framework. He supplements sense-perception with experiences where supposedly 'something more' is involved: the 'penny drops', to use his favourite phrase, and a person experiences the universe as 'coming alive'. Another approach, of course, which has been equally important, perhaps more important, has arisen out of the work of the later Wittgenstein. It could also be represented as having some roots in Waismann and possibly also J. L. Austin: namely, the approach to religious language which attempts to consider what is specific as to its character over against other forms of language. The attempt to apply Wittgenstein and the other people that I have mentioned to religious language has been, I think, fairly fruitful although rather variegated.

MAGEE: In the subject as a whole, to what extent is 'religion' taken to mean, in practice, the Christian religion?

SMART: A lot of the writers in this country in philosophy of religion have tended to equate the two. A clear example is Ramsey's book *Religious Language*, which is almost entirely about Christian language. The same is largely true of the writings in *New Essays in Philosophical Theology* that I mentioned. I would think that in a certain sense philosophers of religion have tended not to do their homework in the way in which they have in philosophy of science for example. There the trend is very much towards looking at the way science actually operates, and reflecting upon that; by contrast, old-style philosophy of science tended to fit science to certain philosophical pre-suppositions. And I think some illumination might be had from widening philosophy of religion towards considering other religions and also, for that matter, views of the world which may to some extent play in the same league as religions; I'm thinking, of course, of ideologies like Marxism.

MAGEE: What is the difference between a religion and an ideology? I suspect many people in the modern world equate the two.

SMART: May I approach this question obliquely? The philosopher of religion in these last twenty-five years has perhaps been over-intellectualist in the sense that the great concentration has been upon taking religious statements – in particular religious doctrines – and trying to see how they could make sense in a largely science-dominated culture. There has perhaps not been sufficient recognition of the way the doctrines themselves are related to other things – practices, like worship, rituals, sacraments and so forth; also to symbolic ways of speaking. To say that Christ died for our sins, for example, which is a fairly central Christian utterance, is to do rather more than utter a proposition about the structure of reality. The notion of sin, for instance, has to do with its converse, the holiness of God, which is expressed above all in the worship ascribed to God. And worship is a practical activity. Now if one wants to adopt good Wittgensteinian practice and, even more, good Austinian practice, then one should see religious statements in their living context. Then one would be drawn to make *some* differentiation between religions and ideologies, like Marxism, in that the practical aspect of worship, and so forth, which is important in a number of religions, is much less developed in Marxism. One can see ways in which it's developing, of course.

MAGEE: A lot of people would say it's already highly developed!

SMART: It's still an open question as to whether, for instance, Chinese Maoism should be treated as a form of religion. It could well develop into a fully-fledged form, in my view. For this reason there is merit, I think, in extending the scope of the philosophy of religion or, if you want it the other way round, the scope of the philosophy of ideology. The only thing is that nobody talks about the philosophy of ideology. There's been very little recognition that there are perhaps special considerations which concern ideologies and religions which could be treated, up to a point, together.

MAGEE: Is the philosopher of religion likely to be more seriously interested in ideologies than are other philosophers, who in fact commonly treat them with contempt? I'm thinking not just of things like Marxism but also, say, something like psychoanalysis – which might be described as a kind of ideology, in that it's certainly a holistic conceptual system.

SMART: In the scientific approach to religion, myths, for example, are a central item to study and their nature is bound too to interest the philosopher of religion. This leads one into the whole world of anthropology and, for that matter, psychology, which is highly relevant to psychoanalysis, etc. I think it's important that philosophers of religion – and I think philosophers in general – should recognize that what appear to be very strange beliefs held sometimes rather firmly by people have a kind of meaning which it's difficult to penetrate to, and which can't be penetrated to by taking them in a very wooden way. Thus that Christ ascended into heaven is part, if you like, of the Christian myth – I'm using the word 'myth' neutrally here as to truth and falsity – but it isn't specially to do with space-ships. It is a banal remark to say there was nowhere up there to go to. One's got to understand the meaning for the people who first produced this belief.

MAGEE: Does this mean then that the philosopher of religion is more likely to be interested in the historical and cultural contexts of ideas than are other philosophers?

SMART: Yes, I think so. Take quite a crude example. I remember one philosopher saying at a conference that the notion of transubstantiation in the classical Catholic tradition was unintelligible and contradictory. Now I'm not going to say that it isn't contradictory; that is a question for debate. But his grounds for saying so were that clearly here was something which was properly described as bread and wine, and was then said to be essentially something else. Now I think this can be a crude comment on it because what the doctrine of transubstantiation was trying to do was to give a sophisticated account of what happened in a particular presentation of Christ to the people. In other words, one would need the cultural context, and in particular in this case the *ritual* context, before the debate really is significant.

MAGEE: What about specifically historical considerations? After all, in most philosophical discussions history is really not very important, is it?

SMART: I'm not so sure that history is so very important in philosophy of religion, except in this sense, that to do philosophy of religion one needs to know about religion; and clearly a lot of the material which you work with is historical material. But one could equally well take a synchronic slice, as it were, of religious cultures, and work on that.

MAGEE: We've talked about the demarcation between philosophy of religion and ideology: what about the demarcation – at the other end of the subject, so to speak – between philosophy of religion and theology? Theology, after all, is a subject which is studied and taught in universities, just like yours. What's the difference?

SMART: If one uses 'theology' in the strict sense of the term (and it's not always so used when people talk about reading theology in universities) theology is essentially the systematizing of a certain set of beliefs and commitments. In this country it's short for *Christian* theology. Karl Barth, one of the greatest theologians of this century, was explicitly doing what he called 'Church dogmatics'; he didn't pretend to be, as it were, a neutral person surveying the religious scene. He was expressing Christian theology; he was expressing a Christian position. That to me is genuine theology. And philosophy of religion I would say differs from this because it's not in its own nature committed to one position rather than another.

MAGEE: Professionally speaking, then, you are a neutral investigator into religious concepts and religious language, and the way they are used. Is that right?

SMART: That's how I regard myself, professionally.

MAGEE: Do you think in order to do this you need to be a believer or do you think an agnostic or an atheist could do it just as well?

SMART: It's interesting that you use the term 'believer', because one of the criticisms that I have of some writings in philosophy of religion since the war is that people assume that there is such a thing as a believer, not further defined. It's quite clear that there are many different sorts of people who may believe different sorts of things. I think the important question is: is it possible to understand a given religious statement or institution or symbol or practice? It can be an *advantage* if you believe in something or other. I was recently discussing the question as to why it is that quite a number of people involved in the comparative study of religion in this country are Anglicans. Answer: because they take rituals rather more seriously than Quakers or atheists, and this is helpful if one's looking at another religion. But it can be a *disadvantage* to be a believer because there are certain people so committed intellectually in certain ways that they'll find it difficult to see the point of alternative positions. So I'd answer your question by saying that the important thing is that a person should be equipped to understand. An atheist or an agnostic can be highly understanding. An atheist and agnostic can also be just as prejudiced as a Seventh Day Adventist, or whoever, when he comes to philosophize about religion.

MAGEE: Philosophy of religion is just about the only branch of philosophy which a lot of professional philosophers don't believe in the legitimacy of. And although I don't think many professional philosophers nowadays are verificationists, nevertheless – on some very much looser version of such grounds – a lot of them simply don't believe that religious propositions have any content that is worth taking seriously, and therefore don't really believe the subject exists. How would you validate it for someone who's inclined to take that view?

SMART: I know that a number of intellectuals are not persuaded of the truth of religion or its importance in their general *Weltanschauung*. But this can on occasions perhaps mislead them. I'd like to use this example. I don't think that we would have any doubt about the importance of the study of anthropology. It is of great fascination, and possibly illumination, to understand the beliefs of a wide variety of different cultures in the world. But most of these beliefs are not beliefs which significantly affect the anthropologist before he goes to live with his tribe. So one's own predilections, one's own commitments and so forth, are not too relevant. Nevertheless I think the climate of opinion in this country among philosophers tends to be rather astringent, as you were saying. As to its importance, I think in any case there's a cultural argument which I've already hinted at in these preceding remarks, that in order to understand cultures, our own culture among them, one has to understand the religious beliefs which have formed so great a part in moulding them. I think there are important philosophical questions about how you do understand beliefs which you don't hold, especially when they're very peculiar beliefs, or seem to you to be very peculiar beliefs. There are, for instance, problems for a Westerner in understanding what it amounts to when the Buddhist says that the Buddha was tempted by Mara. Hence even at this level – of philosophizing about how to do religious anthropology – one can stake out a strong case for philosophy of religion.

MAGEE: Do you think philosophers of religion are led by their subject to take one side rather than another in some of the more traditional philosophical disputes? For instance, are they more likely to opt for a coherence theory of truth than for a correspondence theory?

SMART: That's rather a difficult question to answer. I would answer it somewhat obliquely I think by saying that there is, if you like, a trend towards coherence theory just in the sense that religious concepts do tend to be embedded in wider wholes, so that you can't as it were have a one-to-one correspondence between certain concepts like *grace* and *salvation* and particular conditions in the world or even out of the world. But I'd prefer to say that the philosophy of religion ought to be sympathetic to modern developments in the philosophy of science which have this emphasis upon notions of theoretical concepts and upon the difficulties of too simplistic a model of how scientific theories are true.

MAGEE: Presumably now that the influence of the later Wittgenstein and of Austin is widespread, philosophers of other kinds than yourself are more sympathetic to the philosophy of religion than they were in the foregoing, logical positivist generation.

SMART: I think so. There is certainly a great boom in the philosophy of religion industry, if one looks at it from the point of view of publications these last few years. As to the Wittgensteinian influence, I would detect two different sorts of things that have happened. One is a rather peculiar one, I think. That is the use of certain ideas and hints in Wittgenstein to evolve a philosophy of religion which implies that you have to believe in order to understand, so that religion is either true or meaningless. I am thinking in particular of the work of D. Z. Phillips in his *The Concept of Prayer* and some of his other writings. I mention him partly because he's been influenced by Rush Rhees, who himself of course was close to Wittgenstein. But I am personally not altogether favourable to this approach, because it would put me out of a job, or at least out of half a job, since it would make the study of religions other than one's own, presumably —

MAGEE: — a waste of time?

SMART: A waste of time. Another kind of development is perhaps more Austinian. That is the attempt, shall we say, to get down more closely to the analysis of religious language, rather leaving aside in the first instance questions of truth, and then getting back to them later. An example of that is Donald Evans's book *The Logic of Self-Involvement* which makes heavy use of performatives, and so forth, in the Austinian manner, in a very interesting way.

MAGEE: Is this largely, or even entirely, an empirical investigation into how religious concepts are actually used, and how religious words actually function?

SMART: Let us say it's an attempt to be more descriptive. My own first book, *Reasons and Faiths*, was really an attempt to do that kind of job, for it involved an expressive and to some extent performative analysis of religious language.

MAGEE: To me the two most striking things about religions are, first, they all seem to contain a view of how the world is, an explanatory description of the way things are; and second, they also all seem to contain a moral system, a set of instructions about how we ought to live and behave and conduct our relations with each other. But doesn't this then mean that the philosopher of religion is concerned with epistemology and ethics just as other philosophers are – only from a different standpoint?

SMART: Not in principle a different standpoint, I would have thought. I think though that the contemplation of religion, or for that matter ideologies, might lead to perhaps a greater possible awareness – although I do not say that it's actually evident in practice among philosophers of religion – of the ways in which a view of the world connects up with a certain pattern of behaviour, or certain pattern of beliefs about behaviour. You see it's a bit mysterious really to say that because somebody believes that the world is created by God or that there is a transcendent state called Nirvana which you may attain, you then have to do certain other things like love your neighbour or refrain from using speech wrongly. I think there is interest for moral philosophers in the way in which the bridge is made actually in religions between the *Weltanschauung* and the pattern of moral beliefs. In part it is explicable in the following terms. In Christianity, certain attitudes are inculcated because in worship, and in the story of Christ himself, there is great emphasis upon humility. It is a question as to how far this exists in practice among Christians; but a Christian *ought* to exhibit humility and this connects up with his practices and with the kind of story or ideal that he focuses on. These things in turn are partly reflected in the general *Weltanschauung* or belief that the world is created by God, who is to be worshipped.

MAGEE: Philosophers whom one might broadly call humanists (A. J. Ayer springs to mind as an example) have often written to the effect that there is not, *and could not possibly be*, any logical connection between the existence or non-existence of a God on the one hand and the validity or non-validity of any moral system on the other. Now I take it that what you're saying is that not all important connections are logical connections, and that there *are* in fact exceedingly important connections, though these may not be logical entailments?

SMART: Yes, I would say that they are less than entailments, if you like. I prefer to call them myself 'suggestions', although that sounds a bit feeble – that a certain story or a certain practice may *suggest* a value, but does not entail it. There's a certain amount of logical space, as it were, for other alternative values, but there is a kind of harmony between the story and a certain set of values.

MAGEE: The aspect of your subject which interests me most is the level at which it concerns itself with categories – the terms in which religious believers see the world, and how these differ from the terms in which non-believers see the world.

SMART: The situation is complicated. Strawson in his *Individuals* talks about the analysis of the concept of a person. But some people don't operate with the concept *person* as we understand it in English, just as a kind of neutral concept. For some people the way that the world is chopped up is in terms of living beings; human beings are one sort of living being, animals are another sort of living being, and they're all taken with great seriousness. I'm thinking of course of certain kinds of Orientals who have this way of looking at the world.

MAGEE: So the important thing for them is not that we are persons but that we are livings beings.

SMART: Yes. But on top of that, when it comes to the social sphere, what becomes important is whether somebody is a monk or whether he is a Brahmin or what caste he is, and so forth. These are very important practical categories for people. And I would say the same was true in our own society. So that to that extent we need analysis of a rich set of concepts abutting on that of the person. Some philosophical treatments may be too austere and even culture-bound. Take the concept 'worker'. Not everybody operates with the concept 'worker' – but it does make a difference if you do.

MAGEE: Do you think philosophy of religion has any valuable goods to export to its neighbouring subjects?

SMART: I would think that the philosophy of religion is an important part, among other things, of the study of religion because philosophical question are bound to arise in contemplating the history of religions. And so at one end of the export-interface you can say that the philosophy of religion could help the study of religion to be illuminating by moving in the direction of the social sciences. I believe that the most important growing point in philosophy may well be the philosophy of the social sciences, especially anthropology and sociology, and that the philosophy of religion is really almost of the same substance.

MAGEE: Meaning that you can't do philosophy of anthropology or sociology without philosophy of religion?

SMART: Let's put it this way: that religion and analogous phenomena are so much part of what the sociologist is studying that some of the questions of method that arise, especially in the phenomenology of religion, are highly applicable to them. One of the things that I'm attempting to write at the moment is on the phenomenology of religion precisely because I think it's important, method-wise, for the social sciences, and even for the humanities too. At the other end, the end of philosophy, I am not so sure at the moment. I don't know that the philosophy of religion, unless it becomes more tied up with the philosophy of the social sciences, is going to make very much impact on the rest of philosophy. Certainly in the last twenty-five years the boot has been very much on the other foot – the discussion of questions of religious truth has been highly determined, probably as it almost inevitably is, by the central concerns of philosophy, and in particular of epistemology.

MAGEE: Is the prevailing state of the subject at any one time largely determined by the state of philosophy in general – so that what tend to be the main questions under discussion in mainstream philosophy dominate, or at any rate profoundly influence, what's under discussion in philosophy of religion?

SMART: Yes. But I think what I say about the social sciences and so on is not at all irrelevant to this, because epistemology has been very much influenced of course by the dominant science of a given age: look at Plato and mathematics; and in the modern period physics has really been highly dominant. It appears to me that the fault of certain kinds of philosophical psychology, particularly behaviouristic philosophical psychology, stems from the fact that the attempt is made to use the physical model. The same applies even in practice, I think, in relation to experimental work in biology where it's very much easier to forget about the inner states, so to say, of rats and so forth and simply concern oneself with the behaviour. If we're going to have a unified science, of course (a great dream of the twenties) it's got to take seriously the social sciences, beginning from psychology outwards. They shouldn't be ultimately incompatible with physics, but one's got to redress the balance somewhat, I think, to have a realistic account of man; and I think that the philosophy of religion, precisely because it is or ought to be concerned with the meanings of statements that don't otherwise fit too easily into the general framework, can make a contribution here.

MAGEE: Do you think your subject in its present state has any particular deficiencies, or needs, that you can put your finger on?

SMART: Well I think it suffers from being a sort of bridge subject; the 'philosophy of' is always rather in a tricky position, just as indeed the 'sociology of' is rather tricky, because if it's going to be done in a perfect world then the practitioner of 'the philosophy of X' knows as much about X as he does about philosophy. It's very difficult to create the milieu for this in university institutions and so forth. And I think I'd say a fault of philosophy of religion somewhat in the last twenty-five years has been lack of attention to the facts of religion – to the substance of religious practice, and life. It has also I think suffered in another direction just because it's not been terribly fashionable. It's probably true to say that the people involved in the philosophy of religion have not been so high-powered in philosophy as philosophers pure and simple, so to say. I remember that when I said at Oxford that I was going to work in the philosophy of religion, just after taking my first degree, people looked at me as though I was completely batty and needed my head read.

MAGEE: It was thought eccentric?

SMART: It was thought eccentric then.

MAGEE: My last question is one that arises directly out of that. How would you like the subject to develop, or how do you expect it to develop – not necessarily the same thing – over the next few years?

SMART: I'd like to see more integration between philosophizing and the study of religion basically. I'd like to see also the study of religion more concerned than it has been in the past with treating religion at the phenomenological level and not just at the theological level. Such a programme, of course, is not so easy to achieve because as in a number of areas in intellectual life, you get a certain subject institutionalized, and *defined* by its institutionalisation, so some people count as philosophers and other people count as theologians and others as 'religionists' or whatever ghastly word you want to invent. And I think this is an obstacle. But basically that's how I would like to see things develop, with more contribution to the philosophy of religion from, and from the philosophy of religion to, the philosophy of the social sciences.

11
Conversation with
Richard Wollheim

Philosophy and the Arts

MAGEE: Like moral and political theory, and the philosophy of religion, aesthetics had a bad time of it when logical positivism was the reigning orthodoxy. Since aesthetic statements were neither tautological nor empirically verifiable they were held to be at worst nonsensical and at best mere expressions of subjective emotion – as it might be verbalized cries of exaltation, or orgastic groans, or appeals to share an experience, or grimaces of dislike. No wonder the subject, when viewed in this light, failed to develop much. For decades most of it came down to one of two things: either an attempt to answer the question 'What is art?' (and that of course is little more than a request for a definition – a definition of the word 'art') or an attempt to analyse aesthetic judgments, elucidating what it is we are doing when we say something like 'This picture is beautiful.' Both activities are worthwhile, certainly, but they are also very restricted. However, with the demise of logical positivism the subject has begun to grow again. And it's not just a coincidence that the influence of Karl Popper – who believes that the answer to the question 'Who killed logical positivism?' is 'I' – should be behind one of the most outstanding contributions to the literature of art of recent years, namely the work of Ernst Gombrich. But I'm racing ahead. Before going on I want to put questions arising from what I've already said to Richard Wollheim, a Professor of Philosophy in London University. He's written a much praised book on aesthetics called *Art and Its Objects*, and he's also published a novel, with the title *A Family Romance*, so he speaks with personal experience of the creative artist's standpoint as well as that of the philosopher.

Richard Wollheim, I'd like very much to hear your views as to why the search for a definition of 'art', and the analysis of aesthetic judgment, didn't add up to enough to keep the subject of aesthetics thriving and healthy.

WOLLHEIM: Well, first let me say that I totally agree with the diagnosis which you've given of the state of aesthetics or the philosophy of art in the recent past. It did, indeed, seem to bifurcate into these two enterprises: the definition of art, on the one hand, and the analysis of the aesthetic judgment, on the other – with 'aesthetic judgment' very narrowly understood as meaning judgments canonically of the form: 'This is beautiful.' And even this is true only of the programme which aesthetics found itself saddled with if it took the methodological implications of current philosophy seriously. I'm not talking, nor were you, of what was actually written in the subject, for the simple reason that during this period very little was written in aesthetics. And one of the reasons why so little was written is precisely that people felt that the programme to which they would have had to conform was so peculiarly unpromising. So this takes us back to the question you asked me: what was the matter with the programme?

Let us begin with the first of the two enterprises, the question 'What is art?' understood as simply a request for a definition. About this we may begin by observing that where a question about the nature of something is understood as a request for a definition, this carries with it the implication that we can say something adequate to the nature of that thing in a very brief space. Precisely what does and what doesn't count as a definition isn't very clear, but a definition clearly cannot be anything long. And yet it seems unlikely that we could come up with anything of this sort giving the nature of art. On the contrary, if we are to do justice to the nature of art, it looks as though what we have to do is to take account of a very large number of activities which go on, which are connected in various kinds of way, and which all add up to art, to the phenomenon of art as we have it in our society. In other words, it seems as though we should – at any rate, in the first instance – take our eyes away from what looks like a purely lexicographical problem – what does a certain word mean – and instead look at something quite different, a whole lot of interrelated activities. The sort of alternative enterprise I'm talking about does, I think, bear a very close analogy to something which we can also see going on since positivism in other parts of philosophy, in general philosophy – for instance, in the analysis of the nature of language, as this has developed very largely under the influence of Wittgenstein, particularly of the *Philosophical Investigations* and his writings of that period.

MAGEE: You've now begun to suggest that aesthetics should concern itself with an enquiry into the *nature* of art. Can you say something about what such an enquiry would be – what sort of form it might take?

WOLLHEIM: Clearly I can give no more than a sketch of how a philosophical account of these interrelated activities and of their interrelations might go. Let us first begin with the activities themselves, and which we should pick out. Well, first, there would be those which lie somewhat outside art; nevertheless art in a significant way latches on to them – things like the interest that we take in nature, the way in which we are inclined to find in objects around us reflections of inner states, or to seek out things which correspond to what we feel. And, in this same area, there are the relations of art to current forms of productivity and to man's assertion of himself as a human being. And possibly other things concerned with our feelings about the making and possession of objects. Everything so far belongs to what we might regard as the external relations of art, or its foreign relations. But there are also other kinds of activity which aesthetics must consider, that occur very much inside art, such as expression, representation; though, of course, there is an overlap here in that they can also occur, in another form as it were, outside art. And then there are yet other things which exist only under the shelter or under the concept of art – the aesthetic attitude, or the search for certain kinds of order, or what it is to have certain expectations that are then either satisfied or (as it were) creatively frustrated. These latter activities occur only inside art, and they might be regarded as belonging to the domestic relations, as opposed to the foreign relations, with which the philosophy of art would be concerned.

MAGEE: None of these questions *sounds* new. Obviously it isn't of the first importance if they aren't – but a lot of what you say still sounds to me like a reformulation of the traditional request for a definition. What really is the difference between enquiring into the nature of art and asking for a definition of 'art'?

WOLLHEIM: Well, in the kind of enquiry that I have talked about as being inspired by Wittgenstein's writings, by his investigations into the nature of language, there is in the first place a turning away from the quest for a simple definition, where this is thought of as the quest for something very brief and is moreover very closely geared to a word, and that word may for all we know be comparatively dispensable in the language. We turn away from that and then we are

involved in an examination of certain activities and how they inter-
relate. And now it might look as though we have gone too far away
from the original kind of philosophical inquiry and into something
more like sociology or an empirical inquiry. But our guide-line is
this: that the activities we consider *must* be related in certain ways,
otherwise it would not be appropriate to talk of art, and it is these
relations that we seek. So though we certainly are dealing with phenomena and their connections, we are dealing with connections that
must be as they are if, on a higher level, a certain concept is to be in
place.

MAGEE: That sounds almost Kantian rather than Wittgensteinian –
can you say a little about how it derives from Wittgenstein?

WOLLHEIM: Wittgenstein, in his investigations into what it is for
people to use a language, or what it is for various activities like
meaning something, understanding something, to take place, concerned himself not merely with the elucidation of certain concepts
that we as outsiders, as it were, apply in describing these activities,
nor with the criteria that must be satisfied to a sufficient degree for
us to say of people that they are using language. Not simply that, for
he was also concerned with the concepts that actually guide people
in these activities. More accurately, he was concerned with certain
concepts that are not merely used to describe people when they
speak a language, but are also used by people when they speak a
language to regulate their behaviour, and he was concerned with both
the ways in which these concepts are used. The concepts then are the
same, but they have two uses: a descriptive use, and a regulative use.
Of course, there is this further difference between our use of these
concepts as observers and our use of them when we speak the language and that is that for speakers of the language they play a
comparatively hidden role. We should have to ask people to think a
great deal about what they were doing before they would recognize
that, for instance, they were following a rule – an essential notion in
Wittgenstein's view of language – and they would have to think even
harder before they could begin to give an account of what it was for
them to follow a rule. Nevertheless, we are convinced that this is
what they are doing, we are convinced that they are following rules,
and one of the conditions of their doing so is that they have somewhere or other the concept of a rule.

MAGEE: In talking about what aesthetics should be concerned with
you've shown how the traditional question 'What is "art"?' becomes
absorbed into a wider programme. What part, if any, do you think

G

the traditional investigation into the nature of aesthetic judgment should now have?

WOLLHEIM: I don't know how straight an answer I'll be able to give you. But I could start by suggesting what was wrong with this part of the original programme. I'll suggest three things wrong with it. The first we might put by asking, Why pick on the aesthetic judgment – still meaning by this something like 'This is beautiful'? Because that is only one of a number of judgments that the spectator of art is likely to make. So why ask for an account of only it? Secondly, even if we could get a satisfactory account of the aesthetic judgment, of the judgment expressing admiration or perhaps disfavour, why should this show us all that much about the phenomenon of art and its nature? Things would be different if we thought that the production of art was largely concerned with making things which evoked admiration, if we thought that the eliciting of admiration was a central part of the project of art. Then, to understand what it is for people to admire works of art would show us something important about art. But that is a quite false view, it's a kind of schoolmaster's view of art, as though people make objects of art in order to get high marks. Now, there is an area where we do observe something like this, and this observation has certainly influenced the philosophy of art in the direction it has taken. Moral philosophy has had a somewhat baneful influence on aesthetics. For when we turn to morality, though it is rather grotesque to say that it is central to the project of morality that people engage in actions that are done to be admired, though it's grotesque to put it like this, nevertheless there is a way in which the reactions of approval or disapproval on the part of the spectator are intimately connected with what the moral agent himself is engaged in.

MAGEE: And of course there have been moral systems – the Homeric, for example – in which it was central that you did things in order to be admired.

WOLLHEIM: Precisely, yes. And if I can now take up the third thing I wanted to say, it's this: the aesthetic judgment isn't merely only one of a number of judgments that the spectator is likely to make, or, perhaps better, one of a number of things that he is likely to do when confronted with a work of art. But – this is the point – these various activities are not independent: on the contrary, unless we can be certain that the spectator is engaged in these other activities – and I'll try and say a bit more about them later – we wouldn't really be very interested in whatever aesthetic judgment he came out with.

We're not interested at all in what a spectator of a work of art is doing when he says of it that it's beautiful if we don't think that this spectator has adopted any of the attitudes appropriate to its being a work of art. So just to cut the aesthetic judgment out of this whole gamut of attitudes and ask what it means and what the man who makes it is doing when he makes it – and even this way of putting the question is more advanced than what a great deal of aesthetics has permitted itself, where it has simply asked what the judgment means or what its analysis is – is a way of securing a very partial and ultimately distorted view of the phenomenon of art.

MAGEE: Do you have a view about why we engage in art? Why do we need it? Why does art have a value?

WOLLHEIM: I certainly agree with you this far: that any aesthetic, any theory of art, which left totally open the question whether art had or hadn't a value would be to that degree not merely incomplete, but misconceived. I think that is the implication of your question, and I agree. From the very beginning an account of art must relate art to that which is going to give it justification. And what gives it justification must be something to do with mental states and the human personality. Now I think it's very difficult to give in general a justification of art, but possibly a more successful approach would be to attempt to give, perhaps schematically, some kind of justification of a particular art, and I suggest that, if one did this, one would find oneself doing maybe two things simultaneously. First of all, one would build up one's specification of what the activities that went to the making of that art were, stage by stage. We could imagine this being done by adding various stringencies to the activity after it has been initially and very simply or basically identified. Then one would show how, by a series of successive increments, this activity gained in value for us. Moreover, one would show how each increment in value which is acquired is related to a stringency which has just been imposed upon the basic activity, so the two processes, adding stringencies until we get to something like a recognizable form of an art, and showing how the value of that art is deepened, would themselves be geared one to another.

So, for instance, we might imagine an account of painting, which began, quite simply, with an activity which consisted in the placing of marks on a plane surface. And the value of that activity would consist just in the pleasure to which it gave rise. Then the activity might be further specified as one in which the placing of the marks characteristically resulted in placed marks, there to be seen. The activity would issue in a trace, and that trace could secure for the activity further value and further kinds of value. For the activity could now be connected with the formation of intentions that we carry out or conceptions that we realize. A further stringency would now be added that the placed marks may fall together and form certain characteristic images or patterns: and from this stringency derive the varied values associated with representation and expression. Even in aesthetics, the undertaking would have to be schematic, as I said, but I'm now offering you just a schema of a schema.

MAGEE: If what you're saying is true then aesthetics must be closely bound up with the philosophy of mind, since understanding art involves understanding mental states.

WOLLHEIM: Yes. Any aesthetic philosophy that's at all adequate must draw upon the philosophy of mind, must draw upon whatever understanding we have of the nature of our various mental states, faculties, performances, capacities. But there is a point here to be noted. For, if we look at the philosophy of mind as it has developed, there are certain very general kinds of mental state which have not really been, at any rate in our tradition, very seriously considered, or analysed. And these – well, perhaps 'mental state' is not the term which I should use, but there are certain very general aspects of the mind which have been ignored. You have mentioned idealist philosophy, and these aspects of the mind did find some kind of recognition there, and also, though very often a somewhat shadowy one, inside Marxist thought. I'm referring to aspects of the mind which have to do with the development, with the emergence of the mind, or the way in which we come to acquire self-consciousness, or our conception of ourselves as a person. Now I think that any aesthetic philosophy must bring these aspects of the mind very much to the fore. I personally would say the same thing in connection with moral philosophy, that we can't really understand morality unless we see how it links up with certain ways in which the human being emerges, develops, acquires a conception of himself as an agent, deals with certain types of anxiety, the whole evolution, in other words, of guilt and the integration of desires. That used to be accepted in nineteenth-century moral philosophy, almost the only good thing that could be said about it. But these issues have, I think, fallen somewhat out of discussion in our philosophy of mind, also out of our moral philosophy. Now, the way in which aesthetics is concerned with these aspects of the mind is, of course, somewhat different from the way moral philosophy would be. Aesthetics is concerned in two ways. First of all, through its interest in understanding what it is for someone to make a work of art, and how this work of art can match his mental state. For this takes us to mental states that go through some process of structuring, clarification. If someone can recognize in something that he's made a reflection of an inner state, it is often the case that he would not have been aware of this state except through the object or objects that he makes. And one explanation of this can be that the mental state or condition, though in one sense remaining unchanged, has acquired or developed a structure, a degree of inner articulation that it previously lacked. That is one way in which aesthetics takes an interest in some mental processes otherwise ignored in philosophy. But there is another way too. The making of a work of art is something which we can identify only inside some rather larger process. In other words, it isn't simply an empirical truth, it has a strong conceptual character to it, that works of art are made by artists. If we want to understand art, we are committed to trying to understand this larger process, or the type of process by which someone internalizes a certain technique and so is able to draw upon this technique. The technique itself, once internalized, undergoes certain modifications, some of which will be due to maybe practical things, things to do with the medium. But others will be to do with the way in which the person comes to recognize what he is like through the use of this technique. And he then modifies the technique so that in its further use he will more adequately discover and express himself: his development as an artist.

MAGEE: Doesn't everything you've said up to this point run counter to what so-called New Critics say about the autonomy of the work of art? After all, the New Criticism is pretty widely accepted nowadays (for what that's worth) and one of its central tenets is that considerations of mental states, or motives, or intentions, are not relevant to evaluating art.

WOLLHEIM: I agree. But I think that if we take the New Criticism, at least in the form in which it's often been interpreted by the New Critics themselves, there does seem to be a philosophical error, I'd call it that, included in it. I'll say something about the error itself in a moment. But it is, of course, just because the critical doctrine does include an error, that I am not made uneasy by the fact that the views I am putting forward, which have a philosophical inspiration, come into collision with it. Otherwise I should expect my views to be compatible with it as I should expect them to be compatible with any purely critical doctrine. Now the error, which I attribute to the New Critics, is this: that, when they say that we must ignore intention, that we must look solely at the work itself, they equate intention –

G*

and this emerges clearly in the dichotomy upon which they hang so much – as something totally internal or private, which issues only by chance in a work of art. And if that were a plausible view, then maybe we could be asked to look at the work and ignore the intention – in those happy cases, that is, where there is a work of art. In other words, the New Critics seem to me committed to a view which was also held by some idealist philosophers – though with *them* it expressed itself in a critical doctrine which is the mirror-image of that of the New Criticism. For the view enabled them to say that we should totally ignore the work of art – I mean the object in the outer world – and concentrate upon the inner state. Both these two doctrines share a common assumption: that there exist inner states of a certain kind – states which occur frequently in the process of making – and which can be understood independently of the product in which they issue.

Now this seems to me a totally false view of intention: both generally, and in the matter of art. I do not see how anyone could form an artistic intention unless he had some capacity, varying with the specific medium, to make a certain sort of object. It is a precondition of the formation of the intention that a particular technique or method of making should be one of the person's capacities. And this capacity lies behind the intention, in that it infuses or permeates the intention. So the intention is always the intention to write a certain sonnet, or to undertake a particular piece of carving. In this way, to ask about a particular intention, or to find out about it, is to ask about or find out about some work or other in which, if all goes well, the intention will issue. And now if we reverse this and look at the matter the other way round, we see that, if we ask of a given work of art what is the intention that lay behind it, part of what we're doing, despite the form of words we use, is asking, 'What is really here?' Of course, we're asking the question – if you understand me – on a higher level than we would be if we wanted to know of a picture, say, representing Rinaldo and Armida, what its mythological content was. Indeed, it is instructive to see how the question 'What is here?' asked of a picture can be answered on a number of different levels, and so we get a hierarchy of answers. We get, for instance, an answer in terms of the lie of the pigment on the canvas, an answer in terms of the symbolic representation with which the mythological incident has been invested – and there are intermediate levels on which the question can be taken and answered. And on the top level, as the question rises in generality, the answer will pick up some of what might be thought of as the mental states of the person who made the picture, it will collect the artist's intention. It is much the same as, when we ask the question what a particular man was doing, we can get as an answer to our question a description of the agent's physical or bodily movements, but, as the question increases in generality, we will expect to receive in the answer we get a reference to his intentions. What this shows is that, despite what the New Criticism implies, there is a natural interlock of descriptions of works of art and descriptions of artists' intentions.

MAGEE: The New Critics deny the relevance not only of intentions or mental states but of any background information whatever to the evaluation of art. Do you repudiate that too?

WOLLHEIM: Once again, all depends on how you take the crucial distinction between what is background and what is there in the work. Just as in the case of intention, we can ask what is found in the work in such a way as to produce a hierarchy of answers, and the answers at the top level will take in what counts as background relative to the answers given on lower levels. There is, of course, a cut-off point at the top, such that certain facts that relate to the painting or the poem must be regarded as background, but, if we want to identify them, then we must recognize that the question of whether something is or isn't there in a painting or poem can't be treated simply as a question about how we came upon a certain piece of information about a painting or poem, as though by staring very hard at a picture or poring for a long time over the words we can make the painting or the poem give up its secrets. The test of how much we can find out in this way proves nothing because it all depends on how much initial equipment in the way of knowledge, understanding, sensibility, etc. we credit ourselves with. The question, for instance, Can a man by looking at a building determine its style? is a question which is unanswerable unless you have specified how much the man knows of the history of art or what manner of sensibility he possesses. And when we are dealing say with the earliest Gothic, or with Mannerism, the question raised would be one that depends upon a quite complex sensibility. To arrive then at an absolute notion of what it is for information about a work of art to be background, we should consider not whether we have come by the information by looking at the work but whether, having come by the information, we can see things in the work, things we can then point out, which we would not otherwise have seen. To take an example, say, from *Othello*: the fact or otherwise of Iago's homosexuality. The question whether this is given in the play is not to be answered by considering whether a reading of the text gives us this, for that would be very difficult to answer in that the answer would vary with the kind of psychological understanding that the reader possesses. For instance, the fact that

Iago is very keen that Othello should feel what he himself feels as well as the fact that what he feels is what it is – that is, jealousy – can be interpreted in various ways, some of which would lead us, or some of us, to assume homosexuality in Iago. But what is clear, or it seems to me clear, is that if we do accept this view of Iago, then, when we read the play, certain aspects of it will arrange themselves in ways which independently make an appeal to us and which would not be available without this supposition. Whereas if we were told, say, certain facts about Iago's military record – provided, that is, that it was honourable enough – that wouldn't influence the way in which we look at the play. So here we have a way of distinguishing between what is there, in the work, at some remove or other, and what is irrecoverably background – and all this fits in, of course, with anything like a proper account of perception, for whatever is the appropriate or relevant form or mode of perception. That the distinction between what is there and what is background is always a relative matter, until we come to what I've called the cut-off point, also fits with what I would think of as the proper way of regarding the distinction between what is given and what is inferred, or what is directly and what is indirectly perceived, as this occurs in general philosophy.

MAGEE: So the object isn't clearly distinct from its background – from its cultural, social and historical context?

WOLLHEIM: As I say, in certain cases we might manage to draw a sharp line, because we might be able to show of a certain piece of information about a work of art that, though correct of it, it makes no difference whatsoever to our perception of that work of art. But this would have to be shown, and even then, it is a point always open to revision.

MAGEE: So far in this discussion we've been talking about 'the work of art', in the singular, and we've been talking about 'art' in the singular. But are we right to do this? Can we be sure that aesthetic statements necessarily apply to all the arts? Might it not be, for example, that some very profound truths about music don't apply to painting? And so on?

WOLLHEIM: That is certainly true. And I think that obviously there are certain truths about baroque music which don't apply to the music of the nineteenth century or the music of our day. So there are an enormous number of false or hasty generalizations which we could make. But, of course, simply because we can make a false generalization, because we can project a generalization from one domain to another where it doesn't apply, that doesn't mean that in each case we should observe the line across which the generalization can't be legitimately projected and then use this line as absolute or as valid for all theoretical discussions which we have about art. I think that the question whether we should continue to think of, or to have, a notion of art – as opposed simply to talking about the individual arts – I don't think this is an issue which hinges solely upon the question whether we are likely to make faulty generalizations across the arts. For one thing which is relevant goes back to what I was saying earlier on; and that is that in aesthetics we are not merely concerned to clarify concepts that we use in talking about objects of art, we are also concerned with concepts that are themselves either explicitly or – though difficulty lies ahead – implicitly used in the making of these objects, in the bringing into being of them. And so we must take seriously the question whether there is a concept of art widely or universally used in the production of art. Now, you were saying just now, quite correctly, that there are great differences between the arts, that we ignore these differences to our grave detriment, and these differences it is, I think, natural to account for by reference to the fact that in the different arts different media are employed. It is, then, the differences in media, and their consequences, that are overlooked: philosophers of art and critics fail to take account of them. But when we talk of a medium, hence differences in medium, we don't simply mean such facts as that noises are used in the making of music, and that pigment is used in the making of paintings. For the way of identifying the medium is not simply via the stuff, it is via the use of the stuff. And the use of the stuff can't be specified simply in terms of the physical layout or arrangement of the stuff. It has to do with what is thought to be legitimate – legitimate, that is, as manipulation of the stuff. In other words, it's —

MAGEE: — partly conceptual.

WOLLHEIM: Yes – and this is the point to which I return – the concept that plays a part in determining what is a legitimate, what is an illegitimate, manipulation of the stuff, hence the concept that plays a part in determining what is the medium of an art, is precisely the concept of art. Of course, to show this in a way that would convince the sceptic – that is another matter. But it all goes back to the central point that I've been making, the methodological point, which is how aesthetics needs to have this dual sensitivity, in that it is concerned not merely with concepts that are descriptive of art but also with those which have been regulative in the making of that which we then describe.

MAGEE: Are you, in your own work, trying to develop an aesthetic that will apply to all art production?

WOLLHEIM: To any such enterprise there are limits: limits set themselves. I don't mean that, necessarily, there are limits in that one must always allow that there will be counter-examples to anything one says: that there will be some phenomenon one can't account for. I'm not talking of the essential inadequacy or incompleteness of aesthetic theory. Rather this: that any aesthetic theory needs to be put forward in two parts. First of all, a part which will do justice to the central cases, and then a part which will do justice to the fugitive cases – I prefer to call them this rather than counter-examples, for they are counter-examples only to the first part of the theory. Ultimately the theory as a whole can explain how and why they arise.

The problem relates to something at the back of much of what we've so far considered, and this is the historical, the essentially historical, character of art. This manifests itself in two ways. One way is often neglected in general discussion, but is not all that important: namely, that the actual concept of art is itself an evolving concept. There are indeed a number of scholars who have tried virtually to date the moment at which the concept of art as we know it entered our thinking. A surprisingly late moment. So the concept itself has a history, and in the history of the species a prehistory: just as morality has a prehistory in the history of the individual. But the other way in which art is essentially historical is more important. The concept of art has a history, but, more significantly, it allows for history, so that if we wanted to move from the concept of art to its denotation, to the objects that fall under it, we have to look not merely for certain rather complex relations of resemblance, or association between these various objects, but also for certain purely historical relations, for such relations as would allow us to hang all the objects on different branches of a common family tree. If we are sometimes perplexed by the amazing diversity between art-objects and how it is that they all fall under this single concept – particularly so when we bring in objects of the present or of the very recent past – it is also clear beyond a doubt that, at least within our civilization, if all the objects were very very similar and yet had been produced over the years, we should be totally reluctant to think of all of them as coming under this concept. So though extreme diversity may present difficulties for the application of the concept, total uniformity would be much more of an obstacle. And this is a fact that, in our continued efforts to come to terms with the modern, we sometimes lose sight of. And this is the core of art as a historical phenomenon.

12
Conversation with Alasdair MacIntyre

Philosophy and Social Theory

MAGEE: When one utters the word 'philosophy' outside philosophical circles people think of a wide variety of different things; many, I'm pretty sure, think first and foremost of general ideas in their relation to politics and social affairs. Yet after the Second World War the subject of political philosophy became so etiolated in Britain that by the mid-fifties a number of professional philosophers thought it had withered away altogether. In 1956, under the title *Philosophy, Politics and Society*, a collection of papers appeared whose Introduction included the famous statement: 'Political philosophy is dead.' Personally I think that statement never delineated a seriously arguable view but only the limitations of the people who subscribed to it. But what is certainly true is that now, in the 1970s, there is a great revival of interest in political and social philosophy, especially among the young. In this conversation we are going to consider first why the subject got into the impoverished state it did a couple of decades ago, and second, what are the reasons for its present vigorous revival – or at least the present revival of vigorous interest in it.

Professor MacIntyre, do you think political philosophy ever was dead?

MACINTYRE: I think one can understand what Peter Laslett meant in 1956 when he made this statement. He referred then to two contemporary writers whose work is very heavily tinged with positivism – Weldon and Margaret MacDonald. If one looks at how Miss MacDonald and Weldon did political philosophy one understands why political philosophy had come to seem, not perhaps so much dead, but rather a poor relation of philosophy. For each of them is guided by two maxims. The first is an expression of the enmity to metaphysics of positivism: take traditional political philosophy, and whenever one discovers something that seems to go beyond the simple data yielded by observation, use one's anti-metaphysical razor on it. Secondly, interpret the dichotomy between fact and value as being a dichotomy between that area in which we can have genuine knowledge and in which rationality can operate, and that area on the other hand which is a matter for decision and where principles have to be chosen. When one comes up against concepts such as the concept of natural rights or the concept of utility, or the concept of the state, which, as used in classical political philosophy, appear not to be amenable to this dichotomy, they suggest that here we have a confusion, such that we must rewrite the classics. Miss MacDonald envisaged natural rights theorists as men who may have declared that men do have certain rights, but ought to have declared, if they were to mean anything intelligible, only that men ought to have certain rights. Thus the procedure of most positivists who entered the field of political philosophy was to take over distinctions from their ready-made epistemology and then use them in the field of political philosophy as though political philosophy was almost entirely a field of confusions to be cleared up, and not itself likely to be a source of original insight and understanding worth studying for its own sake. The notion that political philosophy, for example, might throw light on epistemology rather than the other way round is absolutely foreign to them. Of course, it is quite true that when Laslett wrote, not all philosophers took this kind of stand. But it seems to me that even the very different sorts of philosophy that were also then going on in Britain were equally unlikely to breed live thought about the nature of the social sciences, though this for very different sorts of reason. There was for example the massive contribution of Sir Karl Popper whose book *The Open Society and Its Enemies* contributes to and continues classical political philosophy in its discussions, but which is essentially negative in character about the understanding of the social sciences.

MAGEE: But what about Wittgenstein's view that a language is a shared form of life, and that meaning is something essentially social? Surely these should have led to investigations into society across a wide front?

MACINTYRE: Certainly what was mistaken in the way in which positivists understood the relationship between epistemology and social philosophy arose from their failure to see that those established norms which make it possible for us to communicate, to have arguments with each other, to frame our understanding of the natural world and the like, are as much norms that define and enable us to have social relationships as are those norms which underlie political allegiance, kinship relations and so on. Moreover we should have learnt from Wittgenstein that language is not *a* but in one sense *the* form of social life. But the way in which this has been understood, certainly by some followers of Wittgenstein, has led to the use of these insights as a substitute for systematic social enquiry rather than an inspiration to it.

MAGEE: When the turnabout did come, and political philosophy started to get out of the doldrums, what was responsible for the change?

MACINTYRE: I see three influences. The first is probably still un-recognized by many people. One of the most important aspects of British philosophy when it was strongly influenced by positivism was a belief that the history of philosophy was a mere addendum, a source-book of problems. It held that although knowledge of the history of philosophy might be quite useful, one could be a very good philosopher indeed without knowing very much about the history of philosophy. When British philosophers do write about the history of philosophy their method customarily is to treat the historical figure concerned as much like one of their contemporaries as possible and to debate with him as they would with a colleague at the Aristotelian Society. One of the influences in reviving philo-sophical thought on political and social matters has been the number of excellent histories which have been produced, studies of the work of Hobbes or of Locke or of Mill, in which the relationship between the epistemology and political philosophy of a particular thinker has become so clear that the attempt to separate these, or to treat them in the way that the positivists did, becomes very implausible. When we understand how closely Hobbes's political philosophy is linked to his epistemology (and I think here of Mr Watkins's excellent study of Hobbes) or when we realize how systematic a thinker Mill is, so that again one cannot separate his epistemology from his moral and political concerns (as Mr Ryan has shown in his outstanding recent book), then we come to realize that in our own time the notion that we can pursue philosophy as primarily an epistemological subject without worrying about its implications for political and social affairs begins to seem bizarre. Why should we in our time be so different from Hobbes and Mill? It's at least worth taking seriously the hypothesis that we are not.

Secondly, an extremely important influence in reviving political philosophy has been the impact on philosophy of actual political concerns. I think here of Isaiah Berlin's concern about the concept of freedom and allied concepts, or the writings of Richard Wollheim on equality. Freedom and equality are extremely important terms because we use them *both* to evaluate *and* to characterize societies. They are precisely expressions which are not going to be easily disposed of by approaching them with a neat factual-evaluative dichotomy, and trying to find factual elements and evaluative elements and separating them out. Indeed when we characterize societies as more or less free, or as free in one respect and not in another, and when we characterize some society as providing equality of opportunity but not other kinds of equality, then the question of the precise criteria employed in making these judgments, and the relationship between meaning and criteria, and all the other epistemological questions, become central to political and social philosophy. Furthermore, if our epistemological analyses and our conceptual analyses do not provide us with an apparatus which will enable us to understand our use of those terms, then this puts a question-mark against our epistemology and our analysis of concepts. This is the kind of area in which political and social philosophy is a source of epistemological thought and not a mere postscript to it. Thus the coming of the Welfare State, the Cold War and its sequels, did have their impact on political philosophy through the importance which these concepts assumed, and the particular kind of importance that they assumed. If one pursues still further the question about what kinds of concept and what kinds of judgment are involved when we speak about freedom and equality in characterizing and evaluating societies, then one comes to the third important influence. The work of the later Wittgenstein, the work of Austin, the work of Professor Hart, all these bring out the need for patient descriptive labour in answering the question of how concepts of different kinds are used, of how the widely ranging vocabulary of political and social life is deployed. Austin showed us how what some have taken for minute differences between negligence, inadvertence, and irresponsibility of other kinds, can be extremely important in characterizing the way in which an agent's intention was or was not embodied in his actions on a particular occasion. These descriptive labours result, of course, in reports of how people do actually use discourse and therefore they have an empirical basis. They provide some of the data which we need if we are to return to the problems of classical political philosophy. At the core of such enquiries, both of the later Wittgenstein and of Austin, there is the large general question of how we do and how we ought to characterize what a man is doing when he does something. How do we distinguish between his action and its effects, consequences and results? (Notice that the notions of effect, consequence and result are by no means the same notion.) This whole family of questions raises the issue of how we understand the actions of ourselves and others in our social relationships. Thus what contemporary philosophy has brought us to is a realization that we do not as yet understand how to understand what we are doing in those elementary social relationships which are relationships of everyday action and everyday conversation, just because we have not adequately clarified yet our basic concepts.

MAGEE: What sort of concepts are you thinking of?

MACINTYRE: I've already given you two examples: the concept of responsibility, and that of the relationship between intention and effects, consequences and results of action. It is true these are very generally applicable concepts deployed whenever action of any sort takes place. We have not even reached the point of enquiring why any particular action was done in the way it was done. What we are doing is clarifying what would be involved if we were to ask for such an explanation.

At this point in the argument it is profitable to consider the condition of sociology. Sociologists have gathered a great quantity of data and provided us with large amounts of not hitherto available information, which purports to demonstrate, for example, the effects of different types of income distribution, or the effects of different types of educational system, as these have been observed in advanced industrial societies. Yet this accumulation of data, so great an accumulation that we have more facts than we know how to cope with, does not have its meaning written on its face. I suggested earlier that the social sciences do not, just as a matter of fact, seem to be able to formulate any laws in the way in which the natural sciences do. So when we are faced with these interesting facts or alleged facts about poverty, or class, or education, how are we to interpret these data? How are we to understand them? What have we actually been told? What would it be like to frame a theory? The answer as of now is: we do not know. I have already suggested that one reason why we do not know is that we are very unclear how to describe sociological findings about the actions and passions of men in such a way that we might begin to elaborate genuinely theoretical explanations. We do indeed very often make factual discoveries in sociology, but these factual discoveries tend to be of the same order as the factual discoveries that we make in ordinary life, and do not derive from any kind of understanding specific to the social sciences. So we may learn, for instance, as one European sociologist has discovered, that in passing sentence on criminals *some* judges at least tend to have more regard to the social class of the criminal than they do to the nature of the offence. When we ask what follows, what generalizations can be framed, we are not at all clear, because we are not at all clear how we should understand the phenomena of a legal system in such a way as to be able to generalize about them, and this is because we are not at all clear at what level we should be looking for a theory. A theory of evaluative behaviour in general? Or a theory of legal behaviour? Or a theory of the behaviour of officials such as judges? How ought we to group together the phenomena of social life? How ought we to categorize them in such a way that we can begin to frame explanations? We do not know.

MAGEE: Can you yourself see a way in which the minute, almost scholastic verbal analyses of Austin and Wittgenstein – which still have a great influence on the way philosophy is done – might become relevant to the formulation of the kind of generalized sociological theories you're now talking about? Can you see a bridge between the two?

MACINTYRE: I think the way in which one might begin to look for a bridge is by asking at what points the sociologist himself sees his explanations as involved in conceptual difficulties, and then asking what the philosophers have actually been doing that might be relevant to these.

MAGEE: Clearly you think there is a sharp relevance.

MACINTYRE: Oh certainly I do. Two kinds of relevance. The first is negative. Very often, carrying through a philosophical analysis will tell us that a certain kind of theory cannot hope to succeed, and this may be very relevant to the empirical enquiries of social scientists. Perhaps I can give you an example which is not from what you take to be the minuter sorts of philosophical enquiry, but which is to the point here. In his writings Popper has diagnosed the methodological mistake which he calls psychologism – that is, the mistake of trying to explain the social in terms of individual psychological characteristics – and he has argued that his own methodological individualism does not commit him to psychologism. One finds an application for this point in the argument that has gone on between the British social anthropologist Rodney Needham and the American sociologists Homans and Schneider on the question of how we should explain certain kinship rules, and why is it that certain types of cross-cousin marriage and not others are permitted or proscribed in certain societies. Needham has deployed arguments which he developed as an anthropologist, but which are essentially in line with Popper's more general critique of psychologism, showing that no psychologically-based explanations could account for the type of kinship rules which we actually find in the type of society with which Needham, Homans and Schneider are all concerned. This negative work of philosophy is however perhaps not so important as what I take you to be more concerned with, the positive contribution that the philosophy of action, as it has been developed since the work of Austin and Wittgenstein, can make to sociological understanding. What I take to be important here is exemplified best in the work that has been done in the philosophy of law. Consider the fact that when a chain of causation passes as it were through another person, the original author of that chain of causation is often not treated as responsible for subsequent events in the way that he was for events prior to the chain passing through another agent.

MAGEE: Can you give an example?

MACINTYRE: Supposing that I irritate you unpardonably during this conversation by my attitudes, and you as a result lose your temper on the way home and assault a bus conductor, there would be no suggestion that I was responsible for the assault on the bus conductor. You would be held responsible for the assault, even though there was a well-established causal chain which ran from my recalcitrant attitudes during this conversation to your actually striking the man. Why do we treat agency and responsibility in this way? Why do we treat some parts of the causal chain as extremely important in determining who was responsible for what and who ought to be punished for what and treat other parts of the causal chain as irrelevant? The first thing that we have to learn in these matters is what the courts actually do, and therefore a part of philosophical work here is empirical, examining decisions in which responsibility is assigned or negligence is ascribed, and the like. Then there is the question of whether the concepts and criteria of responsibility and of agency that are used by ordinary agents in their transactions with each other, outside the Law Courts, differ from the legal concepts and criteria. There is the question of how responsibility and irresponsibility are assessed in different types of society. And arising from all of these there is the crucial question of how far the norms that we follow could be different. How much of the rest of our social practice either presupposes or is presupposed by our practices in relation to responsibility and irresponsibility? Some determinist philosophers have claimed that we could make discoveries about the causation of human behaviour which would radically change our views about the assigning of responsibility without making any great difference to the practices of human life in general. We find it difficult to say whether this is true or not, because we do not know whether all sorts of other human relationships do not logically presuppose acknowledgment of norms in the relationships between human beings which are tied to our present understanding of responsibility and irresponsibility. What is becoming clear is this, that the kind of understanding that positivistically-minded philosophers had of the relationship between the philosophical analysis of concepts on the one hand, and the concepts employed by ordinary agents on the other, just will not do. The relationship between how philosophers categorize the world, the social world and the natural world, and how ordinary agents in their practices, pre-scientific, non-scientific and scientific, categorize the natural and social world, is a very complex one. This perhaps explains why, in a growing way, Kant and Hegel, who understood this very well, are becoming much more important authors in both philosophy and sociology in the English-speaking world than they were. Because the question of how a categorial scheme is applied, of what justifies using some and not other categories, of what a categorial scheme is applied to, and so on, becomes urgent. Philosophy cannot just record how, as a matter of fact, agents categorize the natural and social world in which they live. Philosophers are bound to ask which elements in their categorial schemes are necessarily as they are, could not be otherwise; and which are just contingently so; perhaps varying from society to society, and perhaps not.

MAGEE: And perhaps which can be changed.

MACINTYRE: And perhaps which can be changed. Mr Strawson's book on *Individuals* and Mr Strawson's study of Kant are both concerned with trying to isolate those elements in our concepts and categories which are so basic to any understanding of a world of persons and things that they could not but inform any categorial scheme whatsoever. This is a question that's going to be very important both for those sociologists who are empirically concerned with the ways in which different societies envisage social reality and also for philosophers. Moreover, just as philosophers cannot only be concerned with how we ought to think about reality, so sociologists cannot only be concerned with how we actually do think about reality. Ernest Gellner, for one, has emphasized the fact that in some societies people think about reality in confused, inadequate and irrational ways. This massive fact has enormous implications. For if we want to treat certain ways of thinking about the world as confused and irrational, then we have different phenomena to explain from those which we have to explain where men's view of the world is rational. The sociologist *qua* sociologist is forced to ask: 'Is this a set of rational procedures or a set of irrational procedures that I find operating in this or that society?' Depending on his answer to this he has a different set of data, a different explanatory problem, and presumably, in the end, if he is very fortunate, a different explanation to offer. So just as the philosopher cannot neglect the empirical question of what concepts we actually deploy in grasping the world, so the sociologist cannot escape the question of what kinds of procedures are rational and what kinds of procedures are irrational. But these are philosophical questions. That is to say, the picture of a social science purged of the old alien dominance of philosophical elements, and now become purely empirical, producing survey analyses and discovering quantifiable data, so that one could construct theories as in the natural sciences, turns out to be illusory. This hope gives way to the understanding that sociology and political science are ineliminably philosophical – ineliminably philosophical because how a society is is in large part a matter of how its members understand social reality, and how they understand social reality is in large part a matter of whether their understanding is rational or confused; of whether they have, to use another idiom, true or false consciousness, how far their vision is ideologically distorted, and the like. We could not deploy any of these notions of ideology or false consciousness unless we presupposed a concept of rationality, and we cannot deploy a concept of rationality in the social sciences unless we are prepared to do philosophical work on what constitutes rationality in different areas of human life.

MAGEE: But, in spite of all you're saying, how much philosophically sophisticated sociology has actually managed to get written?

MACINTYRE: I think the first achievement of philosophically sophisticated sociology in this country has lain in the amount that hasn't got written that would otherwise have been written. Now I'm not entirely happy about saying this. Philosophy does tend to sterilize the mind and the imagination far too easily. For example, it's been remarked that the Popperian philosophy of science, with its crucial and absolutely right-minded emphasis on criticism and refutability, can have a tendency to sterilize programmes of scientific discovery. This is nothing to do with the truth or validity of Popper's contentions and arguments. It has to do with a side psychological effect of philosophy. And in a similar way, I think, to read Austin and Wittgenstein and Hart is for many sociologists an experience that is at once illuminating and dazzling. They see and they cannot see as a result. In this situation I'd expect there to be a need of a re-orientation which would take a long time. But of course it is quite untrue that there is not sophisticated sociological work, very often work that shows no trace of any overt influence of philosophy. I have already mentioned Rodney Needham's writings. Needham is somebody who in his anthropological work produces a good deal of philosophical understanding with great skill. He does not write as a philosopher but as an anthropologist. Mary Douglas is another anthropologist who has worked in the same way. Behind both of them lies the work of Evans-Pritchard, which is extremely acute philosophically in just the way that one would want. We also find this among sociologists. I think here of Professor Tom Burns's inaugural lecture on sociological explanation. The title might lead one to expect a lecture by a philosopher commenting on what sociologists do, but this is a sociologist commenting on what he and other sociologists do, in a way that is at once philosophically clear-headed and illuminating but also very much to the point in guiding actual sociological enquiry. Now it may be that Mary Douglas or Rodney Needham or Tom Burns have not in fact been directly influenced by the philosophical climate at all. I do not know. But what I do know is that the sort of work they are doing is work that could enter into rewarding dialogue with the best contemporary philosophy. Only this will take time.

MAGEE: My impression is that a much increased proportion of the intelligent young are turning towards sociological enquiry, and if this is true it means that a lot of people who perhaps 20 years ago would have become philosophers will not now become philosophers, but will become sociologists. One's hope is that they will be more philosophically sophisticated sociologists. Do you think this development is taking place?

MACINTYRE: I think this is probably true. I have however one large reservation. British sociology has expanded numerically in a quite extraordinary way in the last ten years, and the achievement of British sociologists in coping with this expansion has been remarkable. But in so far as the expansion has been a matter of undergraduate student demand, one has to put a question mark against it. This is not a doubt about the intelligence or the enthusiasm of those undergraduates who come into sociology. It is a question about the expectations that they have of the subject. There was a time when people who wanted a view of the world that would inform their moral convictions, and give them a substance of hope in the work of social reform that they were doing, turned to theology. And there was a time when such people turned to philosophy. The Oxford of T. H. Green is an example. I think that what young people have expected from sociology in Britain in the last ten years has been what their predecessors got from T. H. Green's idealist moral philosophy, and *their* even earlier predecessors got from evangelical theology. Frankly if that is what is wanted, you would do better to have stayed with evangelical theology. That is to say, a great many of the young coming into sociology wish for a theory of society that will legitimate belief in certain sorts of changes in social life. In fact what we have to learn from the social sciences as they now exist is how little understanding the social sciences can give us beyond the everyday understanding of social life that we have anyway. I think that is extremely important. That fact itself invites reflection of a kind that it has not so far received. If this is so, then there is going to be a disillusionment with sociology, just as there was disillusionment with theology and with philosophy. We are going to see people racked with guilt because they have lost their sociological faith. Indeed one has already seen people of this kind.

Conversation with Alan Montefiore

Conclusion

MAGEE: It's time now, in the last of these conversations, to put what we've been talking about in some sort of international perspective. The first and most obvious point to make is that the kind of philosophy that flourishes in England, analytic philosophy, is dominant only in the English-speaking world – plus, for some reason, Scandinavia. If you were studying the subject anywhere else, even in Western Europe, you'd find yourself doing quite different things. We can't go into all the other traditions there are, let alone compare each of them separately with Britain's, but the least we can do is take a look at what's happening on the other side of the Channel.

Alan Montefiore is a man who spends more and more of his time trying to establish relations between what's happening in philosophy in England and what's going on elsewhere – not just intellectually but through the physical exchange of people and information.

Mr Montefiore, why is it that the kind of analytic philosophy these conversations have been concerned with has been virtually confined to the English-speaking world, plus Scandinavia? (And – for that matter – why Scandinavia?)

MONTEFIORE: Well, could I perhaps just enter a minor caveat? Although it is fair to speak of analytic philosophy being dominant in the English-speaking world, plus Scandinavia, and not elsewhere, one does want to remember two things. The first is that at least one of the sources of analytic philosophy lay in a movement created in German by German-speaking philosophers —

MAGEE: — the Vienna Circle.

MONTEFIORE: The Vienna Circle, certainly; although, of course, its members were largely forced to leave Vienna as a result of the rise of the Nazis in the 1930s and went, some of them, to this country and some of them to America, where they tended to turn into English-speaking philosophers. Nevertheless, many of their original productions were in German, and if you look at Wittgenstein's works, for example, you will find that they are published with the German on one side of the page and the English on the other. Secondly, one has to remember that in some parts of the English-speaking world analytic philosophy is only one of the schools of thought which are of influence, and although it may well be true that in the last five, ten, perhaps even fifteen years, it has come to be increasingly dominant, even in the United States there are still today other important schools of philosophy; it just happens that analytic philosophers don't take much notice of them.

MAGEE: Well then, let me reformulate my question in a way that is valid and still says something important: why is it only in English-speaking countries and Scandinavia that the analytic tradition has really flourished in the last two or three decades?

MONTEFIORE: Yes, I think that is true (though, in the last few years, there have been very definite signs of movement). I've often puzzled over this myself. I think that any really adequate explanation must be extremely complex; one would no doubt have to trace it out by reference to cultural factors, social factors, political factors – perhaps economic factors – and the inter-relationships of all these factors with each other. If you go back to the time of the classical British empiricists, who constitute another of the points of origin of the modern analytic school (or complex of schools, because there are, after all, many different aspects or movements within what we are talking about when we talk in this general way about analytic philosophy) you will find people like Locke, who was very much at home on the Continent and had many Continental contacts. There were, too, French-speaking philosophers who did very much the same kind of philosophy as English-speaking philosophers did at that period; and philosophers on both sides of the Channel looked back to a common tradition of philosophy done in Latin. The break seems to have come with Kant, that is to say from the beginning of the nineteenth century. But when one looks to see in detail how this division between continental and British philosophers arose, one has surely to take a very broad cultural, historical canvas on which to paint one's picture. I really don't feel competent to do this. I should say simply that I don't think that the reasons are *purely* intellectual or internal to philosophy, but that they must also have a great deal to do with such institutional factors as, to mention just one example, the structure of universities and the positions of philosophy departments within them, which tend to be very different in this country from what they are on the continent of Europe.

MAGEE: Since analytic philosophy is, and indeed is often called, 'linguistic' philosophy, the following question naturally occurs to one: is the fact that it has flourished mainly in English-speaking countries due to something about the English language? Is English peculiarly amenable to this kind of philosophizing?

MONTEFIORE: Well, this is sometimes said, just as it is sometimes said that English, with its resistance to the construction of abstract nouns, lends itself more easily to hard-headed, analytic philosophy than, for example, German with its natural gift for proliferating abstractions. Nevertheless, I should say quite confidently that it is essentially nothing to do with the nature of the English language. We have already mentioned that one important source-movement of analytic philosophy was created in German and, of course, many of its ideas were worked out in that language. But as a matter of fact, analytic philosophy of one sort or another is by this time being written in a surprising variety of languages. To take a few examples almost at random: not only are there books on analytic philosophy now beginning to appear in Spanish, there are journals of analytic philosophy which use Spanish as well as English as their basic languages. Some analytic philosophy is being written in Japanese; some again in Italian. There are Hebrew-speaking analytic philosophers; Russians write about analytic philosophy, and even if they do not practise it themselves they write about it in Russian. I myself have discussed and even taught analytic philosophy in French, so – no, I really don't think it can be anything essentially to do with the English language.

MAGEE: Is it the case that the other kinds of philosophy being done elsewhere are also divided up according to language – is one sort of thing going on in the German-speaking world, another in the French-speaking world, and so on?

MONTEFIORE: The short answer to that is 'No'. What I think is true is rather that on the continent of Western Europe you will in general find that the mixture of things going on in the German-speaking world is roughly the same as the mixture of things going on in the

French- and Italian-speaking worlds; and that though the range is perhaps somewhat more restricted in Spain, still the same general sort of mixture can be found there too. I should guess that the Spanish 'range' will become even more like that of the other countries over the next five to ten years; and that this will begin to be true even of Portugal.

MAGEE: Do those countries therefore have more contact with each other than any of them has with us?

MONTEFIORE: Yes, certainly. But you will, of course, find within these countries a variety of very different movements, a much greater variety in fact than you would find here. There are, for example, Marxists, phenomenologists, structuralists, people whose main interest is to develop what they see as the implications for philosophy of psychoanalysis, and more or less traditional Thomists; there are violent disagreements within as well as between those movements, and also many philosophers who try to combine features of more than one of them. None of them has had more than a marginal influence on analytic philosophy, not even psychoanalysis – though there has been a certain amount of (largely disapproving) study of its methodology. In very many cases you will find adherents of those various movements exhibiting varying degrees of contempt, often vigorous, for adherents of other movements than their own. But by and large they are perhaps recognizable as belonging to one and the same general family community of quarrelling philosophers. At least, most of them find each other worth quarrelling with.

MAGEE: Before we get down to a consideration of individual philosophies or philosophers, are there any generalizations you can make about the difference between what's going on elsewhere and what's going on here?

MONTEFIORE: Could you give me an idea of what sort of generalization you have in mind?

MAGEE: Yes: for example, although there are many schools of philosophy even in the one university of Oxford, most of them are what an outsider would designate as 'linguistic' philosophy. Is it the case that, by contrast, philosophers on the continent of Europe are on the whole not very interested in language?

MONTEFIORE: No. Curiously enough this is the very reverse of the

H

case. Just at the moment, in fact, I suppose that the theme which arouses most interest among philosophers, certainly in France, but probably elsewhere as well, is precisely this theme of language. Of course, they are interested in language from a number of different aspects. But you could hardly characterize the difference between what goes on here, say in Oxford, and what goes on in Paris, for example, in terms of an interest in language on the one side and a lack of such interest on the other side. It has much more to do with the nature of the interest and with the ways in which the studies are carried on.

MAGEE: This is probably bordering on an impossible question, but can you briefly characterize some of the things that *are* happening on the other side of the Channel?

MONTEFIORE: Well, that *is* rather a tall order. Can we at least come rather closer down to what I know about – with anyhow *some* greater degree of confidence – and talk about France?

MAGEE: Certainly. They're our nearest neighbours, after all, and I suppose theirs is the only foreign language that most educated Englishmen really know any of.

MONTEFIORE: Before talking about France, though, I wonder if you feel I should try to say just something in answer to the question you raised at the very beginning about Scandinavia? I'm afraid I seem to have forgotten about it.

MAGEE: Oh yes, that's right – I forgot about it myself!

MONTEFIORE: It is not that I have very much to say on this topic; I simply am not tremendously knowledgeable about it. Still, it is at least worth reporting what other people have said, namely that an interest in analytic philosophy seems to have arisen almost independently in three different European centres – Uppsala, Vienna and Cambridge. Why this should have happened I really find it very difficult to say; but the point that I should want to make is simply that the emergence of this kind of philosophy in Scandinavia has, so far as I know, been largely indigenous and not merely derived from contact with, and the influence of, the English-speaking world. Of course, the fact that these kinds of movements have arisen has facilitated contact with the English-speaking world; the Scandinavians are very familiar with the kind of philosophy done by

English-speaking philosophers and have themselves made a great contribution to it. They write in English, they lecture in English, they teach in England and America; many of our undergraduate students here at Oxford probably don't realize that some of the philosophers they are reading are Scandinavians. I'm thinking of von Wright particularly.

MAGEE: He is in fact Finnish, isn't he?

MONTEFIORE: Yes.

MAGEE: Let's come back to France now and discuss what it is that's happening there, by contrast with what you've just been saying about Scandinavia and the English-speaking countries.

MONTEFIORE: Well, as I've said, there are a number of different things happening in France, some of them happening in the universities and some happening outside. This may sound a curious kind of point to bother to make, but I think that in the French context it is in fact worth making, because some of the French philosophers who have become best known in the English-speaking world have never, or only for short periods, actually held university posts in France at all. I'm thinking most obviously of Sartre, of Simone de Beauvoir . . . there is an important sense in which their philosophy is not professionally academic. However, if one is to talk about what goes on in French universities, the first thing to say, I think, is that the tradition of philosophical study there remains very closely related to an intense study of the history of the subject. This is true not only of what one might call the academic structure of the subject – the bread-and-butter business of what courses you teach, and of what kinds of fences your students are supposed to jump over in order to obtain their official credentials – but also at the much more fundamental and interesting level of the subject's intellectual structure. Almost all French philosophers with whom one enters into discussions will insist that the problems with which they're trying to deal only emerge as problems for them through their study of the work of those who have preceded them, and through, if you like, the development of their thoughts at the point of apparent breakdown. That is to say, they tend not to do what on the whole many British philosophers do tend to do, both in their teaching methods and in their own ways of approaching the subject – they tend not to see their problems as arising out of some non-philosophic or even wholly non-technical area of study or concern. An analytic philosopher of science might regard himself as

trying to grapple with problems arising out of his efforts to understand scientific procedure and scientific method; analytic philosophers
of mathematics are bothered by problems which they see as arising
directly out of their efforts to understand the nature of mathematics,
philosophers of history by problems arising directly out of their
efforts to understand the nature of history. Somebody doing moral
philosophy might see himself as trying to grapple with problems
arising out of his efforts to understand – to use the title of Professor
Hare's well-known first book – the language of morals. This, I think,
to French philosophers is a deeply naïve way of going on. They see
philosophical problems as historical in their very essence. By that I
mean not that they see them as problems about the history of the
subject, but rather as problems which arise as the result of working
through the history of the subject; problems in moral philosophy, for
instance, would be seen as arising from the history of moral philosophy. This is very characteristic of the work of French philosophers
in general, and particularly, I think, in the universities.

MAGEE: Doesn't this make for a certain sort of academicism?

MONTEFIORE: No, I don't think that it necessarily does. It can do,
of course, and obviously there is a great deal of academicism in what
is done in the French universities; but there is equally, no doubt, a
good deal of academicism in what is done in British universities.

MAGEE: As soon as I had uttered the question I realized that one
could scarcely call British philosophy non-academic!

MONTEFIORE: Yes; and in any case it depends more than a little on
what you mean by academic. But it is perfectly fair to say that this
accusation has been levelled by some French philosophers, or French
philosophical polemicists, against others. One very good example of
this can be found in two books by Jean François Revel, who became
very well known, even briefly notorious in a sense, among professional philosophers for his attacks on the university and on academic
(in the bad sense of the word) ways of doing philosophy and allied
subjects. As a matter of fact those two books showed marked signs
of influence by positivist or, if you like, analytic styles of thought –
or at any rate one so-called analytic style of thought. So, yes, the
point you make about academicism in French philosophy is in a way
true; but I don't think that this is peculiar to France, nor that it is a
necessary aspect of this emphasis on history as a crucial dimension
of philosophy.
    Well, let me now add two rather diverse points to build a little

on what I have said so far. The first is the very evident one that some of the most important figures with whose work French philosophers are concerned **are** writers whose views have been inextricably bound up, not only with purely academic subjects, but also with widely and deeply influential extra-academic movements. Marx and Freud are two very obvious examples. Hegel, another very important figure, was doubtless less of a practical man himself, but has, of course, had a deep influence on Marxism, however controversial the precise nature of this influence may be. So while one can see well enough how a study of Hegel can go off in a purely academic direction, one can understand too how it can be seen to relate to a deeper understanding of problems which have more than a purely inward-looking academic dimension. Another very important name to mention is that of Nietzsche, who, although he did hold a university post for about ten years, could hardly be considered a very academic sort of philosopher; his work too is of great influence among contemporary French students of philosophy.

MAGEE: Let me see if I've got right the sort of distinction you're making. When one reads the works of Ryle or Austin, say, one finds scarcely any mention of the great philosophers of the past. There might be a couple of passing references to each of two or three philosophers, but that's usually as much as you find. Whereas one typical way in which a French philosopher might discuss a live issue is through a study of its beginnings in, say, the work of the early Marx, or something of this kind. Is that right?

MONTEFIORE: Yes, you're almost right, but interestingly enough you've put it in a characteristically English way. You spoke of 'one way in which a French philosopher might study a live issue' as if he first had his live issue, and then said to himself 'How am I going to study this issue? Oh I'll go and get the early Marx to help me.' But that isn't really the way in which he operates. May I take an analogy which would be more immediately familiar perhaps to people who've done some philosophy in English universities than it might be to people who actually work in philosophy at French universities? Someone who was interested in the problem of causation might, for example, tell his students or his professional colleagues, that it was extremely important to study Hume's views on the nature of causation, and after Hume's perhaps Kant's, in order (a) to understand the direction which subsequent controversies have taken and, most importantly, (b) to get some help in our own attempts to analyse the nature of causation from the insights of Hume and Kant. Now, although I am, of course, slightly exaggerating the contrast in order to make the point, I think it would be much more typical of a French philosopher to start by working on Hume and then, out of this already Humean context, to ask 'How do we understand Hume's view of the nature of causation, where does it come from, to what problems does it give rise – and what are we to say if we want to go beyond Hume?' That is, if you want to work on, say, the problems of causality, you are almost bound to articulate the problem to yourself within the terms already set by the work of some previous philosopher. If Hume is the one who is most immediately accessible, for whatever reasons of cultural tradition, then he sets the terms in which you have first to articulate the problem. And then you try and show just how this way of taking it is unsatisfactory.

Of course, as a matter of fact what you have on the Continent is not just one set of prescribed philosophers out of whom everyone agrees to work, but a number of violently competing movements claiming incompatible allegiance, not only in the intellectual philosophical world but in the active institutional and political world too. And this brings me to the second point that I wanted to make. What I was going to say was first that one should remember that in France philosophy has existed within the universities as part of the Faculté des Lettres, that is to say very much as a literary subject and in general cut off from effective working contact with the sciences. This seems to me to have been of very great importance for the development of philosophy at any rate in France. At the same time one should remember that the whole internal structure of French universities, indeed the life of French intellectual society in general, is far more politicized than it is in this country. So that in all sorts of ways which would seem very peculiar and unexpected, and perhaps improper both socially and intellectually to Englishmen, the intellectual stands that one may take up in France, as indeed in other Continental countries, may at the same time turn out to be political stands, stands on matters not only of university politics but *ipso facto* of national politics too.

MAGEE: So there might literally be a direct connection between, say, your epistemological views and your view about the war in Vietnam?

MONTEFIORE: Well, in practice at any rate there is often an inescapable working connection, though whether it is a logical connection, whether it is a *de facto* connection, whether you can make these sorts of distinctions, are all matters of important philosophical controversy. At least one can say that there have been many who have thought that the connection was by no means accidental. It is, for example, very well known that Lenin believed that there was a close connection between the philosophies of what he called the empirio-criticists and the taking of a particular reactionary stand on matters of revolutionary politics.

MAGEE: If one says 'contemporary philosophy in France' to an educated Englishman it's ten to one he'll think of existentialism, and of names like Sartre and Camus – who are also, of course, well known for their political views, and indeed their active participation in contemporary politics. Now I take it from everything you've said that any notion that the prevailing orthodoxy in France is existential-ism is simply wrong. If it *is* wrong, what is existentialism's standing among academic philosophers?

MONTEFIORE: Yes, I think it is wrong, but before trying to explain why, one ought first of all to cast a little doubt on the usefulness or solidity of this label 'existentialism'. The term 'existentialist' has been used to cover a rather wide variety of philosophers, all of whom may, no doubt, have something in common with *some* other members of the group, but who may not as a group share any one characteristic common to them all. (In fact they may be said to exhibit what Wittgenstein called a family resemblance.) Between some members of this group, however, there really existed more differences than resemblances. So I'm a little sceptical about using the term 'existentialism' too easily. I don't know whether you'd like to talk at greater length about this, or whether I should go straight on to Sartre and Camus . . . Let me just say this perhaps – that one of the most helpful little books I can remember reading on existentialism was a short book by Jean Wahl – I think it is much more accessible, incidentally, to newcomers to the subject than his longer book on the same theme – in which he hit upon what struck me as an ingenious and illuminating way of characterizing it. What he did was to pro-duce a list of a number of terms which recur with notable frequency in existentialist writings taken as a rough whole – 'anguish', for example, was one of them, 'bad faith' was another. Not all of the terms that he listed occur in the writings of all those writers who have been called existentialists; but, Jean Wahl suggested, we can say that those who use, say, any four or five of them in a way which gave them a central role can be counted as existentialists for most practical purposes. Moreover, we can conveniently characterize the differences between them by seeing the very different uses which they give to these terms.

But to turn now more specifically to Sartre and Camus . . . Sartre, of course, has been an extremely influential and important figure not simply in philosophy, but also in many other cultural and even specifically political dimensions. Camus, I would have thought, was not centrally a philosopher at all. In saying this I am not in any way giving him a lower rating, so to speak, nor do I want to say that he has had no influence at all on philosophy; in any case there has been in France a far greater continuity than in England between philosophical writing and literary writing and political writing of 'non-literary' sorts. But I really doubt whether one would think naturally of Camus as one of the leading *philosophers* in France. Still, however this may be, the fact of the matter is that just at the moment neither Sartre nor Camus (nor Marcel nor Mounier, if it comes to that) arouse any interest at all among French philosophers. In philosophy, as elsewhere, fashions tend to change very fast, of course. Nevertheless, whatever hold they may retain on their places in the history of the subject (and Sartre at least, I feel sure, has carved out some secure niche for himself) they have for the time being simply fallen out of the focus of discussion. When I think of the people or the subjects which are studied by the students whom I happen to know in the University of Montreal, where I go fairly regularly, Sartre does occasionally occur among the subjects of theses, but offhand I can remember only two students during the last two or three years who wanted to concentrate on Camus; and these were students whose main interests were not, I should say, philosophical as such.

MAGEE: Well then, if professional philosophers are not much concerned with what we think of as existentialism, what *are* they primarily concerned with?

MONTEFIORE: How should I try to give a brief answer to this question? In terms of names of philosophers, or in terms of leading topics of interest?

MAGEE: The way you think is likely to make it clearest to me.

MONTEFIORE: Well, let me try a few names by way of examples, though I am afraid that they can hardly amount to much more than that. Among contemporary French philosophers the most talked about names would certainly include those of Jacques Lacan, Louis Althusser, Michel Foucault and Jacques Derrida. Althusser is a Marxist, Lacan works within the world of psychoanalysis, Foucault's main field is that of cultural structures and Derrida's principal concern is with the nature of language. Though they would refute the label, all four may be said to be structuralists in some wide, if rather vague sense of the term; and structuralism – an approach (rather than a theory) which provides for interpretations of different aspects of

reality as autonomous systems of meanings to be understood in total
abstraction from any individual subjects – is probably most readily
associated in this country with the name of Lévi-Strauss, the famous
anthropologist and one of its leading exponents. Among those who
have been opposed to structuralism with its abolition of 'the subject',
I should anyhow mention the names of Lucien Goldmann, a Marxist
with a special interest in the sociology of literature, who died a short
while ago, and Paul Ricoeur, a philosopher of very wide range, but
whose name is above all associated with hermeneutics or the theory of
interpretative understanding. I should add that translations of at
least some of the works of most of these philosophers are already
available in English.

There are other names that I feel I should also throw in. Some of
them I have already mentioned – big names belonging already to
history, such as those of Hegel and Nietzsche, Freud and Marx; to
which I should add those of Husserl and Heidegger, both of whom,
incidentally, had a great influence on Sartre. But among French
philosophers the biggest name I have left out is that of Maurice
Merleau-Ponty, whose work is, I think, just beginning to become
reasonably well known in this country and in the United States.
Merleau-Ponty was, like Sartre, very much influenced by phenomenology, though unlike Sartre he was very much a professional.
And although interest in his work among French philosophers is
just at the moment perhaps somewhat less intense than it was a few
years ago, he is such an important figure that I ought to add a
further word or so about him.

I said that Merleau-Ponty was heavily committed to phenomenology. Phenomenology covers, of course, an enormous and tangled
area, but I can perhaps indicate *something* of its nature by way of a
quick contrast with what I said about structuralism; for phenomenology provides an approach to the interpretation of different aspects of
reality through the study of the ways in which the mind gives meaning
to the different types or 'regions' of experience – experience which is
only intelligible as such in terms of its relations to the mind as the
subject which gives it meaning. But, you may at once protest, is not
the major part of our experience precisely experience of an independent world of 'objective reality', which exists in whatever way
it may happen to be irrespective of however *we* may happen to
experience it or, indeed, of whether anyone is actually there to
experience it at all? Certainly, a phenomenologist may reply; only
you must remember that this category of 'objective reality' is itself
one of the most important ones through which conscious subjects
conceive of their experience and so make it possible to experience
it as such. The problem of how to do justice to the two-sided fact

that we cannot but think of the world as thus autonomous *and* that to think of it even in this way is to understand it as existing in a certain relationship to our own modes of awareness, is one of very long standing in the central focus of the theory of knowledge. It was, of course, one of Kant's main concerns; it was also one of Merleau-Ponty's. For him the world is constituted of the meanings that we give to it, but at the same time the giving of meaning is rooted *not* in some abstract and disembodied intellect, but in real bodily gesture and behaviour, which of necessity takes place in the very world which in a sense it constitutes. How is one properly to understand this situation? How can we understand the meaningfulness which we confer upon language, but which yet only exists *in* language and not prior to it? How can we reflect upon the unreflective presuppositions of all reflection (including this one)? What is the nature, individual or social, of this creative subject of meaning? These are his problems; the answers are perhaps only to be sought in their best possible formulation – (a thought which is, in very different ways, both characteristically Heideggerian and Wittgensteinian).

MAGEE: Thank you for that lucid characterization . . . Can I now, at this point in the discussion, turn the camera round and ask you how what is going on in Britain looks to the sort of philosophers you've been talking about?

MONTEFIORE: In general I should say that it still looks pretty strange and remote, though it might be more accurate to say that most of them don't really look very closely at us at all.

MAGEE: And I suppose the same would be true the other way round?

MONTEFIORE: The same would indeed be true the other way round. We should remind ourselves in passing, incidentally, that we are here talking about French philosophers rather than about French-speaking philosophers in general; Belgian French-speaking philosophers, for instance, are more often familiar, I think, with what goes on in the English-speaking world than are most of their French contemporaries. Still, what you say is by and large true, that on both sides of the Channel people do not for the most part spend much of their time in being interested in what goes on on the other side. The next thing to say would be, I suppose, that most people who do give it a thought over there still tend to think of what goes on over here as being some form of logical positivism, mixed up with a strange interest in the minutiae of ordinary language.

MAGEE: So their view of us is two generations out of date, not just one.

MONTEFIORE: Depending on how you count generations, yes.

MAGEE: But I suppose it's also true that educated Englishmen with no training in philosophy commonly have the same picture.

MONTEFIORE: That's probably true, yes. As you said earlier on, many educated people in this country still seem to think that all that goes on in France is existentialism. I don't think professional philosophers think that, but many do probably believe that everything is still dominated by phenomenology. On the whole, comparatively few French or indeed Continental philosophers would still actually call themselves phenomenologists, though there remain some very active centres of it. However, just as it remains true that though very few philosophers here would still actually call themselves logical positivists, what they are doing would hardly be intelligible to somebody who had never heard of the logical positivist tradition out of which, and often against which, they are reacting, so I think it is fair to say that many of those French philosophers who regard phenomenology as now largely dépassée fail to give due weight to the fact, which strikes us from across the distant Channel, that their reactions against it can only really be made intelligible by reference back to that out of which they are reacting. (Though with their acute sense of history, they would be the first to take the point once their attention was drawn to it.)

The third point I wanted to make, however, is that there is nevertheless now beginning to be a gradually increasing interest in what is actually going on over here. It is still a comparatively small group of people who are interested in this, but it is for the most part a young group. There are one or two philosophers of the older generation who have done a great deal to stimulate interest in the work of British and American philosophers; Ricoeur is one notable example. Another of the 'names' whom I mentioned earlier on, Derrida, who is much younger than Ricoeur, has played a leading part in helping to organize exchange seminar visits between Paris and Oxford, which we got going for the first time last year on a regular basis, and himself came over to take part in a series of discussions with our graduates on the subject of his own work. And some members of the younger generation are now making themselves very expert on different aspects of analytic philosophy, and producing theses and articles on such authors as Frege, Moore, Russell and Wittgenstein.

MAGEE: What aspects of what's happening here most catch their imagination?

MONTEFIORE: There are perhaps two things of primary importance. One has to do with the general interest in language, which has been created from a number of different perspectives in France at the present time. We are clearly doing *something* about language and therefore it seems worthwhile to come and look a little more closely at exactly what we are doing; and here they may have been influenced to some extent, or encouraged in their interest, by the writings of professional linguists such as E. Benveniste, who has actually written on Austin and performatory utterances and who has had very considerable influence in France. It is likewise characteristic of the present mood that translations of Chomsky can be found in almost every bookshop on the Boulevard St Michel. They have also, I think, been attracted by the apparent concern for rigour and by what might be called the scientific seriousness of some analytic philosophy as compared to the much more open, indeterminate nature of a great deal of French philosophical expression. This may explain why a number of this group have been on the whole more interested in the work of philosophers such as Russell or Quine, whose methods are clearly more rigorous and whose style of philosophy is much more formal and exact than that of apparently ordinary-language philosophers; though Wittgenstein too has aroused a lot of recent interest – and not only through the *Tractatus*.

MAGEE: On the other hand are there some aspects of what's happening in England that seem to even sympathetic outside observers to be mistaken?

MONTEFIORE: Well, not so much mistaken as perhaps superficial and pointless. Of course, it is still not easy for them to discriminate between what is characteristic of English ways of doing philosophy as such and what just happens to be indifferent philosophy of any sort. You have after all to know a movement fairly well before being able to create your own standards on the basis of which to discriminate between what is good and what is bad. Certainly there is a tendency to treat our almost exclusive concern with what is or could be made explicit (or at any rate deliberate) in one sort of discourse or another as strangely naïve, just as there is a tendency to regard too persistent an interest in the details of English idiom as being excessively parochial. But I should not at all want to suggest that they are not interested, for example, in Austin's work. This isn't so at all. Indeed, in the seminars which were held during the last academic year at the École Normale Supérieure in Paris and which were attended by between 15 and 25 people, some of them very very good, the main basis for discussion with the visitors from Oxford was provided by John Searle's book on *Speech Acts*, which contains a development and discussion of ideas that were first worked out by Austin.

MAGEE: As you said earlier, most philosophers over here have really been as uninterested in what *they* are doing as most philosophers over there have been in what we're doing. What have we been missing in recent decades by not interesting ourselves in what they were up to?

MONTEFIORE: I think that what we've been missing most importantly is simply the experience of close and regular discussion with highly intelligent people working out of a different tradition from our own, and this always seems to me to be impoverishing. One of the most interesting questions that arises in such discussions, and which arose quite explicitly and self-consciously in the discussions we had here in Oxford with Jacques Derrida, is that of knowing how to identify a problem (or a theme, if 'problem' is too question-begging a term) as being the same one when it appears to present itself in radically different traditions. How do you measure how different the traditions really are? What are your criteria for intellectual translation from one to the other? Now, these are themselves fascinating philosophical problems. Moreover, the cultural problems, the problems of human communication, are of enormous interest, both intellectual and practical, and the best way in which to tackle them is surely to try and see what criteria for common areas of concern you can establish with people with whom at first sight you appear to have so little in common that you don't even seem to be talking about the same thing. I would say, then, that one of the most important things that we've been missing has been the opportunity to learn how to discriminate more carefully between what is relative to our own particular language and cultural tradition and what is of common concern to people of somewhat different traditions and thinking in somewhat different languages. If it comes to that, I should like to see not only French-speaking and English-speaking philosophers trying to learn how to work together, but both of them exploring the possibilities of working with philosophers of much more radically different cultures and languages, such as Chinese. But that would bring me to another long story.

Suggested Reading

Introduction

GENERAL SURVEYS
Morton White: *The Age of Analysis* (Mentor)
                 Selections, with commentary, from major philos-
                 ophers of the century.
John Passmore: *A Hundred Years of Philosophy* (Duckworth &
                 Penguin)
                 Very detailed and thorough, admirably written.
G. J. Warnock: *English Philosophy since 1900* (O.U.P.)
                 A linguistic philosopher's view, extremely lucid.

RUSSELL AND MOORE
Bertrand Russell: *The Problems of Philosophy* (O.U.P.)
                 A classic introduction both to Russell's thought
                 and to philosophy.
G. E. Moore: *Some Main Problems of Philosophy* (Allen and
                 Unwin)
                 Similar ideas, presented at much greater length.

LOGICAL POSITIVISM
Justus Hartnack: *Wittgenstein and Modern Philosophy* (Doubleday
                 Anchor)
                 A brief and elementary introduction.
A. J. Ayer: *Language, Truth and Logic* (Gollancz & Penguin)
                 The first logical positivist book in English, still
                 exciting.
Victor Kraft: *The Vienna Circle* (Philosophical Library)
                 A clear and reliable survey.

LINGUISTIC PHILOSOPHY
Gilbert Ryle: *The Concept of Mind* (Hutchinson & Penguin)
                 The most substantial product of post-war 'Oxford
                 philosophy'.
J. L. Austin: *Sense and Sensibilia* (O.U.P.)
                 Brilliant and entertaining critique of traditional
                 ideas about perception.

P. F. Strawson: *Individuals* (Methuen)
Powerfully original and systematic; rather difficult.

RECENT DEVELOPMENTS
J. J. C. Smart: *Philosophy and Scientific Realism* (Routledge & Kegan Paul)
Quite technical but reassuringly lucid exposition of materialism.
J. Lyons: *Chomsky* (Fontana Modern Masters)
Helpful brief account of the chief innovator in modern theoretical linguistics.

1. The Philosophy of Bertrand Russell

Bertrand Russell: *The Principles of Mathematics*, 1903; 'On Denoting' (article in *Mind*), 1905; *The Problems of Philosophy*, 1912; *Our Knowledge of the External World*, 1914; *The Philosophy of Logical Atomism*, 1918; *The Analysis of Mind*, 1921; *An Enquiry into Meaning and Truth*, 1940; *Human Knowledge, its Scope and Limits*, 1948; *My Philosophical Development*, 1959. D. F. Pears: *Bertrand Russell and the British Tradition in Philosophy*, revised edition 1968.

2. The Two Philosophies of Wittgenstein

Wittgenstein: *Tractatus Logico-Philosophicus*, with an English translation by Pears and McGuinness, 3rd imp. 1966; *The Blue and Brown Books*, 1958; *Philosophical Investigations*, with an English translation by G. E. M. Anscombe, revised edition 1958. D. F. Pears: *Ludwig Wittgenstein*, 1971. G. E. M. Anscombe: *Introduction to Wittgenstein's Tractatus*, 1959. G. Pitcher: *The Philosophy of Wittgenstein*, 1964. G. Pitcher (ed.): *Wittgenstein: Philosophical Investigations*, a collection of essays, 1966. K. T. Fann (ed.): *Wittgenstein, the Man and his Work*, a collection of essays, 1967.

3. Conversation with A. J. Ayer

A. J. Ayer: *Language, Truth and Logic*, revised edition 1946; *The Foundations of Empirical Knowledge*, 1940; *The Problem of Knowledge*, 1956; *The Origins of Pragmatism*, 1968. J. L. Austin: *Sense and Sensibilia*, 1962.

4. *Conversation with Karl Popper*

Karl Popper: *The Logic of Scientific Discovery*, revised edition 1968; *Conjectures and Refutations*, revised edition 1969; *The Poverty of Historicism*, 1957; *The Open Society and its Enemies*, revised edition 1966.
Bryan Magee: *The New Radicalism*, 1962.
Thomas S. Kuhn: *The Structure of Scientific Revolutions*, revised edition 1970.
Lakatos and Musgrave (eds.): *Criticism and the Growth of Knowledge*, 1970.

5. *The Philosophies of Moore and Austin*

G. E. Moore: *Principia Ethica*, 1903; *Philosophical Studies*, 1922; *Philosophical Papers*, 1959; *Commonplace Book 1919–53*, 1962; *Lectures on Philosophy*, 1966.
P. A. Schilpp (ed.): *The Philosophy of G. E. Moore*, 1942.
A. Ambrose and M. Lazerowitz (eds.): *G. E. Moore: Essays in Retrospect*, 1970.
J. L. Austin: *Philosophical Papers*, revised edition 1970; *Sense and Sensibilia*, 1962; *How to Do Things with Words*, 1962.
K. T. Fann (ed.): *Symposium on J. L. Austin*, 1969 (this contains a complete bibliography).
G. J. Warnock: *English Philosophy since 1900*, revised edition 1969.

6. *Conversation with Gilbert Ryle*

Gilbert Ryle: *The Concept of Mind*, 1949; *Dilemmas*, 1954.
Oscar P. Wood and G. Pitcher (eds.): *Ryle: A Collection of Critical Essays*, 1971 (this contains a complete bibliography up to 1968, and an autobiographical sketch).
J. Beloff: *The Existence of Mind*, 1962.
Alan R. White: *The Philosophy of Mind*, 1966.

7. *Conversation with Peter Strawson*

P. F. Strawson: *Introduction to Logical Theory*, 1952; *Individuals*, second edition 1965; *The Bounds of Sense*, 1966.
Bertrand Russell: *Lectures on the Philosophy of Logical Atomism*, 1918; *Human Knowledge, Its Scope and Limits*, 1948; *My Philosophical Development*, 1959.
W. van O. Quine: *Methods of Logic*, revised edition 1962; *Word and Object*, 1960.

John Kemp: *The Philosophy of Kant*, 1968.

8. Russell v. Oxford Philosophy

A. Flew (ed.): *Essays in Conceptual Analysis*, 1956.
J. O. Urmson: *Philosophical Analysis, its Development between the Two World Wars*, 1956.
Bertrand Russell: *My Philosophical Development*, 1959.
Karl Popper: Preface to the 1959 edition of *The Logic of Scientific Discovery*.
Ernest Gellner: *Words and Things*, 1959.
C. W. K. Mundle: *A Critique of Linguistic Philosophy*, 1970.

9. Philosophy and Morals

Aristotle: *Nicomachean Ethics* (preferably tr. Ross, World's Classics).
Hume: *Enquiry Concerning the Principles of Morals*.
Kant: *Groundwork of the Metaphysic of Morals* (preferably tr. Paton, under the title *The Moral Law*).
G. E. Moore: *Principia Ethica*, 1903.
A. Camus: *The Myth of Sisyphus*, 1942.
R. M. Hare: *The Language of Morals*, 1952; *Freedom and Reason*, 1963.
P. Nowell-Smith: *Ethics*, 1954.
G. J. Warnock: *Contemporary Moral Philosophy*, 1967.
Philippa Foot (ed.): *Theories of Ethics*, 1967.
J. Feinberg (ed.): *Moral Concepts*, 1969.
Wallace and Walker (eds.): *The Definition of Morality*, 1970.
(The last two mentioned books have useful bibliographies.)

10. Philosophy and Religion

A. J. Ayer: *Language, Truth and Logic*, revised edition 1946.
A. MacIntyre and A. Flew (eds.): *New Essays in Philosophical Theology*, 1955.
A. Flew: *God and Philosophy*, 1966.
R. Braithwaite: *An Empiricist's View of the Nature of Religious Belief*, 1955.
I. T. Ramsey: *Religious Language*, revised edition 1967.
N. Smart: *Reasons and Faiths*, 1958; *The Philosophy of Religion*, 1970.
J. Hick: *Philosophy of Religion*, 1963.

F. Ferré: *Language, Logic and God*, 1961.
D. Evans: *The Logic of Self-Involvement*, 1963.
D. Z. Phillips: *The Concept of Prayer*, 1965.
Basil Mitchell (ed.): *Faith and Logic*, 1957.

11. Philosophy and the Arts

Ernst Gombrich: *Art and Illusion*, 1960; *Meditations on a Hobby Horse*, 1963.
Wittgenstein: *Philosophical Investigations*, revised edition 1958; *Lectures and Conversations on Aesthetics, Psychology and Religious Beliefs*, 1966.
S. Cavell: *Must We Mean What We Say?*, 1969.
W. Elton (ed.): *Essays in Aesthetics and Language*, 1954.
Richard Wollheim: *Art and its Objects*, 1968.

12. Philosophy and Social Theory

Karl Popper: *The Open Society and Its Enemies*, 5th edition 1966.
Laslett and Runciman (eds.): *Philosophy, Politics and Society*, First, Second and Third Series, 1956–67.
Peter Winch: *The Idea of a Social Science and its Relation to Philosophy*, 1958.
Ernest Gellner: *Thought and Change*, 1965.
B. R. Wilson (ed.): *Rationality*, 1970.
Emmett and MacIntyre (eds.): *Sociological Theory and Philosophical Analysis*, 1970.

Conclusion

Any short bibliography for so vast a field is bound to involve a somewhat random and scattered choice. The following suggestions offer no more than one out of many possible sets of examples.

The following are all reasonably accessible and reasonably inexpensive:

Lucien Goldmann:	*The Human Sciences and Philosophy* (Cape Editions)
Iris Murdoch:	*Sartre* (Bowes & Bowes, Cambridge, & Fontana)
Jean Piaget:	*Structuralism* (Routledge & Kegan Paul)
Jean Wahl:	*Philosophies of Existence* (Routledge & Kegan Paul)
Mary Warnock:	*Existentialism* (O.U.P.)

Somewhat more difficult and expensive:

Fraser Cowley: *A Critique of British Empiricism* (St Martins)
This is written from the standpoint of Merleau-Pontyan phenomenology.

Stephen Erickson: *Language & Being – An Analytic Phenomenology* (Yale University Press)
About Heidegger, with some comparisons with Wittgenstein.

Michel Foucault: *Madness and Civilization* (Tavistock)

Herbert Spiegelberg: *The Phenomenological Movement*, Vols I & II (Martinus Nighoff)

More difficult again:

Louis Althusser: *For Marx* (Allen Lane, The Penguin Press)

M. Merleau-Ponty: *The Structure of Behaviour* (Methuen)

Paul Ricoeur: *Freud and Philosophy – An Essay on Interpretation* (Yale University Press)

Notes on Contributors

A. J. AYER, born in 1910, was educated at Eton and Christ Church, Oxford, where he remained until the Second World War. He served in the war as an officer in the Welsh Guards. From 1946 to 1959 he was Professor of Philosophy at London University, and in the latter year became Professor of Philosophy at Oxford. He was knighted in 1970. His chief publications to date are *Language, Truth and Logic*, 1936 (revised edition 1946); *The Foundations of Empirical Knowledge*, 1940; *Philosophical Essays*, 1954; *The Problem of Knowledge*, 1956; *The Concept of a Person*, 1963; *The Origins of Pragmatism*, 1968; *Metaphysics and Common Sense*, 1969; and *Russell and Moore: the Analytical Heritage*, 1971. His wife is the journalist Dee Wells.

STUART HAMPSHIRE, born in 1914, was educated at Repton and Balliol College, Oxford. After four years as a Fellow of All Souls he served in the army throughout the Second World War. After the war he held successive posts in London and Oxford, and in 1960 succeeded A. J. Ayer as Grote Professor of Philosophy of Mind and Logic at London University. From 1963 to 1970 he was Chairman of the Department of Philosophy at Princeton. Since 1970 he has been Warden of Wadham College, Oxford. He is a Fellow of both the British Academy and the American Academy of Arts and Sciences. His books include *Spinoza*, 1951; *Thought and Action*, 1959; *Freedom of the Individual*, 1965; and *Modern Writers and Other Essays*, 1969.

ALASDAIR MACINTYRE was born in Glasgow in 1929 and educated at the universities of London and Manchester. He has taught at Manchester, Leeds, Oxford, Princeton and the University of Essex, where he was Professor of Sociology. He is now Professor of the History of Ideas at Brandeis University, U.S.A. His books to date include *Marxism: an Interpretation*, 1953; *The Unconscious*, 1958; *Difficulties in Christian Belief*, 1959; *A Short History of Ethics*, 1967;

Secularization and Moral Change, 1967; *Marxism and Christianity*, 1969; *Marcuse*, 1970; *Against the Self-Images of the Age*, 1971. He has also edited a collection, *Hume's Ethical Writings*, 1965; and, with A. Flew, *New Essays in Philosophical Theology*, 1955.

BRYAN MAGEE was born in London in 1930, and educated at Christ's Hospital. In 1949, after service with the army in Austria, he went up to Keble College, Oxford on an open scholarship in Modern History. After taking his history degree he did P.P.E. in one year (in which he was also President of the Oxford Union). He began post-graduate work in philosophy under the supervision of P. F. Strawson, then held a Henry Fellowship in Philosophy at Yale. On his return from the United States to England he left university life to become a full-time writer and broadcaster, establishing himself as a current affairs reporter on television and a critic of the arts on radio. His nine books have been translated into as many languages. In December 1970 he was appointed Lecturer in Philosophy at Balliol College, Oxford.

ALAN MONTEFIORE, born in 1926, was educated at Clifton and – after army service in Singapore – Balliol College, Oxford, where he read P.P.E. In 1951 he became a lecturer in philosophy at Keele, and remained there until 1961, when he returned to Balliol as a Fellow. His wife is French-born; and in addition to his work at Oxford he teaches philosophy in the French language in Montreal, and takes part in seminars in Paris. He is the author of *A Modern Introduction to Moral Philosophy*, 1958.

DAVID PEARS, born in 1921, was educated at Westminster School and Balliol College, Oxford, where he took Mods in 1940 and – after seven years and the Second World War – Greats in 1947. His books include *Bertrand Russell and the British Tradition in Philosophy*, 1966, and *Ludwig Wittgenstein*, 1971. He is also responsible, in collaboration with B. F. McGuinness, for a translation of Wittgenstein's *Tractatus Logico-Philosophicus*, published by Routledge and Kegan Paul, third impression 1966. In 1970 he was made a Fellow of the British Academy. He is now Student and Tutor in Philosophy at Christ Church, Oxford. He is married and has two children.

KARL POPPER was born in 1902 in Vienna, and educated at Vienna University. From 1937 to 1945 he was Senior Lecturer in Philosophy at Canterbury, New Zealand. After 1945 he was at the London School of Economics, where for 20 years he was Professor of Logic and Scientific Method. He is a Fellow both of the British Academy and of the American Academy of Arts and Sciences. He was knighted in 1965. His books to date are *Logik der Forschung*, 1934 (published in English translation in 1959 as *The Logic of Scientific Discovery*, revised edition 1968); *The Open Society and Its Enemies*, 1945 (fifth edition, revised 1966); *The Poverty of Historicism*, 1957; *Conjectures and Refutations*, 1963 (third edition, revised 1969). He has published over 100 papers in learned journals.

ANTHONY QUINTON was born in Chatham in 1925 and educated at Stowe and Christ Church, Oxford – where his studies were interrupted by three years of war service as a navigator in the Air Force. Since the war he has been at Oxford continuously: from 1949 to 1955 as a Fellow of All Souls, and since 1955 as a Fellow of New College. He is the editor of a collection of papers on *Political Philosophy*, 1967, and author of a forthcoming book on *The Nature of Things*. He and his American-born wife have two children.

GILBERT RYLE and his twin sister were born in 1900, numbers 8 and 9 in a family of 10. Although his grandfather was the first Bishop of Liverpool, his father, a Brighton doctor, gave him a non-religious upbringing. He was educated at Brighton College and the Queen's College, Oxford, where he took a triple first and was Captain of the Boat Club. From 1924 until the Second World War he was Lecturer in Philosophy at Christ Church, Oxford. Like his pupil A. J. Ayer, he served during the war as an officer in the Welsh Guards. From 1945 until his retirement in 1968 he was Professor at Oxford. In 1947 he succeeded G. E. Moore as Editor of *Mind*. His books to date are *The Concept of Mind*, 1949; *Dilemmas*, 1954; and *Plato's Progress*, 1966.

NINIAN SMART was born in 1927 and educated at Glasgow Academy and, after army service in Ceylon, the Queen's College, Oxford, where he did his post-graduate work under the supervision of J. L. Austin. He was successively Lecturer in Philosophy at Aberystwyth, Yale and London. From 1961 to 1966 he was Professor of Theology at Birmingham, and in 1967 became Professor of Religious Studies at Lancaster. He writes and teaches both History of Religion and Philosophy of Religion. His books on the latter, to date, include *Reasons and Faiths*, 1958; *Historical Selections in the Philosophy of Religion*, 1962; *Philosophers and Religious Truth*, 1964; and *The Philosophy of Religion*, 1970. He and his Italian-born wife have one son and two daughters.

PETER STRAWSON was born in London in 1919 and educated at

Christ's College, Finchley, and St John's College, Oxford. After six years of army service during and after the Second World War he taught philosophy at Bangor for one year, since when he has been at Oxford – as a Fellow of University College from 1947 to 1968, and since 1968 at Magdalen as Waynflete Professor of Metaphysics. He has taught and lectured in many countries on both sides of the Atlantic. He was elected a Fellow of the British Academy in 1960. His books to date are *Introduction to Logical Theory*, 1952; *Individuals*, second edition 1965; *The Bounds of Sense*, 1966; and *Logico-Linguistic Papers*, 1971. His wife is a graduate of St Anne's College, Oxford, and they have two sons and two daughters.

GEOFFREY WARNOCK was born in 1923, and educated at Winchester and New College, Oxford, with an intervening spell of war service in the Irish Guards. He has been a Fellow of Magdalen College, Oxford, since 1953, and has held visiting appointments at the University of Illinois, Princeton, and the University of Wisconsin. He is the author of *Berkeley*, second edition 1969; *English Philosophy since 1900*, second edition 1969; *Contemporary Moral Philosophy*, 1967; and *The Object of Morals*, 1971, and is also General Editor of the series of 'Oxford Readings in Philosophy' started by the Clarendon Press in 1967. After the death of J. L. Austin in 1960 he edited, with J. O. Urmson, Austin's *Philosophical Papers*, second edition 1970, and prepared for publication a text of Austin's lectures, *Sense and Sensibilia*, 1962. He is married to Mary Warnock, who is also the author of several philosophical books and articles.

BERNARD WILLIAMS was born in 1929 and educated at Chigwell and Balliol College, Oxford. After serving with the R.A.F. in Canada he was successively Lecturer in Philosophy in Oxford, Ghana and London. In 1964 he became Professor at London, and in 1967 Professor at Cambridge, where he is a Fellow of King's College. He was a member of the Public Schools Commission, 1965–69, and is a Trustee of Sadler's Wells. His wife is the Labour M.P. Shirley Williams; they have one daughter.

RICHARD WOLLHEIM was born in 1923 and educated at Westminster School and – after war service which included being a prisoner – Balliol College, Oxford, where he took degrees in both History and P.P.E. Since 1949 he has taught at University College, London, where in 1963 he succeeded Stuart Hampshire as Grote Professor of Philosophy of Mind and Logic. His books to date are *F. H. Bradley*, 1959 (revised edition 1969); *Art and its Objects*, 1968; *A Family Romance* (a novel), 1969; and *Sigmund Freud*, 1971.

Name Index

Adams, J., 70
Althusser, L., 212
Anaximander, 78
Aristotle, 121
Austin, J. L., 1, 10, 11, 83, 84, 93–7,
   98–9, 111, 115, 116, 133, 167,
   172, 196, 197, 199, 209, 216, 217
Ayer, A. J., 5, 8, 11, *48–65*, 83, 115,
   166, 167, 174

Bacon, F., 72
Barth, K., 170
Beneveniste, E., 216
Berlin, I., 194
Berkeley, G., Bishop, x, 60
Bradley, F. H., 59
Braithwaite, R., 167
Burns, T., 200

Camus, A., 211, 212
Cantor, G., 143
Carnap, R., ix, 47, 48, 49, 50, 53
Chomsky, N., ix, 12–14, 65, 128–9,
   216

De Beauvoir, Simone, 207
Dedekind, J., 143
Derrida, J., 212, 215, 217
Descartes, R., 23, 30, 104, 110
Dicke, R., 71
Djilas, M., 80–1
Douglas, Mary, 200
Duns Scotus, 110

Einstein, A., 53, 64, 76, 78
Evans, D., 173
Evans-Pritchard, E., 200

Foucault, M., 212
Frank, P., 48

Frege, G., 143, 215
Freud, S., 103, 213

Galileo, G., 70
Gellner, E., 198
Gödel, K., 48
Goldmann, L., 213
Gombrich, E., 178
Green, T. H., 201

Hampshire, S., 11, *17–30*, 110
Hare, R. M., 151, 167, 208
Hart, H., 194, 199
Hegel, G. W. F., 14, 15, 81, 83,
   137, 198, 209, 213
Heidegger, M., 213, 214
Hesiod, 78
Hobbes, T., 193
Homans, G. C., 196, 197
Hume, D., 6, 30, 42, 43, 49, 60, 141,
   155, 209–10
Husserl, E., 213

Jennings, H. S., 73

Kant, I., 30, 38, 61, 83, 110, 122,
   123–5, 130, 163, 198, 203, 209,
   214
Kepler, J., 70
Keynes, M., 84
Kraus, K., 45

Lacan, J., 212
Laslett, P., 191, 192
Lazerowitz, M., 92
Leibniz, G. W. von, 6, 17, 19–20,
   55, 123
Lévi-Strauss, C., 213
Lenin, V. I., 211
Leverrier, U., 70

Lewis, C. I., 54
Locke, J., 203

MacDonald, M., 192–3
MacIntyre, A., 167, *191–201*
McTaggart, J. M. E., 59
Malcolm, N., 92
Marx, K., 14–15, 66, 81, 153, 168, 169, 184, 209, 212, 213
Menger, K., 48
Merleau-Ponty, M., 213–4
Mill, J. S., 29
Montefiore, A., *202–217*
Moore, G. E., ix, x, 1, 2–3, 4–5, 6, 7, 9, 25, 27, 29, 49, 50, 59, 69, 83, 84, 85–93, 98–9, 133, 134, 136, 137–8, 151, 215

Needham, R., 196, 197, 200
Neurath, O., 48, 49, 50
Newton, I., 70–1, 72, 74, 76, 78
Nietzsche, F., 209, 213

Ockham, William of, 110
Ogden, C. K., 55

Parmenides, 2
Peano, G., 143, 145
Pears, D. F., *31–47*
Pierce, C. S., 58
Phillips, D. Z., 173
Plato, 4, 17, 23, 30, 66, 79, 100, 110
Popper, Karl, 29, 45, 56, *66–82*, 83, *131–49*, 192
Prichard, H. A., 91, 151
Prodicus, 79

Quine, W. van O., ix, x, 11, 27, 47, 216
Quinton, A., *1–15*

Ramsey, I. T., 167, 168
Ranulf, S., 79
Reid, T., 9
Revel, J.-F., 208
Rhees, R., 173
Richards, I. A., 55

Ricoeur, P., 213, 215
Robespierre, M., 80
Rodin, A., 112
Ross, W. D., 151
Russell, Bertrand, ix, x, xi, 1–2, 3–6, 7, 9, 10, 17–22, 23, 24, 25–30, 42, 44, 46, 47, 49, 51, 59, 60, 61, 64, 69, 83, 93, 103, 105, 115, 117–18, 119, 131, 132–3, 134–140, 141–9, 215, 216
Ryle, G., 10, *100–14*, 115, 209

Sartre, J.-P., 207, 211, 212
Schlick, M., 48, 49
Schneider, D., 196, 197
Schopenhauer, A., 31, 38
Searle, J., 217
Shakespeare, W., 109, 110
Smart, N., *166–77*
Spinoza, B., 55
Stevenson, C. L., 151
Strawson, P. F., 11, 47, *115–30*, *131–49*, 198

Turski, A., 53
Thales, 134

Urmson, J. O., 132

Wahl, J., 211
Waismann, F., 48, 167
Warnock, G. J., *83–99*, *131–49*, 150
Weldon, T. E., 192
Whitehead, A. N., ix, 17, 55
Wilde, O., 111
Williams, B., *150–65*
Wisdom, J., 167
Wittgenstein, L., ix, x, xi, 1, 5, 6–7, 8, 9, 10, 12, 13–14, 23, 27, 29, 31–2, 33, 35, 36–47, 63, 83, 88, 94, 96, 115, 132, 133, 134, 135, 136, 137, 138–40, 141–2, 167, 173, 181, 192, 196, 197, 199, 203, 211, 214, 215
Wollheim, R., *178–90*, 194
Wood, A., 145

Subject Index

aesthetic judgment, 182–3
aesthetics, 37, 179–90
  and philosophy of mind, 184–5
  logical positivism and, 178
  moral philosophy and, 182, 184
  New Criticism and, 185–7
agency, criteria of, 197
analysis, philosophical, 51–3, 55, 57, 127, 134, 196
analytic philosophy, 26–7, 29, 39, 127
  and science, 14
  beginnings of, 206
  in England, 203–3, 204
  in France, 207–8
  in Scandinavia, 202, 206–7
anarchism, 81
anthropology, 171, 175, 200
art(s), 107–8
  and aesthetic statements, 188–9
  autonomy of, 185
  definition and nature of, 179–81
  justification of, 183

behaviour, propositions about, 54
behavioural theory of meaning, 58
behaviouristic philosophy, 10, 55, 60, 104, 176
boundary statements, 39

categories, 108–9
causality, 64, 209–10
common sense, 63, 77, 86–7, 91
  common-sense statements, 50, 51
confirmation, concept of, 53
conspiracy theory of society, 67

definite article, the, 24
demarcation, criterion of, 56, 58
democracy, 80

descriptions, theory of, 23–6, 29, 51, 115, 117, 119, 132, 145, 147–9
discourse, fundamental subjects of, 11
dreams, 106

emotivism, 151
empirical truths, 21
empiricism(ists), 9, 20, 21, 22, 27, 29, 41, 49, 60, 121, 199, 203
  and religion, 167
empiricist-sensory theory of knowledge, 61
epistemological problems, 52
epistemology, 59
  and political philosophy, 192, 193–4
equality, 194
ethical propositions, 49, 54
ethics, 49, 85–6
existentialism, 81, 139, 154, 211, 215
existential operator, 24

factual propositions, theory of, 37–8. See also propositions
falsification, principle of, 56
freedom, 194

grammar, study of, 127–9

happiness, 161
hermeneutics, 213
human nature, 13, 78

idealism, 4, 7, 90, 184
  absolute, 2, 3
  German, 1, 15, 83
identification, 121

identity, concept of, 121
  theory, 12
ideologies, 168
imagination, 101, 102, 105
induction, 58, 70–1, 72
'inner life', 106–8
intention, art and, 185–7
intuitionism, 85, 151
intuitionists, 52

kinship rules, 196–7
knowledge, by acquaintance, 22
  by description, 22
  foundations of, 50
  objective, 74–5
  scientific, 70–2, 77–8
  subjective, 74–5
  theory of, 63
  universal syntax of, 27

language, 216
  and human behaviour, 94–5
  and social relationships, 193
  deep analysis of, 44
  distrust of, 43
  empirical observations about, 41
  human nature and, 13, 78, 137
  limits of, 32–3, 35, 42, 43
  meaning and, 10, 78
  philosophy and, 131–3
  structure of, 35
  study of ordinary usage of, 53
linguistic analysts, 53, 59
linguistic philosophy, 10, 11, 14,
  59–60, 65, 100, 135, 138–9, 142,
  205
  and the English language, 204
linguistics, 12–13, 129
logic, foundations of, 32, 33
  and limits of factual language, 33
  mathematical, 18, 20, 29
  philosophical, 6
  relation to language, 119, 120–1
logical analysis, 27–8
logical atomism, doctrine of, 20–1,
  22, 26–7, 36
logical grammar, 20

logical necessity, theory of, 32,
  34–5, 39, 41
logical positivism(ists), 32, 48, 49,
  59, 78, 83, 132, 178, 214. *See
  also* positivism
  and theory of perception, 11
  and value judgments, 8–9
  and verification principle, 8
  difficulties of, 9

materialism, Australian, 12, 14
mathematical knowledge, 4, 7, 27
mathematical reasoning, 3
mathematics, 4, 5, 18, 20, 143, 148
  and idealism, 3
  and logic, 6, 18, 20, 51, 119
  positivism and, 8, 11
meaning, 22, 23
  analysis of, 58
  criterion of, 56, 58
  investigating, 10
  structure theory of, 36–7
  understanding of, 9
meaninglessness, problems of, 78
memory, 22, 52, 58, 61
metaphysics, 55–6, 59, 126, 133, 192
  descriptive, 125
  revisionary, 125
mind(s), account of, 12, 101
  and the physical world, 4–5
  concept of, 101
  other people's, 52, 54–5, 61, 63, 88
  philosophy of, 10, 42
monads, 19, 123
morality, 33, 182
  sexual, 164
moral judgments, 6, 85, 151, 152
moral questions, 163
moral philosophy, 150–65, 182, 184,
  208
  and aesthetics, 182, 184
  and religion, 173–4
  style in, 164
motives, 101, 102
music, 107–8, 188
myths, 169

names, 23, 24, 25–6
  theory of, 23, 29

naturalistic fallacy, 86
nature, man and, 12, 13
number, notion of, 18

observation, science and, 69–72, 73
  statements, 50
ontology, 58, 61

particulars, 121
perception, 6, 50, 52, 58, 103–4
  phenomenalist theory of, 11
phenomenalism, 11, 60
phenomenology, 213–14, 215
philosophy, 67–9, 95–6, 98, 201
  and analysis, 91
  and philosophers, 67, 68–9, 95
  and philosophy of religion, 176
  continental, 98
  in France, 206, 207–17
  group, 95–6
  history of, 193
  studying, 150
physical world, 4–5
physicalist theory of being, 61
pluralism, 4
political philosophy, 191–3, 199
politics, 79–81
  philosophy and, 210–11
positivism(ists), 59, 193, 208. *See also* logical positivism
  and political philosophy, 191–3
  and technology, 14
pragmatism(ists), 52, 55, 58
prescriptivism, 151
probability, 53, 58, 62
propositions:
  analysis of, 18–20, 21, 26, 88–90
  and fact, 22–3
  and meaning, 6–7
  complex, 36
  elementary, 21, 23
  ethical, 49
  existential, 24
  factual, 32, 33–6, 37–8
  general form of, 120
  logical, 34, 35, 54
  mathematical, 5, 7, 54
  significant, 49

psychoanalysis, 44, 45, 81, 169, 205, 212
psychological atomism, 36
psychologism, 196–7
psychology, 12, 43, 102–3, 176

quantum theory, 64

rationalism, European, 29
reality, positivist account of, 7
  sociology and, 198–9
reason, 2, 4, 7
reductionists, 52
religion, 33, 37, 107
  and Christianity, 168
  and ethical commitment, 167
  philosophy of, 166–7, 168, 169, 171–7
religious experience, 167
religious language, analysis of, 167–8, 173
responsibility, criteria of, 197–8

satisfaction, 161
scholasticism, 138, 139
science, 62, 69–70, 73, 77–8
  and analytic philosophy, 14, 46
  and induction, 70–1, 72
  and philosophy, 64, 135
  dominance of, 46
  logic of, 64
  philosophy of, 58, 199
  positivism and, 8, 11
scientific statements, 50, 56
scientism, 11, 14
sensations, 42, 44
sensation statements, 50
sense data, 90
sense experience, 61
  statements about, 50, 60
sense impressions, 121
simultaneity, concept of, 53
social science(s), 13, 192, 195
  empiricism and, 199
sociology, 12, 175, 195, 198–9, 200–1
solipsism, 33, 92
'speech-act', 94, 151

statements:
  meaning of, 9
  necessarily true, 57–8
  philosophical, 57
  religious, 167
  significant, 54
structuralism, 212–13
subject-predicate form of proposi-
    tions, 19, 24
substantival terms, 23–5
syntax, deep structure of, 19, 26
  logical, 20, 25

theology, 49, 170, 200, 201
thinking, notion of, 112–13, 114
transubstantiation, 169–70
truth(s), contingent, 28
  correspondence theory of, 22–3,
    76
  factual language and, 33
  necessary, 28, 40

tyranny, 80

understanding, 2
universals, 121
  facts about, 4
  realm of, 4, 5
utilitarianism, 160–1
utopianism, 80

value(s), 5
  fact and, 152–3, 154–5, 156, 158,
    159, 192
  judgment of, 8–9, 37, 155
verification, principle of, 8, 54, 56,
    58
  status of, 56–7

words, and meaning, 78–9